Donald Barthelme

Number Thirteen:
Tarleton State University
Southwestern Studies in the Humanities
William T. Pilkington, Series Editor

Helen Moore Barthelme

Donald Barthelme

The Genesis of a Cool Sound

Texas A&M
University Press
College Station

The paper used in this book meets the minimum requirements
of the American National Standard for Permanence of Paper
for Printed Library Materials, z39.48-1984.
Binding materials have been chosen for durability.
∞

Library of Congress Cataloging-in-Publication Data

Barthelme, Helen Moore, 1927–

   Donald Barthelme : the genesis of a cool sound / Helen Moore
Barthelme.

      p. cm. — (Tarleton State University southwestern studies in the
humanities ; no. 13)

Includes bibliographical references and index.

   ISBN 1-58544-119-8 (alk. paper)

   1. Barthelme, Donald.   2. Barthelme, Donald—Marriage.   3. Experimental fiction, American—History and criticism.   4. Authors,
American—20th century—Biography.   5. Barthelme, Helen Moore,
1927-—Marriage.   6. Postmodernism (Literature)—United States.
I. Title. II. Series.

   PS3552.A76 Z58 2001

   813'.54—dc21

                                        00-012208

For my sisters

Odell Moore
and
Margo Vandruff

"I would concurrently be working in fiction like Glenn Miller
in that awful picture, searching for a cool sound."
Don Barthelme to Joe Maranto,
from Korea, September 28, 1954

"The essence of our calling is right behavior."
King Arthur in *The King*

Contents

Illustrations

Preface

"Well, Babe, are you ready for this?" I turned from my desk and saw Don standing there holding a typescript—I knew this meant that his first story was ready for me to hear. Don spoke in a serious, challenging tone, but underlying it was a kind of gaiety that characterized his mood as he worked. We moved into the living room, and I sat on the sofa while he stood facing me and read "Me and Miss Mandible," a short story that he had first called "The Darling Duckling at School." His voice was rich and deep, every word precisely enunciated. I was astonished—I had heard nothing like it before, yet in it I could hear the Don that I knew and loved, his incisive wit and his satirical humor, the matter-of-fact tone and the ironies it created.

On that morning in the fall of 1960, Donald Barthelme had just completed what would become his first published story in the new literary style he was developing. Within a few months it appeared in *Contact.* After that, other stories followed one after another.

I had also been with Don the day he discovered Samuel Beckett's *Waiting for Godot,* the catalyst in Don's search for his own literary style, one that would be different from anything else that had been written. As Don wrote the stories that became *Come Back, Dr. Caligari,* his first collection, I was with him every day and gradually began to understand something of the creative process that was taking place. Later, as he struggled to find a place for himself in the New York literary world, I understood that his immersion in that world was necessary in order for him to gain the recognition that he sought.

I was the only person to whom he could talk every day, who could read his stories as he went through the process of rewriting, who observed many of the influences on his ideas and on his creativity, and who worked with him to achieve recognition for his extraordinary talent.

I met Don in the fall of 1949, but we did not marry until 1956. After his death in 1989, I began writing a memoir of the years that began with our first meeting and ended with the publication of *Come Back, Dr. Caligari* and *Snow White* in the mid-1960s. But as I worked, I realized that there was more to tell of what we shared and of my understanding of his work than I could have imagined. I realized as well the necessity of including in my story the years that followed—years in which Don's personal and literary life moved forward without my regular presence but within the patterns established early in his life.

After 1964, when *Come Back, Dr. Caligari* was published, Don Barthelme was recognized as a new writer whose innovative work challenged the accepted forms of fiction; his style was puzzling but exciting. Within a few years, readers began to look forward to his fiction, the short stories in the *New Yorker* and then the novels, of which *Snow White* was the first. Almost as soon as his work appeared regularly, it began to influence young writers throughout the Western world.

In this account of Don's struggle for recognition in the intensely competitive New York literary world, I describe how he was able to succeed without waiting years to be recognized through the small journals that first carried his stories. I relate how, beginning in 1956, he made a series of choices that led inexorably to his single goal of becoming one of the country's literary elite. Don's quest began early in his life, but it was only after we married that he began to achieve what he sought. I believed that Don was a literary genius, and I wanted for him what he wanted. Thus, I had the unique opportunity of not only sharing the first years of his writing but also of assisting him in his efforts to gain acceptance among the country's literary elite. From 1951 to the early 1970s, I combined business and academic careers, in teaching at the University of Houston as well as Dominican College, and in founding and running an advertising agency in Houston. In 1987, just two years before Don died, I left the world of business and returned to university life as a member of the faculty of the Department of English at Texas A&M University in College Station. With teaching as my sole career and interest, I had a different perspective from which to view Don's work. It was from this personal perspective, now cast into an academic context, that I began this work.

No one else knows this story.

For Don, the process of creativity began with dissatisfaction, especially with his own writing before the fall of 1960. In his dissatisfaction with what he created and in the world around him, Don was impelled to search for perfection—in his work, in his personal life, in every small thing he did. He was intensely engaged in life, continually seeking new ideas; he thrived on change and on whatever was new. He yearned to write fiction that would satisfy not only himself but the literary world as well.

Don's writing talent was apparent even when he was a child. His brothers Peter, Frederick, and Steven all became published writers themselves, and his sister Joan and parents were all remarkably talented individuals as well. In his early career as a journalist, editor of a literary journal at the University of Houston, and then director of the Contemporary Arts Museum in Houston, Don was honing the language skills that he would need to develop his literary style. As his literary career moved forward, Don was never uncertain of his talent with words; he was more concerned with *what* he wanted to say and the literary forms that would best express his ideas.

When he first undertook to create a new style, Don's fiction was derived largely from conscious and unconscious reflections and feelings about his own life. But within a few weeks, he began to bring in more of the world around him. And very early, he sought to find and portray value and meaning in life; in fact, he held out hope for "possibility" to the very end. Don often was able to do just this through what I call "lyrical moments" in his fiction. Not every story offers such value and meaning, but these "lyrical moments" or scenes occur throughout his work and tell more about Don and his inner life than the casual reader might otherwise observe.

Don's high moral sense emerges over and over throughout the years in which he wrote and published. As early as 1957, before he wrote the first of his new fiction, while taking a course on the philosophy of literature, Don noted on a page of Tolstoy's *The Death of Ivan Ilych* that the "sole solution to life and death is *manner of life*," a view of the world that is reflected in his fiction throughout the next three decades.

"Shouldness" was essential to Don's view of how life should be conducted. He yearned for order, for perfection, and although he was clearly not satisfied with the way that his life went, I believe he cared about living it as responsibly as possible.

Although Don's place in Western literature appears certain, the difficulty of reading his fiction sometimes overshadows its significance. I believe my account of many of the literary, intellectual, and artistic influences that were important to his work, together with insight into the kind of person he was—how he responded to people and events, and the values by which he tried to live—will provide the reader with a better understanding of what Don accomplished in creating a new style of fiction.

I have attempted to recount only what I know or learned from Don himself or from later conversations with our very close friends. What Don told me about his life is essential to the story, but I have not tried to tell of events or relationships of which I know nothing. Although I have tried to be objective, I found that—like George Christian, Pat Goeters, Bob Morris, Joe Maranto, and others who knew him throughout his life—it is tempting to recall above all else the compelling enthusiasm and challenging mind of the younger Don, who undertook at the age of twenty-nine to become one of the world's most important innovators of twentieth-century fiction.

There are a number of bibliographies of Donald Barthelme's work, including a *Comprehensive Bibliography and Annotated Secondary Checklist* by Jerome Klinkowitz, Asa Pieratt, and Robert Murray Davis, published by Archon Books in 1977. Later bibliographies will be found both in print and on the internet. Most of the stories mentioned in the text are included in two major collections: *Sixty Stories* and *Forty Stories*. References to stories which are not in either of these collections will be found in the Notes. References to other work, including the four novels, are also found in the Notes.

Acknowledgments

I want to thank colleagues at Texas A&M University who encouraged me to undertake and complete this memoir and biography. I am especially grateful to Jerome M. Loving, William B. Clark, and Jimmie M. Killingsworth, all scholars in American literature who read my manuscript and made suggestions for revisions and for publication. I am also grateful to the department head, J. Lawrence Mitchell, who has supported my work from the beginning.

I owe Samuel B. Southwell, professor emeritus at the University of Houston, a special debt. He not only encouraged me and read my manuscript but was a close friend to Don in the 1980s and shared with me many of their conversations.

I want to thank Pat Bozeman, head of Special Collections and Archives at the M.D. Anderson Library at the University of Houston, for her generosity and assistance in allowing me to go through all the materials on Don at the university. I also want to acknowledge the Manuscripts Department of the Wilson Library at the University of North Carolina at Chapel Hill, which allowed me to review the Walker Percy collection and is now in possession of the Percy-Barthelme letters.

Donald Barthelme

DON WAS A NEW FRESHMAN at the University of Houston when we met for the first time in the fall of 1949. I was alone in the offices of the Department of Journalism and working on a writing assignment when he walked in and introduced himself. It was only after he spoke that I looked up and saw him standing over my desk. He explained that he needed to see a faculty advisor regarding his program. I told him to whom he should speak; after a few more questions, he left and I returned to my work.

Years later, Don confessed that he was walking down the hall when he glanced into the office and thought, "What a pretty girl!" He immediately came in on the pretext of looking for advice. His mother later recalled that day; Don had come home and told her about the "handsome girl" he had just met at the University of Houston.

Don seemed so young that I thought little of our first encounter; besides, I was finishing my classes, involved in student affairs, and engaged to Peter Randall Gilpin, a fellow journalism student. I can still visualize the tall slender boy who quickly became a remarkable presence at the university. He had light brown hair and wore horn-rimmed glasses. I noticed even in our very first meeting his deep and rich voice and the way that he spoke with a distinctly sharp enunciation. And as he looked directly at me, listening closely to whatever I said, his blue eyes were serious and intense. From these first months, I also remember that he was proud and self-assured, with a striding, almost jaunty walk. As I later learned, he could easily become somber and even remote and unfriendly, but for me, it was his laugh and cheerful demeanor that I still find unforgettable.

Although Don was the traditional age of a college freshman, he was almost out of place on a campus crowded with former GI's, many already in their late twenties and early thirties. That autumn in 1949, he was eighteen and a freshman and I was twenty-one and a graduating senior.

I had been a serious, intellectual child, graduating as an honors student from Corpus Christi High School at the age of fifteen. Like Don, I wanted to be a writer and began my journalism career in high school. Shortly after I graduated from high school, my mother and father separated, and I moved with my mother and two sisters and brother to Houston, where I enrolled at the University of Houston the following year.

I enjoyed everything about college. I edited the student newspaper, the *Cougar,* won a lot of honors, and was active in student government. When I first enrolled at the university, I was interested in creative writing, but the curriculum was meager and I quickly gave it up. In the fall of 1949, I was in the final semester of my undergraduate work and had begun graduate courses as well. The day we met, I was engaged in work for the department to satisfy the requirements of a fellowship.

Don always remembered our first meeting, although another year passed before we became close friends. I was slender, five feet four and one-half inches tall, and had dark hair and green eyes. Don described me as "very intelligent and natural." I had a soft voice and a cheerful manner, but I was professionally ambitious, with strong convictions and considerable self-esteem.

The University of Houston in 1949 was an urban university with a diverse student body. With the GI Bill, veterans of World War II were pouring into the university, and the student body now included a large population of former military men. The draft had continued after the war ended; this meant that younger men as well as mature students with wives and families were among the former soldiers.

A sprawling trailer village and enlisted men's barracks provided housing for several thousand men and their families. Unmarried veterans lived in the trailers; families lived in apartments in the wooden barracks.

Notwithstanding that it was a very young university first established as a community college in the 1920s, the institution appealed to a large number of qualified and talented students financially unable to go away to another university. Most established institutions offered few scholarships and, other than menial jobs, few employment opportunities. Ambitious young men and women, many with already established careers in Houston, were anxious to attend classes and work at the same time. And by the late 1940s, the influx of qualified veterans from other parts of the country created an intellectually challenging climate for all students.

Don's writing talent had provided him with an audience of admirers while he was still in high school, particularly because of his interest in bebop and jazz. He was a regular contributor to the teen page of the *Houston Post,* and Joe Maranto, a World War II veteran and now a student who became one of Don's lifelong friends, was among those who noticed his work.[1] Also a lover of jazz, Joe admired both Don's writing and his knowledge of music; he praised as brilliant such pieces as the one Don wrote for the *Post* on the bandleader Stan Kenton. At the university, Don made friends easily; Joe described him as "attracting people like a magnet." Before the end of his first year, Don was known among both faculty and students as an exceptional writer who had read an impressive number of literary works.

Don began at once to cover theater, film, and other fine arts for the *Cougar.* Maranto, five years older than Don, was editor of the student newspaper and had appointed Don arts editor, telling him that he could write anything he wanted. Before long, Don was also writing a weekly column "about everything from alchemy to a dismantling of Dr. Johnson and Samuel Pepys." He used the pseudonym of Bardley, an unabashed linking of his own name to the Bard from Stratford.

In his column, Don began to develop a style of satirical humor that was his own. Even though the subjects for his columns were often typically collegiate, there are glimmers of Don's later style in them. He once wrote an entire article for the sole purpose of printing at the bottom of it, in 24-point wedding type, the word REPENT. Writing on Kate Smith, he suggested that the singer posed a threat to the American way of life, observing in a one-line paragraph, "It is a very real danger." Although intended as humor, one can hear in it a note found in Don's later, mature voice. Don eventually perfected this device of ending a story with an observation, or even a surprising turn in the story, the effect of which was to create an unexpected tone, sometimes somber, even harsh, and at other times wonderfully lyrical.

Most of Don's close acquaintances would have agreed with Joe that even though he was only eighteen, he was already "fully formed, very precocious, but rare in that he was sort of born with a vision and a gift; like some people can play basketball, he had that unique ability to do it. Don did not have to work hard learning it; he worked hard at what he did." In the *Cougar* office, Don "pecked away, usually writing a little something against one of the University departments, just having a ball." Typing fast with two fingers, "he would just break himself up writing those things; he was a joy to be around." As he edited Don's copy that first year, Joe continually chuckled while marking it up.

Joe knew that Don was an avid reader of the *New Yorker* and had read the work of important American humorists, including E. B. White, S. J. Perelman, and James Thurber. He "would quote Dorothy Parker, always in an appropriate way, at the right moment when it fit." He remembered little lines from Robert Benchley and "that funny *New Yorker* writer, Perelman." Joe was "always angry at Don" because he wanted him to become the new Benchley or Perelman, both of whom were "getting kind of tired about that time." Instead, "Don became a Barthelme and there is nobody like him nor has there ever been."

Joe Maranto soon saw what he believed to be a contradiction in Don's personality and his ambition to write. Joe cautioned him that since he did not "really like people all that much," how could he become a great writer? Since "writers like Steinbeck and Hemingway always got into the characters of people," Joe said, he was unable to imagine the direction Don was going to take. Maranto was nevertheless among those who believed Don *would* become a great writer. Admitting that neither he nor anyone else could envision how Don would achieve this goal, he observed that, nevertheless, "Don got around the problem and astonished everybody."

At the university, Don studied creative writing with Ruth Pennybacker, the only writing professor he ever had. He wrote short stories and poetry for her classes and for the university literary anthology, *Harvest.* In "Shrunken Clocks for Small Hours," a poem published in the 1952 *Harvest,* Don looks back on his early undergraduate experience. Although he was clearly in control of what he wrote, the poem does not yet hint at the originality that was to come later:

> At once knowing and naive
> We came in diligence,
> Shining epigrams, coining
> Rich bits of paraphrase,
>
> Mining the fresh veins.
> . . . .
> And now, the clock has spun round
> Two years, and it is
>
> Later, our bright
> Triumphant promised never never
> Later.
> And—We crouch in our empty cups
> And wonder.

During the year following our first meeting, after receiving a bachelor's degree, I worked in public relations at the university, then left to start a career in corporate public relations. Within a short time, however, the university invited me to return as director of the information office, a position that I eagerly accepted. This was in January, 1951, Don was in his second year, and before long we had a chance to see each other more often.

At this point, I knew very little of Don's earlier life or of his family, only that he was the son of a prominent architect. But the staff I supervised included several journalism students, younger than I but more familiar with Don's background and family life. Later, of course, after I learned about Don's life and family, I could see the influences that contributed to his intellectual brilliance and the unique nature of his writing talent.

Don was born in Philadelphia, Pennsylvania, on April 7, 1931, the first child of Donald Barthelme, Sr., a native of Galveston, Texas, and Helen Bechtold Barthelme, a native of Philadelphia.[2] When they met, Don's parents were students at the University of Pennsylvania. He was studying architecture, and she was studying English and drama and preparing to be a teacher. She was tall, slender, and elegant, a lovely blonde with green eyes. Like her first son, she possessed exceptional wit, what Don, Jr., later called a "wicked wit." Donald, Sr., was strong-willed and outspoken, confident of his talent, and destined to be a rebel and architect of immense originality throughout his career. They had met when he came with a friend to Helen's sorority house for a blind date. When he and a fellow architectural student came into the foyer, Helen turned to her sorority sister and said that she hoped "the tall, dark, and handsome one" was her date. Instead, it was Donald Barthelme, "the short, red-headed one."

Donald, Sr., first studied architecture at Rice Institute, as Rice University was then known, where he also was the editor of and a writer for the *Thresher,* the student newspaper. He left Rice because of an editorial prank that occurred during his tenure as editor. When told that he was to be suspended for a year, Donald, Sr.'s indignant father came from Galveston to speak on his behalf, but he found the conservative administration of the Institute unyielding. Instead of waiting twelve months to continue his studies at Rice, Donald, Sr., applied to the University of Pennsylvania, was accepted, and completed his studies there.

At both Rice and Pennsylvania, Donald, Sr., studied traditional architecture, but independently he was attracted to and studied the work of the Bauhaus movement in Europe. He soon recognized that herein was the future. He also understood the significance of the work of Frank Lloyd Wright, such that in his own architecture the functional lines of the Modernist movement were enriched by the influence of Wright.

In June, 1930, despite growing economic uncertainties in the nation, the couple married soon after Donald, Sr.'s graduation from the University of Pennsylvania School of Architecture. They were both twenty-three years old. Helen, who lived in Philadelphia with her mother and sister, had graduated the previous year and, unable to find a job in teaching, worked for a short time in an office at Gimbel's Department Store. Her father had died when she was twelve, leaving a comfortable income for his wife and two daughters, but Helen wanted a career that would provide her own support. When Donald, Sr., and Helen met, she was interested in an acting career; she also made what she later described as an "abortive attempt" at creative writing. However, when she married, Helen gave up all plans for a career. Later, both she and Donald, Sr., would encourage the creativity of all five of their children, but she more than anyone else inspired each of them to excel in writing.

At first, Donald, Sr., was able to practice architecture with a firm in Philadelphia, and during that time he worked on the Department of Justice Building in Washington, D.C. However, before long, the deepening of the Great Depression made it impossible for a young architect to practice in Pennsylvania. At that point, Donald, Sr., accepted an offer from his father, John Barthelme, to join the family lumber business in Galveston. In December, 1932, the couple and their young son moved to Galveston, arriving there shortly before the birth of Don, Jr.'s only sister, Joan, on December 31, 1932.

The grandparents, natives of New York state, had moved to Galveston soon after their marriage in 1900 and were now a prominent family in the city. For the next few years, Donald, Sr., worked in his father's business, but he wanted to practice architecture, and as soon as possible he joined a firm in Houston. The younger Barthelmes then moved permanently to Houston, and Don, Jr., always thought of himself as a Texan.

In the early 1930s, Don and Joan were the only children, and they were together constantly. An attractive pair, Joan had blonde curls and Don was a smiling, friendly older brother. By this time, Don was known by the family only as Bo.

Don was three years old when his father left Galveston to join Staub and Rather, a prominent architectural firm in Houston. In Galveston, Donald, Sr., had opened an office to practice architecture but during that time designed only one home. After moving to Houston, he spent two years with Staub and Rather, during which time he worked on the Hall of State building for the Texas State Fair in Dallas and on a brief assignment in the small city of Big Spring. After that, he opened his own office in Houston and, both locally and internationally, he gained prominence for his innovative work. He not only brought Modernist theories in architecture to Houston but also developed theories of his own. He became renowned as a formidable professor of architecture as well, at both the University of Houston and Rice University.

The younger Don enjoyed a rare and privileged upbringing, and he sometimes alluded to it in his work. The world in which he lived was one of uncommon intellectual and cultural experiences, a world further enriched by the extraordinary humor and wit of his entire family—his mother, father, sister, and three brothers. It was an environment of music, literature, and art, along with modern and contemporary architecture and design—all of which would influence not only his lifestyle but his fiction as well. As his father had done in architecture, Don would later feel that he had to create "new" forms in literature, unlike anything that had been done before. And throughout his literary career, Don drew on the resources of this world.

In one of his first stories to appear in the *New Yorker,* "A Shower of Gold," Don provides through the persona of Peterson a brief but brilliant image of himself and of his childhood and youth. On a television show called "Who Am I?" Peterson concluded that "in this kind of a world . . . absurd if you will, possibilities nevertheless proliferate and escalate all around us and there are opportunities for beginning again." And then in conclusion, " 'My childhood was pastoral and energetic and rich in experiences which developed my character. As a young man I was noble in reason, infinite in faculty, in form express and admirable, and in apprehension . . . ' Peterson went on and on and although he was, in a sense, lying, in a sense he was not." [3]

Three other children were born in Houston. A second son, Peter, was born in 1938, a third son, Frederick, in 1943, and the fourth son, Steven, in 1947. In 1939, they moved to West Oaks, a small neighborhood "in the country" on the western outskirts of Houston. The elder Barthelme designed and built the home, a contemporary wood-and-glass structure, the wood later covered in copper. He then furnished it with the Modernist designs of Alvar Aalto, Eero Saarinen, and Charles Eames; shortly after Charles and Ray Eames designed their famous chair, Don's father purchased one in beautiful rosewood and leather.

Within a few years, the area was developed for several upper-income residential neighborhoods, but in the 1940s much of the land was still a prairie, and families often spent Sunday afternoon driving out to look at new neighborhoods and new homes. The design of the Barthelme house was novel enough that on weekends, people who came to see the house either drove by slowly or parked along the street to stare at the strange structure. Finally, one Sunday afternoon, the Barthelme children started what was to become a weekly entertainment for their drive-by visitors. When they saw cars stopping and their occupants peering at the house, they went outside and formed a chorus line, dancing across the lawn for their curious visitors.

The Barthelme house was at 11 N. Wynden Drive and was home to the Barthelme family until 1977, when encroaching office buildings and high-rise condominiums began to take over. The neighborhood was nestled in a secluded area off South Post Oak Lane and just across the street from the neighborhood in which George H. W. Bush would build his Houston residence after completing his presidency in 1993.

The Barthelme home was on a single level except for a second-story room with a circular stairway leading from the living area. Designed as a study, the room instead became a secluded and private domain for Don until he was grown; after that, in his turn, each brother moved into the second-story room.

When Don took over the upstairs, he used it as a retreat in which he could practice his drums. The beat reverberated throughout the house, however, so Don moved his drums to the family area that was originally intended as a garage. Then it was the neighbors' turn to complain, but they negotiated specific times during which Don could play. Don's family as well as his friends recognized Don's considerable musical talent, but he learned to play only the drums, which he finally gave up in the early 1950s. He sometimes wrote musical scores, but the only composition that anyone recalls is for a student variety show at the University of Houston in the 1950s.

As a teenager, Don and his high school friends attended concerts by such artists as Peck Kelly and Erskine Hawkins. He loved jazz, and in the years that followed, he seldom missed any chance to hear visiting musicians. One of his first articles for the *Houston Post* was on bebop, the music of his generation, evoking such names as Thelonius Monk and Dizzy Gillespie.

Don and his family were members of St. Anne's Church on Westheimer Road; they later became parishioners of nearby St. Michael's Church on Sage Road. Don stopped attending mass by the time he was a teenager, but rejecting the church was more difficult for him than he ever acknowledged.

During his ten years in parochial schools, Don was an excellent student, and he developed respect and admiration for aspects of the Catholic church. Even though he eventually rebelled, Don certainly respected the priesthood as well as the orders of teaching sisters. Through the eighth grade, Don and his sister Joan, who was two years behind Don in school, were pupils at St. Anne's Elementary School. After St. Anne's, Don attended St. Thomas Catholic High School for boys through his junior year. He then enrolled at Lamar High School for his senior year. Because it was closer to the Barthelme home than the Catholic school for girls, Joan, too, attended Lamar. But the younger sons attended only Catholic schools, and Steven was one of the first to graduate from Houston's new Jesuit school in the 1960s.

Sister Huberta Gallatin, who was principal of St. Anne's Elementary School while Don was there, doubled as a teacher during World War II; Don was in her seventh grade class in 1943. With "a room overcrowded with lively boys, very interesting characters from affluent neighborhoods," Sister Huberta knew that she was being challenged:

> In the fourth row toward the back or at least half way sat Donald. Never troublesome, I was aware that he was studying me when there was a little flare up of some kind. He would peer over his glasses at me with a wry little smile. I remember that because he never fit into the rank and the file, and he got my attention as unobtrusive as he was. Teachers enjoy bright students, the deep thinkers, who tend to surprise them. Don was certainly one of these.
>
> This was a student who loved to write, something special in my experience. Always I was eager to read his compositions. Looking back on it I am sure it was because there was originality and always an element of surprise. . . .
>
> This was during World War II or the beginning. Three of my brothers were in the thick of it, one in Australia, the younger two in Europe. One day my youngest brother in his early twenties came to visit me, on a furlough. There was no way I could take the day off to visit so I invited him to spend the day in the classroom with me. Those were the days when there were self-contained classrooms and one or two teachers taught all of the subjects. I put Jim in an empty desk right across from Don.
>
> We had had a State Fair in Houston and practically all of the students had attended on a day off for schools. On that day I thought what a neat subject for a composition "My Day at the Fair." As I look back I am sure I gave meager instructions but the class went to work. Don wrote a paragraph and handed it over to Jim. Now Jim was quite literary himself and was an avid reader. I cannot remember what Don wrote but Jim thought it hilarious and brought it to me. Don grinned and waited. When Jim returned it, Don continued to write and Jim waited eagerly. The two became

friends over the two days Jim was there. I recall he told the Sisters about his experience and remarked that he was amazed that a boy so young had such insights and was able to articulate them so well. . . . Every once in a while he [Don] would pen some philosophical observation, roll it up and when he passed my desk he would toss it to me. Dignified teacher that I was, I dared not read it until I was in the clear. I had to maintain discipline! I wish I had kept those tidbits because now I cannot remember the contents except that I was delighted with a sheer delight. I do remember how heartbroken I was to give up that class at the close of the semester.[4]

In spite of Don's rejection of Catholicism, the church was a significant influence on his life and on his writing. Much of the time, there is a pure idealism and a seriousness at the heart of Don's writing that is often obscured by the satire and parody in his stories. The world he saw around him, often reflected in his fiction, is frequently in contrast with Don's own commitment to life and to his idealistic belief in "possibility."

By the time he was in his junior year, Don had already developed such an implacable will that he was certain to encounter difficulties as a brilliant and forthright seventeen-year-old Catholic. The first disappointment came when, as a member of the staff of the St. Thomas *Eagle,* Don learned that he was to be denied his turn as editor of the newspaper. Don believed that the priests overseeing student publications thought he was too strong-willed for them to risk turning over the responsibility of the newspaper to him. And then in one of his classes at St. Thomas, his writing style and the originality of his work was such that the instructor, a priest, told him that he did not write his own papers, they were too well written, and Don must have plagiarized them.

Deeply wounded by these events, Don decided to run away and invited a fellow student, Herman F. "Pat" Goeters, a year older and then editor of the newspaper, to go with him. Pat had stopped by the newspaper office to pick up a column that Don was writing when Don abruptly suggested, "Let's go to Mexico." This was February of 1948, only two months before Don's seventeenth birthday and four months before Pat's scheduled graduation.

Although the two did not know each other well at this time, Pat liked the idea, and they left almost immediately. First, Don wanted to stop by his home to pick up something and to leave a note for his parents. The note read, "We've gone to Mexico to make our fortune." Then they departed with only thirty dollars between them, part of which they had to spend for clothing and miscellaneous supplies. From Houston, they caught a ride in a truck to San Antonio, where they spent the night at the YMCA, and then the next day hitchhiked to Mexico City. At the border in Laredo, while the driver took the car through the customs checkpoint, all of the car's passengers, including Don and Pat, walked across the bridge. The two boys later learned that the others in the group were smuggling copper.

In Mexico City, the family with whom they had traveled provided a temporary place for them to stay while they looked for jobs. They soon found employment in a jukebox factory, where they filed the slots in the American machines so they would accept Mexican coins.

Meanwhile, Don's father and grandfather set out from Houston to search for them. Because he thought Pat might plan to visit his father in Mexico City, Donald, Sr., immediately checked the border at Nuevo Laredo, where customs officials told him that the two had indeed given Mexico City as their destination. After that, Don's father and grandfather returned to San Antonio and then flew from there to Mexico City.

Once they arrived in the capital city, the elder Barthelmes sought out street photographers, who traditionally snapped pictures of all tourists; they hoped to learn if anyone had taken a picture of Don and Pat. After this effort failed, they registered at the Hotel Reforma and began to walk around looking for them. Finally, on a Saturday evening, more than a week after the young men left Houston, Don's father suggested that undoubtedly they would be downtown on a Saturday night. Within a short time, on Reforma Boulevard, they saw Pat and Don across the street. After a cheerful reunion, the four of them went back to the hotel to call Don's mother in Houston and then to have dinner.

Pat had met neither Don's father nor grandfather before this chance meeting on the street in Mexico City; uncertain who they were, he was nervous that Don "was willing to talk to these two older men and to go back to their hotel with them."[5] The next day, Pat and Don flew home with Don's father and grandfather.

In his story, "Overnight to Many Distant Cities," Don recounts this story, concluding, "After about a week of this we were walking one day on the street on which the Hotel Reforma is to be found and there were my father and grandfather, smiling. . . . I have rarely seen two grown men enjoying themselves so much."[6]

When he returned from Mexico, Don did not want to go back to St. Thomas High School, and it was then that his parents agreed that he could transfer to Lamar High School. Don was then enrolled in a public school for the first time. Attended by the children of Houston's affluent west-side families, Lamar was situated on Westheimer Road near the exclusive River Oaks neighborhood. At St. Thomas he had worked on the high school newspaper. Now, at Lamar, he was an editor and contributor for the school's literary magazine. That same year, he won the Poet Laureate of Texas award with a poem entitled "Inertia." And with a short story entitled "Integrity Cycle," Don placed fourth in a *Scholastic Magazine* contest.

Meanwhile, Pat Goeters returned to St. Thomas High School to complete the term and to graduate as planned in June, 1948. After their adventure in Mexico, Pat became Don's closest friend. Like Don, Pat planned to be a writer, but he thought Don would not be the one to succeed in writing because "he was not interested in serious writers and great ideas." Instead Don read "all the humorists, especially S. J. Perelman . . . the first writer Don imitated." [7]

In the spring of 1949, Don graduated from Lamar High School, and after an argument with his father, who would not give his approval, he became the drummer for a small band and went on a brief tour of engagements in southeast Texas. In September, against the wishes of his parents, who wanted him to go back East to continue his education, preferably to an Ivy League college, Don chose to enroll at the University of Houston. Just as he rejected the institution of the church and its authority, he seemed now to be unwilling to submit himself to the authority and discipline of a more traditional university. Even at the University of Houston, Don was never to be a conventional student.

IN HIS FIRST YEARS AT THE University of Houston, Don developed friendships that were to last throughout his life. Besides Joe Maranto, they included another journalism major, George Christian, and before long, Herman Gollob, who had been a fellow student at Lamar High School.

Herman was a little older than Don and had graduated from Texas A&M and gone to Korea as an air force officer. After his return, he enrolled in a graduate program in theater arts at the University of Houston; it was then that the two met again in a literature class on Restoration drama. They immediately became close friends, but neither knew that Herman would eventually be responsible for the publication of Don's first collection of stories, *Come Back, Dr. Caligari,* as well as his first novel, *Snow White.*

Even in high school, Gollob had been impressed by Don's sophistication; there was something "very Ivy League about him" with his "button-down oxford cloth shirts. He was exceptionally well read and expected of his friends the same quality of thought and conversation that he expected of himself." To Herman, he was "your intellectual conscience." [1]

Don was enrolled in the Restoration drama course for his degree program, but he liked neither the class nor the professor and would "revile" Herman for his enthusiasm, both in the classroom and in preparing for class. Herman found the professor to be a nice guy who told of his father's admiration for George Bernard Shaw and who had "his own little whimsical jokes." Don, however, had the utmost contempt for the professor and called Herman, who wrote his essays on time and turned all of his work in, a sycophant. Herman denied being sycophantic, telling Don that he "liked the guy" and just wanted to get good grades.

In another incident, Herman and Don were leaving the River Oaks Theatre on West Gray one day when Herman innocently observed that the cafeteria across the street had good apple pie. Don did not say a word but "froze" Herman with just a look, probably at what he thought was the banality of Herman's remark.

Although Don was well liked by his friends, his disapproval could be devastating. These friends, usually men, felt his displeasure in the form of Don's often sharp wit. But Gollob knew, as his other friends did, that such remarks from Don were never "meanspirited." In fact, they usually accepted and even laughed at Don's censure. "Unwilling to suffer fools" was how Gollob and others described him. Because Joe Maranto, Herman Gollob, George Christian, and other close friends understood Don and admired him, they did not feel rejected by Don's harsh judgments.

Don was even more intolerant of what he believed to be "phoniness"; he seemed to intuit it and to turn away from acquaintances he found "phony," even those he thought to be talented. Maggie Maranto, Joe's wife, felt that Don simply had "no patience whatsoever for anything that was not genuine; he saw through things very clearly." [2]

Actually, Don's arrogance was often tempered by kindness when he was talking to friends. As we became better acquainted, I found him to be singularly kind and sensitive, especially with someone he thought vulnerable. He remarked about a friend one day that it was "too bad that he had so much talent and was trapped in such an unattractive body."

Autocratic rather than arrogant is how I think of his manner at times, particularly in a relationship with a friend. During his first years at the University of Houston, Mary Blount, then a freshman journalism major and later a prominent author of children's books, was working in the *Cougar* office one day when Don walked in and abruptly suggested that they "take a walk." They walked over to the reflection pool in front of the Ezekiel Cullen Building and as they strolled around it, Don explained what he wanted.

Mary was then dating George Christian, but they were not yet engaged and she had accepted an invitation from another student to attend the senior prom. On behalf of George, Don told Mary "to call this fellow and cancel your date with him," assuring Mary that this was what George wanted. Mary laughed but willingly broke the date. Mary also recalls that while she and Don were walking around the reflection pool, they found a ten-dollar bill lying on the sidewalk and agreed to share it. Neither of them was working, but Don was living away from home and needed the money more than Mary, who lived at home, so they divided it, giving Mary two dollars and Don eight.

Not only was Don articulate and witty, but he had an open, friendly manner that was attractive. His demeanor, especially with women, was polite and attentive, a characteristic that he had throughout his life. He smiled often, was open and unpretentious, and had a forthright earnestness that sometimes surprised me. At that time, I don't think it occurred to him not to tell the truth or not to say what he thought, unless to do so meant to wound a friend or a colleague unnecessarily. And he was a good listener, whether you were a man or a woman, an appealing trait to women in the 1950s. Women were expected to defer to men, especially in discussing ideas, but one did not have to do this with Don.

A characteristic that I noticed early was that Don's public demeanor reflected an insistence upon privacy. With strangers, he often became remote, even aloof. Contrary to his manner in private life, he would discuss nothing personal nor would he answer questions that he felt were intrusive. This was especially true when he was with people for whom he did not care or about whom he felt indifference. He would withdraw into a polite silence or answer questions or comments in a formal, restrained manner.

Don's fiction a decade later would mirror these two aspects of his personality. He used wit, irony, absurd situations, and complex metaphors to create stories that were free of sentiment and from which he could separate himself. He was fully aware that his style enabled him to eliminate most emotion in his stories. But from the beginning, he often introduced a lyrical phrase, or comment or aside as if he were speaking out of his heart to those who knew him.

At the university, Don worked toward earning a bachelor's degree in liberal arts, studying literature, philosophy, and journalism along with creative writing. On his own, he read widely in psychology, sociology, and anthropology, but he was not interested in the rigorous academic study of these disciplines. There were a number of serious scholars on the faculty of the university, but Don found only a few that he could admire. Among these was Maurice Natanson, a member of the faculty of the Department of Philosophy from whom Don later took classes. I am not certain, however, that Don would have been satisfied with the faculty of any university, nor would he have been interested in the kind of scholarship essential to the academic world.

During this period, Pat Goeters also returned to Houston. He had gone off to study for the priesthood at the University of Toronto, but during his second year he decided against becoming a priest and returned to Houston. Before long, he enrolled at the University of Chicago, where he stayed for a year and then came back home and enrolled in architecture at the University of Houston.

Pat Goeters and Don continued to see each other during holidays and summers and then resumed their close friendship when Pat began studying architecture. Don's father by this time was with the faculty of architecture at the University of Houston, and he became Pat's professor and mentor. Before long, a father-and-son bond began to develop between them, a bond that may have had a subtle effect on Don's feelings toward Pat as well as toward his father.[3] The elder Barthelme frequently mentioned Pat's talent to Don, whereas he seemed to always withhold approval from his son. Don sought to achieve in his own work the kind of perfection that seemed to be his father's professional goal, yet he felt that his father always expected something more of him.

Since their first meeting at St. Thomas High School, Don and Pat were competitive and engaged in a competitive kind of writing game. Sometimes they even vied for the same girl, with Pat usually winning out. Pat was a handsome young man; he was slender, tall, and blonde, with a dry, laconic wit in contrast to Don's sharp, but usually more humorous wit. Joe Maranto, who met Pat through Don at the university, recalled that Goeters "would just cut you with a couple of words," but that the rivalry between the two was "always friendly."

During the year after our first meeting, I talked to Don occasionally, but it was not until I returned to the campus as director of the university news service that we became closer. The staff included several students in journalism, so when we needed a writer for fine arts copy, I asked Don if he would be interested. He accepted and started working on the first of March, 1951, covering fine arts at the university, including productions of the university's Attic Theatre.

Don was enthusiastic about writing on the theater and was usually exuberant, almost ebullient when he was in the office. His humor was a bit sharp at times, but his wit and intellect were hard to resist; even those with whom he was most severe were admirers. As he wrote his articles, Don was thoughtful and meticulous; he sometimes erased to make changes, but he often started over on a clean sheet of newsprint.

He continued to write his Bardley column for the *Cougar* as well, gaining recognition off campus as well as on campus. Several members of the daily press had by this time recognized his talent, so it was not surprising that within a few months his work was noticed by the *Houston Post,* and he was offered a position on their fine arts staff starting July 15, 1951. He was to join his friend George Christian, who was already with the *Post* and who had recommended Don to Hubert Roussel, the newspaper's editor of amusements and a notoriously demanding writer himself.

Thus Don was twenty years old when he became a full-fledged professional journalist writing film reviews and covering openings of new theatrical and musical productions. His work for the *Post* also included a weekly column called "Stage Business."

A perfectionist in his role as one of the country's reigning editors of fine arts, Roussel was an ideal instructor for Don, and he as well as George enjoyed the prestige of being on Hubert's staff. They both lived in fear of Roussel's caustic criticism of their work, however, and especially of the harsh buzzer—one buzz for George and two buzzes for Don—that would summon either of them to his office for some kind of dressing down.

When he was first shown his desk at the *Houston Post* and was told that it had belonged to O. Henry, who had actually worked at the *Post* at the turn of the century, Don recognized the story as a joke but wittily embellished it and frequently told of finding O. Henry's initials carved into the top. It was just one of the continuing jokes fostered by George and Don.

Another concerned Ambrose Bierce, whose name George introduced into a story one day; shortly afterward, Don mentioned Bierce in his column. Other colleagues followed, and finally, Joe Maranto, now a *Post* staffer whose assignments included a post exchange newsletter for the military in Korea, was about to leave for a new position at the *Houston Chronicle.* He signed the final edition of the newsletter, "Ambrose Bierce, Editor." Harry Johnson, who was city editor of the *Post* and later Atlanta bureau chief of *Time,* overlooked it with a chuckle. But at this point, Arthur Laroe, managing editor of *Post,* asked what "this Bierce business is about" and brought the joke to an end.

In describing the way Don worked on his articles for the *Post,* Joe said, "He always wanted to write tight, short sentences, except when he wanted to write a long one to impress you and he thought you'd know that's what he was doing."

Don also believed that no one else could improve his writing. One day, after Don first started his new job, he said to Maranto, "George is editing my copy." Roussel, as editor of fine arts, wrote a column covering some of Houston's major events, but George was responsible for editing most of the section. Because at that time Don had been at the newspaper just a few weeks, Joe pointed out that George had been there longer. Don, however, was certain of his own talent and said simply, "He should not be editing my copy."

The *Post* was a morning newspaper, which meant that the day was often starting to dawn as Don and George left work. They would tiredly stumble out of the building, thrusting their arms out to push back the first glow of the pink-and-orange sky coming up over the buildings of downtown Houston's eastern skyline, while shouting "back, back." But it was mostly joy that they were expressing; they knew they had enviable jobs covering the city's cultural events.

During this period at the *Post,* Don learned to hastily read critical studies and other works on the arts so that he would be knowledgeable in his reviews and critiques of whatever he was covering. It might be a performance by a pianist or a violinist, sometimes a theatrical production, or a new film. He and George shared a joke that "given forty-five minutes, they could master anything." This particular talent, what George later called the ability to "don a false face," was probably useful as Don began to read and "take in" the work of philosophers, poets, and scholars for his short stories. He could quickly find relevant chapters or passages and glean the text for salient information or even difficult philosophical ideas. Don's mastery of what he read is reflected throughout his work. For example, a reader of "Kierkegaard Unfair to Schlegel," a story that Don wrote in the early 1960s, needs to know something of Kierkegaard's work on irony and Friedrich von Schlegel's *Lucinde* to fully understand the story.

In working for the *Post*, Don saw and reviewed numerous motion pictures; from this experience, he developed a lasting interest in the creative aspects of the industry. He acquired a store of knowledge on the talents of individual directors and actors, on theories of acting, and on general film studio lore. Even in his early years, Don seems to have been a keen observer of everything that was happening around him, so it was natural for him to draw on this material later for his fiction. In fact, one of his first stories, "The Hiding Man," is filled with movie allusions and takes place in a motion picture theater.

When he enrolled at the University of Houston, Don was living at home, but after going to work for the *Post* he decided to move out and live on his own. He apparently had had a disagreement with his father that was serious enough for him to leave. So along with friends Joe Maranto, Pat Goeters, and Henry Buckley, Don rented a large old house on Leek Street near the university. It was just off Cullen Boulevard and not far from the Gulf Freeway.

The house was in such need of remodeling that Don and his friends decorated the entire house with newsprint. Don was sufficiently pleased with their handiwork that he invited his father to come by and see it. The only good piece of furniture that they possessed was an expensive Eames lounge chair that Buckley had purchased. They managed, nevertheless, with an assortment of miscellaneous furnishings as well as a hi-fi system and plenty of records.

Don did not own a car and frequently walked the two miles home from the *Post*. Since he was heading home in the early morning hours, no buses were running. Although it was an easy walk for Don, and in the early 1950s the area was not as fraught with violence as it is today, it was sometimes uncomfortable because the route took him through an older industrial district and the decaying east side of the inner city.

Joe was then engaged to another university student, Margarette (Maggie) Stubblefield, a former music major and then an art major at two other universities before transferring to the University of Houston, where she was now an English major. Because they were usually broke, Maggie each week prepared a large pot of vegetable soup or a big pan of spaghetti and sauce that the trio ate for several days. When Joe and Maggie were married, they moved to a nearby apartment, but Maggie continued to cook for the group. Just a couple of blocks away on Cullen Boulevard there was an all-night restaurant where, on his way home from the *Post,* Don stopped for blackbottom pie and grilled cheese sandwiches. Their student life milieu also included a 1950s drive-in situated just across the street from their house; food and drinks were served to students in their automobiles by pretty girls wearing short costumes, but the neighbors remember that music was piped out to the cars until late at night. Joe and Don and their friends especially liked the Johnny Ray records, as well Rosemary Clooney singing "Come on-a My House."

When Joe and Maggie were married, the others gave a wedding reception, and for a wedding gift, a molded Eames chair along with a bottle of champagne. The chair was regarded as special because, as Maggie explained to me later, they were all "totally impecunious, nobody had two pennies to rub together."

Before long, the house was demolished, and Don, with Henry Buckley and Pat Goeters, rented a large apartment on Cullen Boulevard.

DON HAD WORKED FOR THE *Post* for more than a year, when in September, 1952, he married Marilyn Marrs, a graduate of Rice University and a first cousin of George Christian. I had met Marilyn but knew little more than that she and Don were dating. After he joined the *Post,* I heard about Don occasionally from Mary Blount, who later married George, but I seldom saw him except at a play or musical event that Pete and I also attended. They were married only seven months when Don was drafted into the U.S. Army, and just before he left I saw him at a farewell party. This was in April of 1953, and within a few months he was sent to Korea.

He received basic training at Camp Polk, Louisiana, with Company M, 145th Infantry Regiment, 37th Infantry Division, known as the Buckeye Division. From Camp Polk, on April 6, he wrote to Maranto about life in the army:

> well boss it isn't such a good deal really the food in this place isn't fit even for the likes of me and there isn't enough of it to bloat a cockroach. . . .
>
> geeters [Goeters] is writing regularly and says he's disgusted with everything i maintain i could teach him a few things about disgust perhaps a few of the niceties i didn't make it home for easter as maybe you noticed a lieutenant [or] some other higher animal inspected the barracks and said everything was filthy you could have eaten off the floor actually had you anything to eat but he wore some special glasses with built-in dirt and the whole outfit was restricted but as they say here that's the way it goes a homily i am in no position to argue as it sure as hell went that way two guys from this company are awol right now and if they don't start feeding me and letting me have a little sleep say fifteen minutes every other day I might very well join them except for the fact that after this couple of years is up i'll never join anything again not even the w.c.t.u.
>
> bardley [1]

In June, 1953, Don completed basic training and, after spending his leave at home in Houston, departed on the first stage of his journey to Korea. From Houston, he traveled to the West Coast, where he spent about two weeks at Fort Lewis near Tacoma, Washington, waiting to cross the Pacific.[2]

While stationed at Fort Lewis, Don read, went climbing on Mount Rainier, and did very little work. Finally, as a member of the 2nd Replacement Company of the 2nd Infantry Division, he embarked on what he called "the grand cruise," expecting to arrive first in Japan, but instead arriving in Korea on the day the truce was signed, July 27, 1953.

Before arriving at his permanent assignment with the headquarters of the 2nd Infantry Division in Korea, Don was given several temporary assignments, including guard duty and setting up a tent city at Sasebo, Japan, and then more guard duty and painting latrines at Pusan. It was at Pusan as a perimeter guard that he first saw what he described as the "grimy hills of Korea." For a while, the army wanted to send him to a bakers' school; they did not know what else to do with him since there were no writing jobs available. Even by the late 1950s when we married, Don could still scarcely make a cup of coffee, so of course he enjoyed the irony of the army's notion. But finally, by insisting that his "weapon was a typewriter," Don got himself assigned to the public information office at division headquarters. He recalled this as lucky since there were twenty thousand men in the division and only eight men in the information office.

After a journey of more than eight thousand miles since leaving home, Don reached 2nd Division headquarters—just over the 38th parallel in North Korea—on a Sunday in late August, 1953. The life he described in Korea was one of comparative luxury; men in the PIO had no inspections, pulled no guard duty, made reveille "in an offhand way," and worked a seven-to-five day, except when there were night assignments. A Korean houseboy did the laundry, cleaned the weapons, and heated water for shaving in the mornings. And they had hot water for showers as well. The men kept two cases of beer in the office, another luxury even though the beer was warm.

Don's job entailed writing news releases for the division and working on the *Indianhead,* the division's authorized publication. He worked on radio and television scripts and even helped produce a thirty-minute script for a battalion battle problem. In October, he wrote to Joe that a television unit in Seoul "comes up here to the front and films things if we do the scripts. Needless to say, this is marvelous experience."

A few years later when he was telling me of Korea, he recalled his fellow staffers admiringly. They all had either a college or newspaper background, and several among them were scholars. He had written to

Maranto that the people in the office included "a Master from Columbia and a Master from Wisconsin, the latter with a degree in drama; also a Southern Cal type and a Kansas U. type, and one from Minnesota and one from Pitt. We're getting a new one from CCNY this morning; he's a lawyer and looks to be pretty much of a bomb." While writing this letter, the "new man" came into the office and began reading Don's letter over his shoulder. "I turned around without thinking and asked him if he always read other people's mail but he is expendable since I don't like him already anyhow," he added to his letter.

After discussing problems he thought their mutual friends were having at home, Don wrote, "I have difficulty in summoning the proper superficial tone for all of this; I'm not, of course, deliriously happy . . . feel that everything is going to pot, can't write worth a damn (tho well enough to show these people)."

On Thanksgiving eve, Don wrote to Joe and Maggie again. Maranto had sent copies of book reviews that he had written, and Don began his letter by commenting on them: "To pay your book reviews the highest compliment of which I am capable, they remind me of me. There is a certain intensity, plus a reaching for the word that is not merely the mot juste but also has a cluster of overtones; in fine, they are very, very good. As is my custom, I say not that they *seem* good to me, but flatly that they are good."

Feeling the lack of "good music" in Korea, Don wrote that "strangely enough the most consistent source of good serious music our Zenith can pick up is Radio Moscow, which sometimes gives us Tschaikowsky [*sic*], sometimes propaganda in English."

Don had been invited to a Thanksgiving party "at the Dutch CP— a whole gang of bigwigs are flying in from the Netherlands and there is a promise of much liquor." He also described the kinds of stories he wrote for the army, explaining that "we run into a lot of stories, better stories, that we can't write—had half-a-dozen of EM attempting to blow off their officers' heads in the last month. Despite sunny pictures being painted in Stateside publications, morale is lousy. In indoctrination classes they're asking us to report anybody who bitches about the army or expresses a desire to go home. . . . Remember 1984."

Then on December 29, he wrote to the Marantos and told them of the new books he had received and was reading. He mentioned Saul Bellow, Dylan Thomas, Ezra Pound, the *Partisan Review,* the *New York Times* and the *Herald Tribune* theater and book sections, the *New Yorker,* and *Theatre Arts.*

He also wrote that Francis Cardinal Spellman had "choppered in on

Christmas Day to say mass . . . along with the [chairman of the] Joint Chiefs of Staff Arthur Radford." That afternoon, someone produced a couple of bottles of "vin terrible from somewhere, and the Thais chipped in with a bottle of Mekhong, a whiskey that is peculiarly their own and tastes remotely like anti-freeze. Not that anti-freeze of whatever kind isn't welcome at the moment—it's been snowing (I had a WHITE CHRIST-MAS!)." The weather was then around 9 degrees and was expected to get down to 60 below zero in January and February.

In this letter, Don mentioned that he was "pedagogging two nights a week at the TI&E Education Center—English (on a very elementary level), about 15 students, $1.25 a hour. One of my students is an aged Negro M/Sgt. who hasn't been inside a classroom since 1930 and 5." This must have been Don's first teaching experience, something he enjoyed enormously. Later, when he was a guest lecturer for my classes at Dominican College, he was a splendid lecturer. Eventually, with the help of John Barth, he received teaching appointments at several major universities on the East Coast.

Don also told of progress on his novel: "THE GREAT AMERICAN NOVEL is moving forward steadily. Two chapters, about 12,000 words, have been written, and an addition[al] 1400-word beginning for Chapter the Third. It's hard work, especially as all I can tell about it right now is that certain portions are terribly bad."

About this time, he wrote to his father that he had seen *From Here to Eternity,* and although "they emasculated half the characters," the film "nevertheless had some wonderful moments." He goes on to tell the senior Barthelme of the "multi-million luxury hotel S. Rhee is building in Seoul with American gold." Don knew one of the architects, "who is not really an architect at all but an artist who used to design sets for the 'Kukla, Fran and Ollie' TV show and is a PFC belonging to our 9th Regiment." The "main architect is equally not a real architect but some kind of a bastard designer who went to MIT and parades around in Seoul looking weirdly out of place in Ivy League uniform." Don described the product of their labors as a "14-story Babel in which the interiors are all very chichi in . . . what they fondly believe to be the modern manner. They are being very arty about the whole thing and that's quite a trick because it's almost impossible to be arty in Seoul since the city is all bombed-out ruins and poverty."

In January, he wrote that he was now a corporal and that he had finished the first draft of the fifth chapter: "When the sixth is done I will go back and make drastic revisions on it and the preceding chapters, which will comprise the first half of the book and run to about 36,000 words. It's a very peculiar book to date; it keeps changing its form."

In writing to his parents about his novel, Don told them that it was not a "deeply disturbing novel of the south, or a persecuted artist-type thing, or the record of somebody's miserabboble [*sic*] adolescence." It was a love story, but "more accurately, an unlove story, like the unbirthdays in Disney's 'Alice in Wonderland.'"

At this point, Don clearly did not identify with the literary styles and genres that were prominent in the late 1940s and early 1950s, especially that of the Regionalists as well as the fashionable style of pessimism and suffering. Don thought of Faulkner as a genius, and he admired the work of Carson McCullers and other major writers of the South, but he was never interested in the "gothic" or in writing about the "historical past."

In his letters, Don usually gave some news of what was happening in Korea. In December he had written that Syngman Rhee had been "down for a small fiesta" on Monday and that "Vice-President Nixon visits us tomorrow." In January, 1954, he wrote,

> They're exchanging the 22,000 POWs right now, as you have probably read, and as a consequence we're having a series of alerts and false alarms all along the front.
>
> I spent yesterday afternoon in a foxhole on a hill, steel helmet on my headbone and all. Tremendous anti-climax. Nothing happened.

Within a few months, he was much further along on his novel. He wrote to Joe,

> No I am not satisfied with it, not by a couple of miles, but I have seven and a half long chapters on paper now and am nearing 50,000 words and that's more words than I've ever laid end to end before in my life on one subject. I fear it is a terribly bad novel but hope to do a rewrite that will correct the most glaring faults. I haven't tried to write the thing paragraph by polished paragraph, and make each paragraph a jewel as I tried to do with the pieces for the *Post*. I would never have gotten more than a few gilded pages on paper if I had.
>
> As it stands the thing has a million rough edges and I will never get all of them smoothed out but perhaps it's better that way.

When Don returned home from Korea, he did not ask any of his close friends to read the novel he had written. And although he later talked about his previous attempt to write a satisfactory novel, he was not working on it when we married in 1956 and has left no record of it. Nevertheless, Don's departure from conventional fiction in this early effort in 1953 and 1954 is suggested by his description of it as an "unlove story."

Don also told Joe that he had purchased a lot of paperbound books during a trip to Tokyo, including George Orwell's *Down and Out in Paris and London,* Andre Gide's *Strait Is the Gate,* Sergei Eisenstein's *The Film Sense,* Albert Camus's *La peste,* and "the Hortense Powdermaker study of Hollywood," as well as "a lot of stuff by the various Sitwell's, including the *Canticle of the Rose.*" In Tokyo, he also saw *The Robe* and *The Moon Is Blue.*

In this letter, he mentions Goeters, who had returned home from the University of Chicago and was now enrolled in architecture at the University of Houston. Don wrote that "Goeters is still writing the obscurantist prose he was writing when I left. I am pervertedly happy that such things remain constant." And then on April 22, 1954: "The first draft of the novel is finished and I have launched a radical campaign of revision. It is a new attack which could conceiveably [*sic*] erase the major difficulties. It will in any case likely go into a third draft. Right now it's just under 50,000 words, and that's kind of slight for what I want."

Finally, on September 28, Don wrote, "The current novel is better than anything I've ever done but not finished and I can't get a typewriter after hours to nurse it on here and so will have to wait until I get home. I don't think I'll want to publish it when it's finished, but I do want to finish it and see how it comes out. It's been tremendously good exercise and has taught me much."

During his service in Korea, Don traveled to Japan several times, the first time to the headquarters of *Stars and Stripes* in Tokyo to study their operation for two weeks. He marveled at the "old line Japanese" architecture, especially the Imperial Hotel, which he admired "more than any other building" he saw there. Once he traveled there with Sutchai Thangpew, a friend from the Thai Royal Battalion; together they saw the ballet and the kabuki, as well as the national theater. Sutchai was an army lieutenant who had gone to Tokyo in connection with publishing his battalion's history. He was nearing the end of his Korean assignment and would soon leave for Bangkok, where he was to marry his twenty-year-old fiancee, Kalaya.

One of the experiences that Don later used in stories was his friendship with Sutchai. The Thai Royal Battalion was attached to the American division and was made up of about one thousand of Thailand's elite men, including a prince named Chitancok Gridakorn. They were renowned for their skills with the bayonet. Don's friend, who was taller than his fellow Thais, expected to play an important role in Thai politics and hoped to become prime minister of Thailand. Don described him as gentle and intelligent and thought of him as a close friend. Although Don sent Sutchai and his bride a wedding present and later talked to me of going to visit them, as far as I know, Don did not hear what happened to Sutchai. For years, he watched the news hoping to hear of his election to a prominent office.

Although he tried to put aside the past of his own life, Don's stories often reveal his inability do so. In "Thailand," Don provides a glimpse of his experience in what he called the "Krian War"; he created two perspectives of his own life: an old sergeant recalling the war and a younger soldier who is bored with the sergeant and his memories. The sergeant tells of Sutchai and his ambition to be prime minister of Thailand. After describing a Thai feast day and thirty-seven wastubs full of curry that included the "delicate Thai worm," the older sergeant has the last word when the tells the younger man that "they don't really have worm curry. . . . I just made that up to fool you."[3]

During one of Don's trips to Tokyo, an earthquake occurred in the middle of the night. He was at a hotel with a Japanese girl when this happened, and, as Don described the experience later, her skin "turned white" from terror when the tremors began. Spending the night with the girl posed a moral dilemma for Don as well as for a fellow soldier who had made the trip with him. They discussed whether when you were married but forcibly separated like this, it was immoral to be with another woman. It was a dilemma that Don seemed not to have resolved when he told me the story a few years later. In "Visitors," a story published in the *New Yorker* in 1981, Don used the experience with the Japanese girl, but although he embellished the story by extending the relationship, he did not introduce the moral aspect of his experience.

Just four months before the end of his tour in Korea, Don considered applying for duty with the U.S. Military Advisory Group in Thailand. Hanoi was about to fall and the Americans were getting more involved in southeast Asia, doubling the size of the advisory group. Through his friendship with Sutchai, Don had developed a special interest in the country and its people. However, he finally decided against applying and instead continued his plans for a career in journalism.

Even though the everyday problems of working in the PIO had become a burden, Don had decided that he would be a journalist "for better or worse, all my life." He said he could not "imagine anything better." Even though he had at times been disenchanted with wire service reporters, he was now enthusiastic. In addition to reporting on the top military figures who came to Korea, he covered the visits of such people as Cardinal Spellman and Marilyn Monroe. In March, 1954, in a letter to Maranto, he described Marilyn Monroe's visit: "Just before the show I was backstage and the door to her dressing room was open. . . . we watched her warming up for the show, complete with bumps & grinds and wiggles in tune to the music being played on the stage, and she was winking & blinking at us and smiling a more or less girlish smile and in fine giving the damnedest preshow show you've ever seen."

Throughout the months in Korea, Don planned his future. He had met "television people, AP & UP people, stage people, political scientists and chemists and militarists and every other kind of people except female people." He said that he was "even being swayed away from theatre criticism to straight news" and talked about working as a wire service correspondent outside the United States. Shortly afterward, he wrote home and explained that he was still aiming at "literature" and that nothing else would do. He explained that since he could not live off "literature," he was planning a newspaper career.

About three months before Don was to leave Korea, he became more and more anxious as he waited for an early release. Although he later talked of friends and experiences in Korea with considerable pleasure, he was becoming increasingly cynical about some of what he observed during the last days of his tour. He described VIP visits, especially those of congressmen, as a farce, as a tour of the Far East with "two weeks of living it up with the brass in Tokyo," then several days of wining and dining in Seoul. The tour of the front "averaged ten minutes on line," and the national commander of the Veterans of Foreign Wars "was clocked at seven minutes." As he described these events, Don was feeling extremely left out of events at home. Goeters was marrying a friend of Marilyn's, and he would not be there. However, he had applied for an early discharge based on his return to college and was now counting the final days.

Don was then working on the farewell edition of the division newspaper, the *Indianhead,* for which he did what he called "jumping designs"— sixteen pages of radical layouts that had everybody "either scared to death" or convinced that he'd "gone ape." When he wrote home about it, he recalled that although some of the layouts were not quite what he wanted, the overall design "shook up the printers" at *Stars and Stripes,* since they "think in terms of straight newspaper makeup." He had to fight with "everybody in sight all the way." Don said the editor, who was young and outranked by Don, went through what was probably "the most nerve shattering experience he ever had." Don had to do a good job against the editor's will, which was made more difficult because Don was supposed to be a consultant, not the publisher charged with doing the overall makeup of the newspaper. Rather than "pull rank," Don "just browbeat the poor devil to the point of madness." Don told of having had rank pulled on him once by a lieutenant who didn't like the lead on a story that Don had written, but Don would not change it until the lieutenant finally gave a direct order.

All this furor about the design of the final edition was caused by design innovations that are familiar today. Don's experimental layout of the *Indianhead* had headlines across the middle of the page, with stories and photographs displayed for visual effect. Throughout his editing and writing career, Don continued to experiment with the visual content of his work, but more important, this episode early in his career gives an insight into Don's strong will and the role it played in enabling him to achieve what he did in the brief period between 1956 and 1964.

This final Korean edition of the *Indianhead,* volume 2, number 22, was published on September 12, 1954. The newspaper tells the story of the 2nd Infantry Division in Korea, beginning with the division's arrival in 1950. In a series of narratives written by staff members, the newspaper recounts highlights of the four years, concluding with an account of a farewell review, in which almost six thousand men marched, on the morning of August 28. Don was not only layout editor for this edition; he also wrote an article on what was happening in the trenches of the 38th Regiment during the last minutes before firing was to stop at the 38th Parallel on July 27, 1953.

Because he had arrived in Korea after the cease of hostilities, it was necessary for Don to ask other soldiers what it was like in those final moments when long months of shooting were to end abruptly for both sides. The story, signed "SFC Don Barthelme," appears on page seven of this final edition, and the scene he created is touchingly realistic:

> At 2200 hours, men of the division were told, the ceasefire was to go into effect.
> After that time, they were instructed not to fire unless attacked.
> The Communists opposite the 38th Regt's sector wanted to slug it out until the final bell. Round after round came into the 38th trenches. This fire was returned.

At 2154 hours, regiment ordered all shooting stopped.

At 2200, despite many warnings, men dashed from their bunks, shed their flak jackets, and stood in little groups on the edge of a no-man's land that was suddenly safe.

On the opposite side of the line, the Chinese poured out of their bunkers and caves by the hundreds. They waved and shouted unintelligible English words and phrases. Many wore peculiar dead-white garments. Many sat out in the open and began to eat.

Men got the feeling that something, or a part of something, was finished.

KATUSAs began singing quietly among themselves.

Although Don's original assignment in Korea ended in the fall of 1954 when part of the 2nd Infantry Division sailed from Korea, he was among those in the division who were reassigned to the Public Information Office of the Eighth Army in Seoul in late September. Don had become acquainted with the staff of *Stars and Stripes* in Tokyo and had expected an assignment there, but at the last moment it was decided that there was too little time left in his tour, which was to end in December. During one of his visits to Tokyo in connection with his work on the division newspaper, he had been elated to find the names of enlisted men Harold Ross and Alexander Woollcott on the masthead of the 1918 Paris edition of the army newspaper, with Woollcott listed as a sergeant and Ross as a buck private. Ross became the legendary editor of the *New Yorker,* and Woollcott—who served as the model for *The Man Who Came to Dinner*—was already drama critic for the *New York Times.* Don was in awe of the possibility of working for *Stars and Stripes* as Ross and Woollcott had and was disappointed when he was assigned to Seoul instead. However, he later assigned one of his characters, Bishop, to the copy desk of *Stars and Stripes* in his story "Visitors."

In December, 1954, Don finally returned to the states for early release on reserve status and was back home in time for Christmas. But it was not until 1961 that he received a full discharge from the U.S. Army.

During the eighteen months that Don was in the army, his reading list was impressive. He mentioned American and British authors, apparently more European literature than before, and numerous studies in literary criticism. For his twenty-third birthday on April 7, 1954, he requested a copy of Erich Auerbach's *Mimesis.* He also read Bellow's *The Adventures of Augie March,* Mark Twain's *Life on the Mississippi,* plays by Bernard Shaw, Oscar Wilde's *The Picture of Dorian Gray,* collections of

Shakespeare's plays, Henry Steele Commager's *America in Perspective,* Will Durant's *The Story of Philosophy,* Suzanne Langer's *Philosophy in a New Key,* a work on Socrates, a life of Ralph Waldo Emerson, and novels by Andre Gide, Stendhal, Alberto Moravia, Aldous Huxley, Evelyn Waugh, and William Faulkner. And he read numerous anthologies and collections of short stories, poetry, and essays as well.

Don wrote to his mother that he had read Truman Capote's *Grass Harp* and that he "found it wanting Capote's earlier magic." Envisioning theater and film criticism as the field to which he would return, Don read Eisenstein on the cinema, Max Beerbohm's theater criticism, a work by Mark van Doren, several other scholars, including G. Wilson Knight and G. B. Harrison on Shakespeare, major works on the theater, and a number of modern plays by Karel Capek, Gerhart Hauptmann, August Strindberg, Jean Cocteau, and Luigi Chiarelli. Many of the books that he read were sent by his wife Marilyn, who also sent, among others, Lionel Trilling's *The Liberal Imagination* and Edmund Wilson's *To the Finland Station.* Don also studied French and read many of the French novelists and poets, some for the first time.

In March, he had written to Maranto about job prospects and was hoping to hear of a new publication in Houston. In April, he again asked for information from Joe. He did not want to return to the *Houston Post;* Marilyn had received an appointment as a teaching assistant at Rice Institute and he did not want to work nights with his wife teaching school during the day. Don wanted to know if there were "any rumors of new newspaper or mag ventures that sound remunerative?"

He said that he had in mind "the old business of starting a weekly mag a la Harold Ross." He then suggested the possibility of something like the *Allied Arts Review* but finally concluded, "I am still dreaming this old dream but sans any quality of hope; it can only be created in despair."

In June, after hearing that Maranto was thinking of leaving the *Houston Chronicle* to work for an advertising agency, Don wrote in a tone of despair that Joe frightened him "with this ad agency lick. . . . Your present lick is no good either but at least it's better than the cess pool." After all kinds of suggestions, he concluded, "THE OTHER THING IS DISASTER."

Don was interested in advertising as a phenomenon, especially the mythology that was created through graphics. He wrote to his mother that he had noted in a "late *New Yorker* that the Man in the Hathaway Shirt, surely one of the more profound figures in the new American mythology, is carrying an oboe these days." Later, although Don's attitude toward advertising as a career softened, his interest in it was largely as an observer.

It became part of the surface of American life that he put into his stories.

In this letter to Joe, Don also sounded despondent about his own situation, that he was suffering a "mammoth inferiority thing" from not having a good education and from losing something by being in the army:

> Whatever you can say about the army you can't say that it doesn't take something away from you. . . . It will take me six months to get back in shape at least. Maybe something is permanently gone. I don't know. I'm afraid to look. Perhaps the army has given me something too but if it has I don't know what it is, except that it has kept me earthy and close to the soil all right.
>
> But is that a virtue? I almost said here in cold b&w that 'only time will tell.' You see what I mean. I'm damn near done for. I think perhaps a high opinion of yourself and your talents is a condition of the kind of writing I used to do. . . . probably something that I'll never do again. You see from all this that I'm desperately conscious of my inadequacies. Novel begun as a defense against this, among other things. I just threw the first two chapters of the draft away, by the way, and am trying to concentrate on the refurbishing of the rest. I have no juice, no fire. Banality. I think I told you *Stars and Stripes* in Tokyo offered me a job and that an obscenity of a first john here wouldn't let me go. Even in the two weeks there I came to life as I never have here.

Don ended the letter with an admonishment to Joe about leaving his newspaper job to work in advertising: "DO NOTHING TILL YOU HEAR FROM ME."

Maranto did not reply to this letter, and finally Don wrote to him again on September 28 to tell him that his division had gone home but he was still there, "resettled in a relatively plush berth with the Korea Civil Assistance Command, which administers the flow of US aid to Korea, as an information specialist. . . . I will be here for another 60 days and then I will come HOME."

In this letter, Don outlined his plans for "finishing up at the so-called University." He explained that Marilyn, whom he called Maggie, would need to stay at Rice for two years before going somewhere else. He said that after the fall semester of 1955, he would

> consolidate my gains and head for Stanford, an MA and a job with the *San Francisco Examiner* or *Chronicle,* which is my next objective, newspaper-wise. The plan is to spend two years in that area

and then whip off to the Yale Drama School for two more years, say, and a Boston or Philadelphia paper, at which time I'll be ready to take a crack at NEW YORK. This is my five year plan, anyhow, at the finish of which I hope to have an MA in English and a lot of related work in drama and the cinema (perhaps a year at the CCNY Film Institute could be worked in, or at the Southern Cal equivalent), and nine years' experience in journalism. The latter would break down as two years on the *Post* pre army, two years in army writing jobs, another year on the *Post* or some allied job in Houston, two years on a Bay area paper and two years on a Boston or Philly paper.

This master plan is of course subject to being screwed up by a number of things: recall into the army, for one, a third world war, the fall of the H bomb, divorce, anything. But it has a lovely sound and it is one of these lines that I'll be working. All this time, incidentally, I would concurrently be working in fiction, like Glenn Miller in that awful picture, searching for a cool sound.

Now that he was ready to return home, Don once again asked for information on job opportunities in Houston other than with the *Post*. But he was back in Texas before he learned that the only position available was the very same job he had had at the *Post*.

In January of 1955, after taking a brief holiday following his return from Korea, Don went back to covering fine arts for the *Houston Post*. There is little doubt that in Korea Don had had one of the most intense experiences of his life. Not only had he encountered cultures other than his own but also, for the first time, he met and shared experiences with colleagues who were intellectually challenging to him. And the concentrated reading that he did while in Korea, in drama and in literature, unquestionably enriched his writing after he returned home.

Don's reviews and critiques now revealed the satirical style of the teenage Bardley giving way to a more mature wit and intellect. Allusions to other productions of a play or to earlier examples of an actor's work served to further strengthen his belief in his own critical acumen.

Soon after Don's return from Korea, I began running into him at arts events that he was covering or sometimes at a friend's party. In 1951, shortly before Don had originally joined the *Houston Post,* I had married Pete, also a student at the university and now on the staff of the *Houston Chronicle*. We were always together when I saw Don, although Don's wife Marilyn was never there.

Don had also enrolled for classes in the spring semester, and before long he began dropping by my office at the university to talk. It had been less than two years since he departed for the army, but I began to realize he was an attractive man, not just the brilliant student I first met in the fall of 1949. He not only looked older, but his demeanor was also more somber in 1955.

We frequently had coffee together in the Cougar Den snack bar, and one afternoon in the spring of 1955, a friend stopped at our table and asked to join us. He was a professor of psychology and had recently established a reading clinic, an event that merited news coverage through my office. I could see that Don was annoyed at what he saw as an intrusion; when I introduced them, the professor remarked in a friendly tone that he and I were friends as I handled "public relations" for him. I saw then for the first time, the more somber, less tolerant Don, as he replied with restrained anger, "Yes, there are apparently a great number of people who think that." He was both protective and indignant.

I continued to see Don during the spring and early summer, and then one afternoon in July he came by in a serious, thoughtful mood. He explained that he was searching for a daytime job so that he could leave the *Houston Post* and asked if he might join our staff in a full-time professional position. As a reviewer, he was still working late each evening, until after midnight, a schedule that had not changed.

He later told me that he thought working during the day might help him to save his marriage. Don did not, however, give any indication that day that he and his wife were having difficulties with their marriage; only later did I learn that he believed Marilyn no longer wanted to be married.

In asking about a job at the university, Don was unaware that just a few days earlier I had informed the president that I was leaving to accept my first position in advertising. I explained this situation to Don and urged him to talk to Farris Block, a former newspaper journalist who was already on the staff and had just been appointed to take my place. Don said he was not interested in working for anyone else at the university and did not want to pursue the job further. I was certain that he and Farris would respect each other and could become friends, but Don was hesitant and said he would think about it. Soon after that, however, they met and talked, and Farris offered him a position that he accepted.

Don undertook his new job in public relations in the fall of 1955, a position that enabled him to immediately propose the founding of *Forum*, a literary and scholarly journal. Though I was unaware at that time of its significance for Don, I knew that he had imagined a literary magazine of his own. I soon found, in fact, that editing such a journal often seemed as important to him as writing fiction. And it was characteristic of Don that he began campaigning for *Forum* within the first few weeks of joining the university staff.

In spite of Don's change from the *Houston Post* to the university with its conventional daytime hours, within a few months he and Maggie had separated and Don had moved into another Victorian-style home with Herman Gollob and two other friends, Henry Buckley and Maurice Sumner. Both Buckley and Sumner were graduates of the University of Houston's School of Architecture and now worked for architectural firms.

Gollob, who was taking classes at the university, remembers the house as a "big old, two-story Victorian place that had a boarded up door to the attic we were too scared to unboard." Situated on Burlington Street in a beautiful early 1900s neighborhood west of Main Street and near Hawthorne Street, the house had been neglected and was now somewhat dilapidated. Gollob recalls that he and the others "fantasized all these horrible things that were up in that attic, and finally made a pact that no one could leave anybody else in the house alone. It was terrifying." Gollob described this experience with the boarded attic as symbolic of Don and his work, what he called "the ultimate Barthelme story . . . funny, but dark and unknown too."

Furniture for the entire house consisted of three chairs and four cots or single beds and four hi-fi sets. They each had record collection consisting of symphonic and jazz music. Later, when the Southwest Freeway was extended into the midtown area, this home along with others on the east side of the street were demolished. No one knows if the doorway to the attic was ever unboarded.

Don and his friends listened to jazz groups whenever they had the chance. Gollob credited Don with educating him in jazz. "We heard any group that came to Houston," Gollob said. "One evening Don, Buckley, and I heard Dave Brubeck at the City Auditorium. The Catalina Lounge was a popular spot for listening to groups. We heard Sonny Marx, Danny Becker, and Herbie Brochstein there." And Gollob remembers Don's frequent discussions of movies: "He would recall special scenes. . . . 'The Man with the Golden Arm' was one of his favorites."

Around the first of February, 1956, Herman left for California to study in a fine arts program affiliated with the Pasadena Playhouse. Don and the others stayed in the Burlington house a few months longer, and this is where he was living when I separated from my husband and moved into an apartment on Harold Street just blocks away.

In the late summer of 1955, just before Don began working at the University of Houston, I had started what was to become a long career in advertising. At that time, I was feeling hopeless about my marriage to Pete, whom I had married in 1951 at the Palmer Memorial Episcopal Church when we were both twenty-three years old.

Pete was a talented journalist who joined the *Houston Chronicle* just after graduation and was now experienced in both reporting and editing for the newspaper. The *Chronicle* was an afternoon newspaper at that time and had a series of early deadlines, a schedule that put intense pressure on the staff throughout the morning and lunch hours. Pete soon grew accustomed to a routine in which he joined his friends for drinks just after the final deadline. Now, however, four years after our marriage, I could see that he was in danger of becoming an alcoholic.

In the 1950s, alcoholism was assumed to be the individual's problem; although Alcoholics Anonymous had a chapter in Houston, it was necessary for Pete or someone else to recognize that his drinking was a problem.

Few people were willing to do so at that time, and even friends assumed that the individual should be strong enough to drink moderately. Pete's doctor was sympathetic but offered no advice. But Pete was the son of affluent parents who married in the 1920s; when he was just three or four years old they took him to clubs and speakeasies where they sometimes let him drink from their glasses on the table. Such behavior was reckless and careless—and undoubtedly affected Pete—but no one understood this.

I felt quite alone in my marriage, and communication between us was now impossible; finally, in early 1956, I decided there was nothing further to do. My husband had gone with other journalists to a national meeting of Sigma Delta Chi, a newspaper fraternity, and when he returned, I told him that I was planning to leave as soon as possible. A few days later, I moved into an apartment with Betty Jane Mitchell, a young woman advertising executive who worked for Boone and Cummings, the agency that I had joined after leaving the university.

Not long after this, in March of 1956, Don and I were among the guests at a dinner party given by a couple we knew from the University of Houston. Shortly after dinner, as we talked in small groups, I was alone with Don when he abruptly asked about my husband and our marriage. He had heard about our separation and asked if I thought there was any hope for my future with Pete. I told him there was nothing left for me to do to save my marriage, that it was too late—I wanted only to be free. With scarcely a pause in our conversation, Don startled me by asking if I would marry him in the event I should get a divorce.

He was quite serious. At that moment, I had not the least doubt about his seriousness. And I knew that he and Marilyn were separated, but I was not at all prepared for such a proposal. I could only reply lightly that I felt he was too young for me—as in fact I did. Then addressing me as "old girl" for the remainder of the evening, Don insisted that he was serious and set about to persuade me that he was indeed as mature as I.

The next morning, just after I had arrived at my office, Don telephoned from the university and invited me to dinner that night. I accepted, and we were soon seeing each other almost every day. Although I was aware of Don's attraction to me, I never imagined falling in love with him. I truly believed he was too young. I had not yet made a decision about my marriage even though I had been distraught over it for a long time. This was the 1950s, and divorce was a difficult alternative to an unhappy marriage. At the same time, I had made a big career change the previous year and until that week would not have taken seriously the possibility of leaving one marriage and beginning another.

For the next seven months, Don and I saw each other almost every day, usually in the evening when we had dinner at a romantic and often expensive restaurant. Sometimes we had dinner at my apartment, or occasionally, we spent an evening with friends. Among them were Buckley and Sumner, as well as Lillian Crittenden, a friend and colleague from the university. My sister Margo Vandruff and her husband Roy invited us to an afternoon party. Joe and Maggie Maranto invited us to dinner. And occasionally we saw George Christian and Mary Blount; they were now both on the staff of the *Houston Post* and were planning to be married on September 22 with Don as the best man. Evenings with these friends consisted mostly of conversation about books, movies, and plays. These gatherings were far more interesting than the lavish social events that were popular with many of the journalists. Perhaps as important as anything else, no one was particularly interested in talking about sports, a godsend that I perhaps irrationally cherished.

On weekends, we saw a film or sometimes a play. And several times that summer, we heard the Houston Symphony in an outdoor concert at Miller Theatre in Hermann Park in the museum district. The beautiful wooded park provided an ideal setting for symphony concerts and plays. At other times, we took drives in Don's Austin-Healey sports convertible or long walks in our neighborhood. The streets were wide with sidewalks, there were many trees, and most of the houses were surrounded by well-kept gardens and lawns. In the late evening, there was very little automobile traffic and few other people were out walking. Even though street lamps provided very little light, we always felt secure.

The apartment that I shared with Betty Jane Mitchell was on Harold Street not far from Don's house on Burlington and was in the same area in which Don and I lived after our marriage. It was in a large home that had been converted to flats, and there was a swimming pool that we shared with two other tenants. One evening, Don and I invited friends from the news service at the University of Houston to a swimming party that lasted most of the night.

But such occasions were rare; more often, we sat on the terrace by the pool and talked about our lives and our future. Don told me of his experiences in Korea and Japan and that he hoped to return to Japan. We always discussed the university; Don had begun to create the first issue of *Forum* and was searching the country for contributors. Financing the magazine seemed an almost insurmountable task, but Don approached the entire endeavor as a challenge. He was excited and happy about it.

Throughout the spring and early summer, neither of us was absolutely certain of the future. I agreed once to a reconciliation with Pete, but after just a few days, I gave up and made no further effort. Don then told me that what he had done from the beginning of our courtship was to "imagine the worst possible thing that could happen," which was that I would return to my husband, and he had for this reason been able to endure the uncertainty of our future. "Imagining the worst" was what he continued to do all his life.

On a brilliant night in August, as we sat on the terrace where I lived, Don suggested that we set a date for our marriage. Neither of our divorces had yet been granted, but we chose October 12. In September, Don became concerned that his wife would postpone the divorce; she had received a Fulbright Fellowship to study abroad and suggested to Don that they wait a year for the divorce—until her return from France. He was afraid at first that she would insist upon the delay; however, Marilyn agreed to the divorce, and it was granted.

And then on Monday, October 5, my divorce from Pete Gilpin was granted, and Don and I went ahead with our wedding on Friday, October 12.

Don talked of the kind of life that he thought we could have together. He really wanted nothing less than an ideal relationship. I was startled one day when he said that we "should have met and married when we were nineteen . . . we missed a lot by not having those years together." When I think of this conversation all these years later, I continue to be astonished by the perfection that he desired.

I knew that Don would have liked to erase our earlier marriages, especially mine. He wanted to recover the past, what he thought of as our "innocent" years, whereas I felt no loss and was happy with the possibilities for our future.

Don told me that he felt some envy of my marriage to Pete, that we had seemed very happy. This was during the brief period in which Don first worked for the university's news service, just before he joined the staff of the *Post*, but he still had a vivid memory of it. He described how his friends Georgia and Pat Goeters sat close to each other when they were in the car and how they held hands in public. He wanted that too. He was as demonstrative as he could be without causing us embarrassment.

I was more realistic than Don about our previous marriages, and at times I was a little uneasy about his belief in the possibility of perfection for ours. However, being with Don was so intensely romantic that I soon believed that the life he imagined for us was indeed possible.

When I married Pete, my name Helen Moore had already achieved some local professional recognition, and now my married name of Helen Gilpin was very well known. But just before my divorce from Pete was granted, Don asked if I would be willing to have my name legally restored to Helen Moore. I had no doubt that he was trying to change the past, yet for me this was an important concession. Nevertheless, I returned to my maiden name as he asked.

At the time of our marriage, Don was concerned that his mother should understand that we both had grounds for divorce, reasons acceptable to her, although not to the Catholic church. (In the 1970s, I learned that Don's youngest brother, Steven, had not known of my marriage to Pete Gilpin.) Nevertheless, Don seemed to want more than anything to live as if neither of us had been previously married.

What I did not know during these first months was that Don understood the psychology of love much better than I. He had read the work of Freud, Jung, Jones, and other leading psychiatrists, but he had also read in the year before our marriage *The Many Faces of Love,* Hubert Benoit's study of the psychology of one's emotional and sexual life.[1] One passage in particular that Don had marked is found in a chapter titled "The Fear of Loving." There is little doubt that marrying me represented the end of a quest for him, that he believed he could make a total commitment to me and to our marriage. As he told me over and over how much he loved me, I was wholly caught up in the intensity of his feelings and began to believe in our future in the way that he did.

In remembering our first years, I inevitably think of F. Scott Fitzgerald's Gatsby and Gatsby's efforts to recapture the past. Throughout our marriage, Don would walk through the rooms quoting Fitzgerald's epigraph for *The Great Gatsby* that begins with "Then wear the gold hat, if that will move her."

Don expected more than just a successful marriage; he wanted the ideal girl. It was unrealistic, but he desired both the beauty of the mythic Helen and the promise of his own "Daisy." The "mystery" of a girl became a recurring theme for Don, but I'm not certain that he ever fully accepted the notion that in marriage it would be impossible for her to retain the mystery for which he yearned.

We chose the First Unitarian Church for our wedding and met with the minister a few days before the ceremony. We planned a brief rehearsal the evening before and then had the wedding ceremony itself at eight o'clock on the evening of October 12 with just members of our families present. George Christian and my younger sister, Odell Pauline Moore, were our attendants.

We spent the first night of our marriage in Don's apartment on Hawthorne Street, truly blissful as we sat there drinking champagne and listening to modern jazz. In the previous few months, after Gollob's departure for California, Don moved twice, each time to an apartment in the same neighborhood. The first one he shared with Maurice Sumner, and the second place he shared with Henry Buckley. It was in this last home that we were to live. When we arrived there following the ceremony, I saw that Don had filled the entire apartment with flowers. There were huge bouquets wherever I looked, on the tables, on the floor, upstairs as well as downstairs. On the previous weekend, Don had painted some of the rooms, and then on the day of our wedding he spent hours cleaning the house and making other preparations. Later, I found Don's list of things to do that day.

The next morning, October 13, we drove to New Orleans for our honeymoon. Before we left, Don gathered up all the flowers and took them next door to our neighbor, an attractive young woman and the mother of two small children.

When we arrived in New Orleans, we drove to the French Quarter and found the small courtyard hotel at which Don had made reservations. But when we discovered that the room had twin beds, we explained to the manager that this was our honeymoon. Apologetic and embarrassed, he telephoned the Hotel Monteleone, which was just a short distance away, and reserved a room for us without difficulty.

The New Orleans French Quarter was authentic in its historic architecture and atmosphere, a beautiful place for long walks and browsing through antique shops and bookstores. We visited St. Louis Cathedral, the oldest cathedral in the United States, sat in Jackson Square watching people, and walked along the street looking at paintings that artists had placed along the fence. Behind wrought-iron gates, we could see courtyards everywhere, most of them lush with plants and flowers as if it were summertime. At one of the bookstores, we purchased a collection of the writings of D. T. Suzuki on Zen Buddhism, the first book that we bought together. We later put it in our library, but I don't think either of us ever read more than one or two selections.

We walked down every street in the Quarter, much of it residential rather than commercial. Once or twice we had breakfast at Brennan's and lunch at the Court of Two Sisters. During the days as well as in the evenings, we found the area endlessly appealing. Crime and pornography had not yet blighted the Quarter, so that in the evenings after dinner at Antoine's or one of the other famous restaurants, we strolled through the area, even Bourbon and Royal Streets, stopping in the small clubs to hear Dixieland and modern jazz.

In the afternoon or evening, we usually spent an hour or more at Pete Fountain's or some smaller place that had a group of jazz musicians and sometimes a blues vocalist. Preservation Hall was not yet established, but a group of older black musicians had formed the Preservation Band and we heard them one evening in a decaying building that provided a few benches and chairs for its audience. We also visited Pat O'Brien's on Bourbon Street, a club famous for a special drink called a hurricane. Before returning to our hotel each night, we walked to the French Market for café au lait and fresh, hot beignets.

When Don and I returned home from New Orleans, we had to face our financial problems. At the end of the summer, I had moved to a small advertising agency owned by the young woman with whom I had worked the previous year and with whom I had shared an apartment. Although she had acquired several large local accounts, they did not bring in enough income for both of us, and I was now without a job.

When Don suggested that I not look for another job but try to live on his income, I was at first reluctant. This was a new concept for me; I had been reared to be a professional person, even in a world that gave little recognition to a woman's career. Marrying Don within such a short time was a possibility that I could not have imagined just a year earlier. Relinquishing my professional status for domestic status was equally unimaginable. In my work at the university, I had occupied one of the most desirable jobs then available to women in Houston.

I had built a reputation as director of the university's news service and as an instructor in journalism. When I left the University of Houston the previous August to become director of public relations for a prominent regional advertising agency, I accepted new challenges and earned more money. While at the university, I had received other career offers as well, sometimes unexpected. I was even invited to run for a county political office, which was unique since women were seldom candidates for any elected public office.

Except for the women's department, obituaries, and other ancillary areas, few writing jobs at major city newspapers were open to women. Kathleen Bland Smith, a *Houston Post* reporter married to a labor union attorney, was education editor for the newspaper and a woman who defied tradition by working through nine months of pregnancy. Another exception was Betty Ewing, who covered "hard" news for the *Houston Press,* a Scripps-Howard newspaper. When the *Press,* a union newspaper, closed its doors, Betty became society editor of the *Houston Chronicle,* a position she held until the late 1980s. Ann Holmes, amusements editor for the *Chronicle,* was also an exception. Ann Hodges became radio and television editor for the *Chronicle,* an unenviable position in the 1950s, but one in which she became one of the country's prominent television reviewers and critics. These were, however, unusual women and unusual positions. It would be at least another decade before women were seriously and routinely considered for traditional news jobs.

Nor was television news yet open to women. KUHT-TV, the country's first educational television station, opened at the University of Houston in 1953. I was responsible for introducing the station to the community, but KUHT-TV had no professional positions open to women. The news was written by men, the announcers were men, and the professors in the university's radio and television department were men.

The world of advertising and public relations was much more amenable to women, and salaries were more equitable. In the summer of 1955, when I first advised Gen. A. D. Bruce, the president of the University of Houston, that I was resigning my position to accept one with the Boone and Cummings advertising firm, he proposed a counteroffer. But when I told him that my new salary would be double what I was earning at the university, he exclaimed with remarkable innocence, "But that's more than some of our male faculty members earn!"

Even in the 1950s his observation was so blatantly discriminatory that I continue to be astonished when I recall that day. However, no one acknowledged such discrimination and no one challenged it. My departure from the university was in itself a challenge to the system; none of my friends or colleagues could understand why I, especially as a woman, would give up such an important university position. In reality, my work for the news service had become a burden, providing very little challenge. Later, I regretted giving up my teaching position as well, but at the time I was more concerned with my public relations career.

Ironically, in recalling this era, I've been even more appalled that even though Don's beginning salary at the university exceeded what I was earning when I resigned, it did not seem unreasonable at the time. The general's reaction was only an expression of what no one talked about, an accepted practice interwoven into the structure of our society. A husband usually earned more money than a wife, and she was always expected to give consideration to his career over hers. Much later, when we found ourselves in this predicament, Don as well as I assumed that I should be the one who compromised for our marriage. Our relationship was in this sense contradictory. I was an especially pretty girl, but I'm certain that my professional achievements appealed to Don as well. Don was known as a talented writer, but he was a little younger than I and had received very little recognition for what he had done.

For the next few months, through the early spring of 1957, I attempted to become a housewife; even as a temporary arrangement, it was radical and strange.

At first, Don suggested that I develop a newspaper column that might be syndicated. He sometimes mentioned the "authority" that I brought to conversations and to my work. He talked about what he described as my "clear and distinct ideas." So with his urging, I made a serious effort for about three months to develop a series of articles that could become a column. But by early spring, I knew that I was not interested in writing anything that might appeal to a broad newspaper audience.

In December, unable to accept a life of just homemaking, I enrolled in classes in philosophy and art at the University of Houston. Don was still working on his degree and registered for two classes as well. Both of his courses were in philosophy, one with Maurice Natanson, with whom he was becoming good friends. Through his work on *Forum,* Don was becoming more and more absorbed with philosophy. Even though we talked briefly of moving to a university on the East Coast where Don could study philosophy and I could work on a doctorate in literature, his interest in philosophy was primarily a source of ideas for his fiction.

At the beginning of our courtship, Don's writing consisted almost solely of the work that he was doing for the university. Although he usually had some kind of manuscript in progress, he had very little time for writing fiction and seldom worked on it. He kept this manuscript and anything else creative that he was working on in a single letter-size file folder that he sometimes carried back and forth to the office.

As far as I know, none of Don's writing from the time before our marriage has survived. He was ruthless in judging his own writing and in discarding whatever he thought imperfect. We did, however, discuss his writing, what was happening in avant-garde drama, and occasionally what Don wanted to do in his own work. We were lucky in that we shared an interest in almost everything that was important to either of us. In fact, an incident in the summer of 1956, a few months before our marriage, held extraordinary significance for the future.

ONE AFTERNOON IN AUGUST OF 1956, as Don browsed through journals and magazines at Guy's Newsstand in Houston, he opened a new issue of *Theatre Arts* and began to read *Waiting for Godot*. As he read Samuel Beckett's revolutionary play, which had just been produced in Miami, Don experienced an overwhelming affinity with Beckett; this Irish genius was giving Don his first glimpse of what he might do with his own view of the world.

When Don came over to pick me up for dinner later that day, he walked in with his copy of *Theatre Arts*—eager to talk about *Godot*. I had seen the magazine as well and had just finished reading the play; I found it exciting but did not foresee the implications for Don. He was deeply moved and ecstatic about the language and the author's ironical and tragicomic stance. Each time we were in a bookstore after this, Don looked for work by Beckett and immediately read whatever he found. It seemed that from the day he discovered *Godot,* Don believed he could write the fiction he imagined; it would be from an ironical perspective of the world and he could use his wit and intellect in a way that would satisfy himself.

Now, however, in the first year of our marriage, Don was engrossed in *Forum,* his new journal at the university. His work was introducing him to new ideas in philosophy and the social sciences, and he was particularly interested in the work of Maurice Natanson, a phenomenologist and Edmund Husserl scholar. So in December, when we enrolled in philosophy courses, both were taught by Natanson. I registered for a class in the philosophy of aesthetics in which we studied the work of Suzanne Langer. I found Natanson to be a brilliant teacher and lecturer and could understand why Don admired him and sought his friendship. Don enrolled in Natanson's class on modern European philosophy.

Don was interested in Existentialism and had read the work of Jean-Paul Sartre and Albert Camus. Phenomenology seemed to give him a philosophical basis for what he perceived as significant in the immediate world, especially the importance of what was to him the ideal in thought and behavior.

In another course that he took from Natanson on philosophy in literature, Don read a collection of short novels, one of which was Tolstoy's *The*

Death of Ivan Ilych. In his copy of the book, Don wrote a note in the margin of chapter 9 in which Ivan Ilych, gravely ill and near death, is examining his life. Don observed that the "sole solution to life and death is *manner of life.*" In Don's own work, "manner of life" would become a recurring theme. Don also noted that what Ilych called "lightheartedness, friendship, and hope," as well as "love," were "plus factors." He made a further note to indicate that "love *vs* sensuality" was important.

Included with the text that Don was reading was a critical commentary on *The Death of Ivan Ilych.* Don wrote in the margin, "Couldn't leave it consistent because there has to be an answer — so we slap that in." With a background that included reading the work of Modernist poets and theorists in Formalism, Don was like many other writers and objected to such analysis. He felt a literary work should stand alone without need of interpretation.

In the fall of 1957, Natanson accepted an appointment with the Department of Philosophy at the University of North Carolina, leaving Don academically stranded. Don had talked to Natanson about universities in the East at which we might study, especially the New School in Manhattan and Brandeis University in Massachusetts. I wanted to consider a graduate school on the East Coast and at first believed the right academic environment would be exciting to Don. But as he worked on *Forum,* reading in several disciplines at one time, I could see that he could never have adapted to an academic life of traditional scholarship. He earned a distinguished professor designation at the University of Houston in the 1980s, but it was for his work in creative writing, not in scholarly research and publications.

With Natanson gone, Don was more isolated than ever and attempted at first to become friends with other members of the faculty. He even accepted an invitation for us to have coffee and dessert at the home of Edmund Pincoffs, who was interested in the philosophy of language and the work of Ludwig Wittgenstein. Despite Don's interest in what Wittgenstein, Kenneth Burke, and even Walker Percy had written about language, he was not a scholar in philosophy nor was he truly interested in becoming one. Since he felt obliged to enter into the discussion, which was largely concerned with Wittgenstein, the evening turned into an uncomfortable two hours, especially for Don. He was clearly miserable, and we escaped the gathering as quickly as we could. I was sure that Don thought the entire affair was a bit phony; he could not speak as an authority, and with a group of young committed scholars, he was unwilling to draw on his own ironical and often deadly wit. In this sense, Don could be very kind; he knew we were among serious philosophers and that he was simply out of place. Much later, I came to feel at home among academics and found that such an evening was not uncomfortable if you were among colleagues who shared similar interests.

Although Natanson was now in Chapel Hill, North Carolina, he continued to suggest contributors for *Forum* and to respond to Don's requests for advice on the format of the journal. During the next few years, they corresponded frequently, and Don's interest in philosophy persisted.

In our first year of marriage, we spent a lot of time furnishing our apartment. How we lived and where we lived were central to Don. He had known fine modern architecture in the Barthelme house and always wanted ours to have a contemporary look. He usually had a clearly defined notion of what a room or house should look like, so that it was useless to argue with him whenever we disagreed. Sometimes, I felt we should have a few more furnishings and even a little clutter, but our home was always comfortable and attractive, so I invariably yielded to his concept.

Our first residence was a two-story New Orleans–style apartment facing a central courtyard, with an upper verandah overlooking the gardens. Don had painted the interior a stark white, and then to give it more texture he covered one wall with stained redwood paneling. This paneling was the only structural change he made in that apartment, but it was typical of the alterations that he undertook wherever we lived. As a bachelor apartment, it had been sparsely furnished, and Don had been adamant about not decorating with anything from my home with Peter Gilpin.

For our new home, we bought an unfinished bedroom chest, which Don then finished with a walnut stain; after that, we found a Danish walnut couch and chair to replace a narrow sofabed that Don had been using in the living room. Shortly before we were married, Don suggested that we purchase fabric so that I could sew a spread for the bed. I was shocked at his request as I had few sewing skills, but I decided to make an attempt. As it turned out, the spread was a simple task, and after that I sewed curtains for the windows.

In creating a comfortable, handsome living space, Don thought only of the present. If we did not have enough room or there was some other reason to give up unnecessary furnishings for our current flat, he would give up whatever seemed inappropriate, even recordings and books. And he did so with little sense of loss. At the same time, we found new furnishings that were appropriate. Don had no desire to own possessions for the sake of possessions; once an apartment or house was furnished, he was not compelled to add or to change anything.

We always had lots of houseplants and cut flowers. My mother grew them, and wherever we lived she brought plants over that were appropriate. From her garden, she cut whatever fresh flowers I wanted. It was a luxury that I later missed.

We soon acquired Bertoia chairs and later an Alvar Aalto lounge chair and Prague side chairs. In the fall of 1957, we spent an entire afternoon looking for a small dining table and finally found a Paul McCobb walnut breakfast table. Later we scoured antique and junk shops for a dining room table and found a late-nineteenth-century oak pedestal table at Trash 'n Treasure on Westheimer Road. After the owner delivered it to our home on Kipling, he called back over the patio wall as he was leaving, "Glad to get rid of that old piece of junk." We laughed because we had found it covered with lamps and other pieces, but when Don refinished our piece of "junk," it was transformed into a handsome dining table.

We bought as many books as we could afford, and when we could not buy a book, we usually borrowed it from a "lending library" at one of the booksellers. Lending libraries were quite convenient; the store charged a small rental fee, but the books were almost always in stock and thus available. It was ideal for novels and other books that we didn't feel needed to be added to our library.

Don had a large library when we married, even though in the spring and summer of 1956, to pay for our courtship, he had sold hundreds of books to a used book dealer. I had now added my own library, and our collection continued to grow. Because he usually read everything as soon as he bought it, Don was always searching for things to read. During the week and on weekends, we browsed in every bookstore in downtown Houston or on the west side of the city. For our library, Don built and stained redwood or walnut bookshelves in each of our apartments, so that these too were part of our decor.

After returning from our honeymoon in October, 1956, we began daily routines that changed little during the next few years. For our first Thanksgiving, I prepared a traditional turkey dinner for just the two of us and a single guest, Henry Buckley, who had been Don's roommate in the apartment in which we now lived. From the beginning of our marriage, we ate most of our meals at home. I was a good cook, but now I was attempting to become a gourmet cook. Don could cook very little and had difficulty preparing even coffee. When we were no longer together and cooking became a necessity for Don, he boasted to me that he had become an accomplished chef. I found it difficult to believe.

In December, between Christmas and New Year's, we gave our first party. We invited all our friends, from the university, from the *Houston Post,* and from the advertising business. We had more than a hundred guests, too many for our apartment, but it was the only time that we invited a large number of friends and acquaintances at one time. Not only did we want everyone to know of our marriage, but I believe we both wanted to boast of it. The holiday party provided the first opportunity for our friends to see us as a couple.

Don's colleagues at the university gave us as a wedding gift a painted golden apple along with a poem alluding to the mythological tale of the winning of Helen of Troy by Paris of Greece. Although we were a little embarrassed by the extravagance of the gesture, we were experiencing such hubris at having fallen in love that it seemed entirely appropriate.

As we settled into the routine of marriage, we received frequent dinner invitations, but most of the time I prepared dinner at home. Pat and Georgia Goeters, who now had their first son, invited us to their apartment on Graustark, an upstairs flat in what had been his grandmother's home. The house was located on a small island of land in Vassar Place, a site on which Howard Barnstone would soon design and build one of Houston's first group of two- and three-story Modernist apartments. The property was just a few blocks from the Museum of Fine Arts.

One of the evenings I especially remember was when we drove down to Baytown, where Guy Johnson, a painter and art instructor, and his wife Nancy lived. It was at their home that we first heard a recording of Kurt Weill and Bertolt Brecht's *The Rise and Fall of the City of Mahagonny.* That same evening, we bought two of Guy's paintings, both satirical comments on contemporary life. One was a collage with a lonely, solitary figure playing a guitar against an isolated, almost desolate shoreline that evoked an image of the flat coastal plains along the Gulf of Mexico. I assumed it was Guy's comment about the isolated world in which he lived as an artist in Baytown. The other was a comment on urban life, with a scene of a stylishly dressed man and his dog in Manhattan's Central Park.

When we ate at home, Don cleaned up afterward, washing and drying the dishes. This was a custom at his family's home, so he assumed the same responsibilities in ours. Don was also adept at quickly straightening the apartment, and in this way he shared in some of the housework. On weekends, we ate dinner out occasionally, but more often we went out for lunch on Saturday afternoons, usually at El Patio on Kirby Drive or at Alfred's Delicatessen on Rice Boulevard.

Saturday was a day for browsing at bookstores and Guy's Newsstand, the only place that sold scholarly and literary journals, including the major "little magazines"; visiting the Museum of Fine Arts and art galleries; and searching boutiques and decorating shops for contemporary furnishings. On these excursions, we took in colors, textures, and shapes wherever we went. We bought small things, a Chagall poster from the Museum of Fine Arts, a piece of pottery from an art studio, and books from Brown's Bookstore or Rita Cobler's Book Shop. On Sunday mornings, we had a late breakfast and listened to recordings of Bach's music, especially Concertos for Two Harpsichords, along with recordings of sixteenth- and seventeenth-century Gregorian chants.

No matter how much work we each had to do, we went to see new films, to the theater, and to concerts. Leopold Stokowski became the conductor of the Houston Symphony Orchestra, and after he left, Sir John Barbirolli. Nina Vance directed the Alley Theatre, then a theater-in-the-round, and produced one classic after another. There were other theaters producing newer work, such as Jack Gelber's *The Connection*. Sometimes we just stayed home and listened to our own hi-fi system, either to jazz or to a symphony, occasionally an opera. Maria Callas recordings were among our favorites. Often lying on a rug near the speakers, we were able to concentrate on the music. Whenever possible, we heard live jazz; there were local groups that gathered to improvise on Sunday afternoons or sometimes a jazz great would play at one of the clubs. Don had recordings of the work of every important jazz musician, and he knew who was playing which instrument in every piece.

These first years were mostly idyllic except for one frightening experience in March, 1957. I had recently learned that I was pregnant, but there was no reason to change my usual routine. I was home alone one day when I suddenly had a miscarriage. I began to hemorrhage and immediately tried to call the doctor; I panicked when I could not reach him and then called Don at the university. He telephoned one of our neighbors and asked her to look after me while he was en route home. By this time, I was lying down in an attempt to stop the hemorrhaging, but nothing helped and I became so weak that I needed an ambulance to get to the hospital. However, in Houston, a city ordinance prohibited ambulances from carrying a pregnant woman to the hospital. A pregnancy or miscarriage did not qualify as an emergency.

Fortunately for me, our neighbor arranged for an ambulance through a friend, and they took me to St. Joseph's Hospital, about three miles from where we lived. Just after I called Don at the university, he reached his father and asked him to go to our apartment. His architectural offices were on Brazos Street, less than a mile from where we lived, so he arrived in minutes. Don then reached our apartment in time to help the attendants carry me downstairs on the stretcher. I began to lose consciousness, so as the ambulance drove to the hospital, Don urged them to drive faster and to turn on the siren. But the driver, obeying the ordinance for nonemergencies, would not use the siren and had to stop at all the signal lights. I arrived at the hospital with an extremely weak pulse, barely surviving the loss of blood.

My experience with the ambulance service that day is indicative of the kind of discrimination that women experienced in the 1950s, a discrimination so deeply rooted in American society that neither Don nor I ever expressed our anger about what had happened. We just felt fortunate that our neighbor had a friend who worked for an ambulance company. I recovered quickly and we went back to our usual activities; this was early in our marriage and we had no doubt that we would be able to have children.

Our routine throughout our marriage usually included Sunday afternoon with the Barthelme family at their Modernist home reflecting the influence of both the Bauhaus movement and Frank Lloyd Wright. The living area facing the rear through an expanse of glass was a spacious, open room in which it was possible to sit and read quietly apart from others who engaged in conversation in a separate group.

We usually read and listened to music through much of the late afternoon. The Barthelmes played symphonic music most of the time, classical and modern. Don's mother and father both read extensively and had introduced Don to modern and classical authors when he was in his early teens. Don later recalled that his father had given him Marcel Raymond's *From Baudelaire to Surrealism* when he was just fourteen. And when the senior Barthelme saw that Don was imitating writers in the *New Yorker,* he introduced his son to Rabelais's *Gargantua and Pantagruel* with the admonition that "if you imitate another writer's style, always choose the best."

At first, I found these visits uncomfortable, chiefly because of harsh arguments between Don and his father. After our arrival there was a brief cocktail hour in which the conversation was general enough, but before dinner started Don and the elder Barthelme always began to disagree about something.

At dinner, his father usually gave an account of his latest professional battles; at that moment, it was the Adams Petroleum Center that he was fighting to complete. His client was Bud Adams, who later became owner of the Houston Oilers.

During this period, the elder Barthelme was also on the architecture faculty of both the University of Houston and Rice University. Academic politics, first at the one school and then at the other, immediately became a principal topic of conversation during our Sunday visits.

When the School of Architecture at Rice lost its professional accreditation around 1960, the senior Barthelme — then at the University of Houston — was invited to join Rice to help restore its recognition. Within a brief time, Rice regained its professional ranking, but during these years, Don's father proposed radical changes that were untenable in a traditional academic institution. Among his suggestions was the reassigning of senior tenured faculty to lower-level teaching assignments. I soon learned that the elder Barthelme set impossible goals for himself. Don was undoubtedly influenced by his father's need for some kind of ideal that he could never attain.

We also talked about political, business, literary, and often family matters. I was struck by the repartee that would take place among the entire family, including Peter, who was in his last year at St. Thomas High School in 1956 and planning to enter Cornell University the following year, and Rick, a handsome youth whose rebellious years were just beginning. Joan's wit, like Don's, was sharp and sometimes biting when directed at her father. Don's mother was articulate and witty but always kind. In 1956, Steve was only nine years old and treated with a special affection. He was gentle and mild mannered and, like his older brothers and sister, acutely observant as well.

Even though I was often unsettled by what I felt were harsh discussions between Don and his father, I realized from the first that these brilliant, witty afternoons and evenings gave Don's life a dimension that he could not find anywhere else. During our visits, Don would always relate a story concerning *Forum.* The entire family took part, but these conversations were largely between Don and his father.

Don and the elder Barthelme were usually quite cheerful at the beginning of the afternoon, with Don laughing at his father's adventures. But as our visit proceeded, they began to argue, not only about ideas or writers, but also about how to rear the younger sons. Don felt his father was too rigid in the rules he set for Pete and Frederick. Don believed that his father's continual disapproval, what his brothers later described as "withholding approval," was a harmful way to rear a child. The entire family was very careful of what was said to Steve, so that Steve's relationship with his father seems to have been quite different from the others. Rick, too, was apparently less concerned than his older brothers and sister with their father's disapproval.

After a while, I became accustomed to the argumentative tone that prevailed and began to feel that their disagreements emerged from the forthrightness of their relationship. But Pete later told me that his father had been a "verbal bully" with all the children, leaving little doubt that Don's inflexible will and ability to challenge anyone at all came from his relationship with his father.

Although Donald, Sr., disapproved of Don's interest in "new" literature, and was not interested in reading the avant-garde work with which Don could identify, Don must have suffered even more than I realized from this incessant disapproval. Don was confident of his own originality, but he could do nothing to win his father's approval. Even the work that Don began doing for the Contemporary Arts Museum failed to interest the senior Barthelme.

I liked Don's father a lot, so in the late 1950s I asked if he would talk to the owners of Bruce and Mitchell, the agency for which I then worked, about designing a mid-rise building on the San Jacinto Street property where our offices were located. After conferring with the two principals, who were also my friends, he undertook the preliminary design without charging a fee. Although Don said he had never done this before and that he taught his students always to charge fees for such projects, in this instance he made an exception. It was a generous gesture that, as Don explained, was simply because "he likes you."

Don was pleased that I liked his parents and that his father and I seemed to get along well. From the first, I was not intimidated by his father; in one of my early visits, when he showed slides of the family—something he did occasionally—he included a photograph of Maggie, Don's first wife. I simply ignored it, so he omitted her photographs after that.

From the first, I saw that Don was close to his mother and seemed never to question her strictures. Once, while Don's parents were away on a trip, we stayed at the house with his brothers. During their absence, we took Rick, who was then sixteen, to dinner and Don asked if he wanted to have a beer; Don felt that this was the proper way to treat a young man who was already drinking beer. But when his mother learned of the incident, she sternly reprimanded Don. He was crushed but deferred to her authority. She insisted upon a code of behavior for her sons and daughter of which they seemed always aware. Don sometimes explained his actions in a way that he believed she would find acceptable, but I do not believe that Don was ever able to escape the influence of his mother's opinions.

Don's mother was an especially attractive woman, a gracious, gentle person, usually cheerful and always kind. She had considerable intellect and wit and seemed to possess great wisdom in being a mother and wife.

During these years, Steven Barthelme was a young boy who loved exploring the woods and bayou to search for snakes that he would bring home as pets. Helen Barthelme would help him take care of his snakes or other creatures, and during our visits she would take me into his room to see whatever he had in captivity. She was tender with Steve, and I do not recall ever hearing her say anything harsh to him. Like his brothers and sister, Steve was a talented writer, and sometimes his mother showed me essays that he had written for school.

In that first year, we once drove with Don's parents to Galveston to have dinner with his grandmother Mamie Barthelme and aunt Elise Hopkins. Mamie, who continued to live in their Galveston home after her husband's death, was short and plump and a good storyteller. She too read widely and loved music. Don had spent his early years in Galveston and still enjoyed going to one of the Galveston beaches on the weekend. He had particularly loved his grandfather and recalled visits to their ranch near Kerrville; you could see the Guadalupe River from the verandah of their home. He was still sad that he was in Korea when his grandfather died. In Don's story "Bishop," the narrator, who is close to despair and focused every day on waiting for the girl with whom he is not really in love, tenderly recalls the ranch at the end of the story—a moment of lyrical meaning.[1]

Don was the first person I had known whose interests, other than our careers, were almost solely in literature and the arts. Since neither of us cared about sports, this alone made our marriage attractive. What was perhaps even more important, in my life with Don our friends shared what we enjoyed as well, and I seldom had to bother with cocktail conversation. The friends who invited us to dinner were artists, architects, and writers. Boring social evenings were rare in our new life.

New acquaintances were often in the art world—Jack and Ann Boynton, both artists; Robert Morris, an artist, and his wife Gitta, a journalist who now writes for newspapers in New England and New York; Jim Love, a sculptor whose avant-garde work is found not only in Houston and Dallas museums but also in the Museum of Modern Art in New York and other metropolitan collections; and Guy Johnson, an artist then teaching at Lee College in Baytown, and his wife Nancy, a public school teacher.

We continued to see Pat and Georgia Goeters, Joe and Maggie Maranto, as well as George and Mary Christian. Mary was to become an author of children's books and George stayed with the *Post* and then moved to the *Chronicle*. Within a few years, however, the Goeterses, Morrises, and Johnsons were among our friends who moved to the East Coast.

We sometimes had dinner with members of my family, especially my sister Margo and her husband Roy. Margo and I frequently had lunch together, and the four of us occasionally attended museum affairs.

The late 1950s and early 1960s were an exciting era for art in Houston, a time in which Don became intensely involved in contemporary art. In the 1950s, the Contemporary Arts Museum was responsible for all of Houston's major exhibitions of modern art, and art patrons Dominique Schlumberger de Menil and her husband Jean de Menil made possible the exhibitions of modern art in Houston. They arranged for a Van Gogh retrospective as well as the first museum exhibition of Max Ernst in Houston.

I recall especially an exhibition of surrealist art that included a small egg-shaped object covered in fur, the inspiration for what became Don's favorite line in his fiction. It appears in one of his first stories, "Florence Green Is 81." Baskerville replies "grandly" that the "aim of literature . . . is the creation of a strange object covered with fur which breaks your heart."[2]

There were also shows at New Arts Gallery, Joan Crystal's Louisiana Gallery, and exhibits staged by Jermayne McAgy at the University of St. Thomas. McAgy had been director of the Contemporary Arts Museum in the late 1950s and then head of the art department at the University of St. Thomas. Before long, the Menils would also help Rice University to establish the Institute for the Arts, but in the early 1960s the only such exhibits at Rice were those installed by the Contemporary Arts Museum in large, gallery-like spaces.

In March, 1957, we attended the national meeting of the American Federation of Arts hosted by the Museum of Fine Arts, Houston. A reception was held in a new wing of the museum designed by Ludwig Mies van der Rohe, its galleries eventually housing the museum's major collections.

It was during the AFA meeting that I saw for the first time Don's sensitivity to being "Don, Jr." He was invariably introduced as "the son of the architect," which he appeared to accept gracefully. Occasionally, he offered a witty retort, but this time, he just acknowledged that he was "indeed the son of the great man" and then withdrew into a kind of aloofness.

In the late spring of 1957, Don and I moved into our second apartment, in an old home that was being converted to contemporary flats and situated not far from where we were already living. The apartment had several levels, and there was no need for Don to alter the decor of the interior. But he built a coffee table suited to our new living area. It was a black lacquer square table on which he worked for several days, applying numerous coats of lacquer to achieve a high gloss finish; finally, he was unhappy with the results and took the table to a professional finisher.

The new apartment was on Richmond Avenue near Montrose Boulevard, and around the corner on Montrose was the city's first coffee house. While on our evening walks, we frequently visited the café. The museum district had just begun to emerge, but the coffee house, along with most other ephemeral landmarks of this era, disappeared long ago.

IN THE EARLY SUMMER OF 1957, not long after we moved into the apartment on Richmond, I went back to work. I became an account executive for an advertising agency owned by two friends, Bill Bruce and Betty Jane Mitchell. Bill was a former news reporter and editor with the *Houston Post,* and Betty Jane was already a veteran in advertising who had worked on the account of a famous over-the-counter medicine known as Hadacol. It was with her agency that I was working just before Don and I were married. Thus, we again had not only Don's professional life to consider but mine as well.

After I began working for Betty Jane and Bill, one of the accounts I handled was Dominican College, a four-year Catholic college for women. Within a few months, the dean invited me to teach classes in literature and in journalism. Preparation of lectures took a lot of my time, but I was delighted to return to teaching after giving it up when I left the University of Houston in 1955.

During the next few years, Don often visited my classes as a guest lecturer. His reading background was already such that he brought an understanding of both the work itself and critical approaches to understanding it. He was a superb public speaker, but a self-conscious one as well. As he faced an audience, he assumed a public manner, distancing himself from the audience with a formal, slightly autocratic manner and shaping his lips to pronounce each word with great care. This mannerism was a way of dealing with the slight discomfort that he seemed to feel in speaking to a group, but then it was also effective in giving dramatic emphasis to everything he said. After a lecture or a reading, Don returned to his informal manner, interjecting warmth and humor into whatever he said.

At Dominican College, he was especially sensitive to his audience and unfailingly considerate of the students as young women, many still teenagers. In his deep, clear voice, he lectured on and read from contemporary works that he admired. He liked giving public readings; when he first read for some of my college classes, his interest in the dramatic qualities of writing was apparent.

Don's reading of "Jerry and the Dog" from Edward Albee's *Zoo Story* was a favorite of the students, some of whom were semicloistered novices from the Villa Matel Convent. Among them were beautiful girls from Ireland who saw very little of the world outside of the convent and the college. To protect them from any kind of verbal offense, Don deleted a number of words and phrases as he read Jerry's long soliloquy. In our copy of *Zoo Story,* from which he read, he marked the phrases to be deleted:

" . . . almost always has an erection . . . of sorts."
"That's red, too."
" . . . he wasn't half-assed, either."
" . . . malevolence with an erection."
"She had forgotten her bewildered lust."

Don was invariably sensitive to anything concerned with the church. His teachers in parochial schools through both elementary and junior grades had been Catholic nuns, and he clearly felt a special affection for them. In later years, he always asked about the "sweet nuns" at Dominican College.

In spite of having left the Catholic church, Don admired many aspects of it. He talked about the priesthood with respect. When one of the students at Dominican College was disturbed by Graham Greene's whiskey priest in *The Power and the Glory,* Don pointed out that a young priest replaces the elder, a tradition that Don continued to admire in spite of his disappointment in individual priests at St. Thomas High School. What interested me was the tone in which Don talked to the students about the novel, revealing nothing of his own withdrawal from the church.

In the early summer of 1957, I was pregnant again, and we began planning for our child. Expecting a child did not alter our lifestyles; it never occurred to either of us to change anything. Three years earlier, when I was married to Peter Gilpin, I lost a little boy born prematurely. He was a handsome dark-haired child, and the loss still haunted me. Although my doctor seemed to think it would be possible to avert another premature birth, he did not advise that I change my routine. In the 1950s, being pregnant and having a career were an uncommon combination, but I was unwilling to give up a professional life.

However, near the end of October, I lost the child. He was another little boy just under two pounds, too small to survive. I never knew what he looked like. After the delivery, when I awoke in my room, still drowsy from anesthesia, Don talked to me about turning the baby over to the hospital for medical research. He thought this was the best thing for us to do and I agreed at once. The child I lost in my first marriage was buried in our family cemetery plot in Houston, and I did not want to face that experience again.

In the spring of 1958, we decided to find a less expensive place to live. We were always short of money and had borrowed as much as we could. Every month we paid bank fees on several checks returned for insufficient funds. Don was never concerned about writing checks that our bank account would not cover; he simply wrote new checks to replace those returned. Sometimes checks were returned twice, but eventually we had funds to cover them. At the beginning of our marriage, he said that we should buy whatever we needed and then find the money to cover our expenses. This was a new approach to budgeting for me, and one that became increasingly stressful.

Don had lived in a more affluent world with greater economic resources than I had known; although he did not see himself as a member of the "carriage trade," we were treated as such by merchants. Don was accustomed to writing checks for whatever he wanted and had very little experience with credit. Later, as we used credit more and more, it became increasingly difficult to manage our expenses. Don, however, seemed not to understand, and by the summer of 1962, we were very close to being overwhelmed by debts.

Don had already explained that he was poor in mathematics, that he had extremely high verbal skills but very poor quantitative talents. When he was a teenager, his upper lip would sometimes tremble uncontrollably; it finally stopped only after he underwent a series of aptitude tests and his parents were advised to "let him be." They were told he was a verbal genius but that he would never be able to balance a checkbook, that they should not expect him to do so. I understood Don to mean that his parents, especially his father, should encourage his creative talents and not expect him to excel in other areas.

While "balancing a checkbook" was intended as a figure of speech, in reality he did not bother to keep checkbook balances. Every day or so, he listed the checks he had written—with estimated figures—and deducted this amount from what he recalled as the balance in our bank account.

After worrying constantly about our bank balance and checks that were being returned for insufficient funds, I assumed responsibility for keeping up with our bank account. Nevertheless, I could never get from Don anything more than a list of checks with estimated amounts; I was unable to record all of our checks until the bank statement and canceled checks arrived at the end of each month. Don was not indifferent to our financial condition; he was just certain that somehow we would have enough money and so he made a practice of writing checks at any time, whether we had a bank balance or not.

It was in order to economize that we moved from Richmond Avenue to a small group of new apartments on Emerson Street just a few blocks from where each of us had lived in the spring of 1956. Our flat was tiny, but it had interior brick walls and the complex provided a swimming pool. There was little need for any kind of structural addition or change other than bookcases. Although the apartment was small, we entertained often. Once, while Don's mother and Steve were visiting her sister in Pennsylvania, we invited Don's father to dinner. When I asked his opinion of our apartment, he cautiously replied that it was "ingratiating." It was the kindest thing he could think to say.

Joe Maranto, who had joined Mobil Oil Company and was living in Dallas, also had dinner with us one evening. Joe was one of the very few people with whom Don could discuss his writing and the new fiction.

We stayed in this intimate little apartment for six months, through the summer and early fall of 1958, and then moved across the street to a 1920s house on Emerson Street owned by Linn and Celestine Linnstaedter. Linn was Herbert William Linnstaedter, a native Texan who had been only a teenager when he was with the 99th Infantry Division in the Battle of the Bulge and who then studied architecture at the University of Houston. After that, he went on to the Harvard Graduate School of Design before returning to Texas to teach at the University of Houston. Celestine, member of a prominent Mississippi family, was a doctor of psychiatry who practiced at the Veterans Administration Hospital in Houston. They lived in the house next door, which Linn had remodeled and they had decorated with antiques and contemporary furnishings.

We especially wanted a house because once more we were expecting a child and needed more space. But not long after we moved, it became apparent that the interior was not amenable to the changes that Don tried to make and he was never satisfied with it. To provide a small entrance foyer for the house, he constructed a Japanese rice paper screen to hang from the ceiling and serve as a room divider. We also tried using one of the bedrooms as the living area; this arrangement was awkward and uninviting, but we stayed there until the following spring.

As it turned out, we were in the Linnstaedter house just a month when I lost our second little boy. This was not long after Don asked if I would still love him after the child's birth; we had not imagined losing it. Throughout the preceding months, I had worked as much as ever, at the advertising agency and in managing our home and our social life.

Again, Don suggested that we give the baby to the hospital for research, and once more, I gave my approval. But I have often regretted this and over the years have been haunted by images of what happened to the two infants. Don too must have had doubts later. He used our experience in one of his stories in 1973. In "One Hundred Ten West Sixty-First Street," first published in the *New Yorker,* Don begins with a scene in which Paul is trying to console Eugenie by giving her "a very large swordfish steak for her birthday."

> He had tried. Paul and Eugenie went to a film. Their baby had just died and they were trying not to think about it. The film left them slightly depressed. The child's body had been given to the hospital for medical experimentation. "But what about life after death?" Eugenie's mother had asked. "There isn't any," Eugenie said. "Are you positive?" her mother asked. "No," Eugenie said. "How can I be positive? But that's my opinion."

I have no doubt that Eugenie was speaking for Don. Don knew that the Catholic church would not have approved of what we did, and he later told me that his mother talked to him about it. Giving the bodies to the medical school for research was, I believe, an attempt to leave the experience in the past. The presence of two tiny graves would not let us do this. And as always, he was driven by an implacable will to make decisions independent of all authority, in this instance both the church and his mother.

Nevertheless, Don often regretted a decision and felt guilty about whatever he had done. However, I don't think regretting an earlier action or feeling guilty made Don any less determined to make decisions independently. And turning experiences into fiction seemed to enable him to live with his decisions.

In using events from his life, Don did not necessarily develop a story around a single episode. More often, as in "One Hundred Ten West Sixty-First Street," he drew from several events and experiences. Characteristically, he used whatever worked in the story, and although he altered details, anyone who shared the experience would be able to recognize it.

We spent Christmas Eve of 1958 with my family and Christmas day with Don's. The youngest Barthelme, Steven, was only eleven that year, and Frederick was fifteen. Joan and Pete were older; Joan was working and Pete was in college, but both were home for Christmas.

Don's father drove to Galveston to bring Don's grandmother to spend the day with the family. A prominent Galvestonian, Mamie Barthelme told us stories of families in Galveston and recalled incidents from the past with Don's grandfather John, whom she called Bart.

In her version of Don's impulsive trip to Mexico City, Mamie recalled the three male Barthelmes as Bo (Don, Jr.), Don (Donald, Sr.), and Bart (her husband John). When Don ran away to Mexico, she and Bart were in Kerrville at their ranch on the Guadalupe River, a place that Bo had loved. It was the first time she had gone there without a complete wardrobe and did not have what she needed for travel. For this reason, she could not accompany them to Mexico City to look for Bo, clearly a disappointment for her.

She was articulate and witty, and sometimes, in a spirited mood, she would burst out singing operatic nonsense. On at least one occasion, Joan sang in reply. Short and heavy, Mamie often fell asleep after dinner, still sitting in an Alvar Aalto lounge chair.

We opened gifts in the family room; dozens of gifts were placed around a large tree, and we took turns opening each gift. Also, throughout the afternoon, Don's father took informal photographs of the family. At some point, he brought out film slides from previous years to show. He was a talented photographer and had a darkroom in which he developed film and made prints from his negatives. From the beginning of their marriage, Mr. Barthelme had taken both still photographs and 8-mm films, so that by this time he had a large collection of slides, photographs, and home movies.

We spent New Year's Eve in 1958 with the Linnstaedters; after dinner, we sat on a rug in front of the fireplace and drank champagne. That evening, we argued about the abuse of free or government-sponsored medical facilities; Celestine told stories of men of apparent means, even wealth, who came to the Veterans Administration Hospital for free treatment. She felt the benefits should not be free to veterans who could afford to pay for them. The discussion turned to excessive welfare benefits and the dangers of socialized medicine.

When the Linnstaedters built a group of fashionable apartments on Memorial Drive, they asked if we would like to occupy one of the apartments as resident manager. It was a small but expensive property and would have been easy to manage. Don was at first interested in the offer because the apartments were exceptional in design and the arrangement would have given us an important supplement to our income. Then Linn added that this would be an ideal arrangement since we were such a "chic" couple. I don't believe Linn could have said anything that Don would find more offensive. He visibly withdrew, assumed his aloof expression and firmly said no. It was characteristic of Don that a single word could provoke such feeling. We lived graciously, and the decor of our home was often striking, but for Don, "chic" evoked a pretentious world with which he did not identify.

One day not long after we were married, Don had told me that he believed we "should be committed to becoming part of the intellectual and artistic elite rather than the wealthy elite." Of course, there was no way that we would become a member of the "wealthy elite," but Don was simply describing the kind of life he wanted for us. I agreed with him about having an intellectual life and was surprised that he felt we should "choose" one life over the other. He later told me that he believed his mother was disheartened over having a less affluent lifestyle than any of her friends, the kind of life that one could have expected from an architect as famous as his father. Several of their early friends were now quite wealthy, but it was not a world that Don envied.

In the spring of 1959, we found a two-story apartment on Kipling Street where we both wanted to live. Our friends had grown accustomed to our moves and joked about them, but Don was uncomfortable in telling the Linnstaedters that we were leaving. On the day that we told them, the four of us were outside in the yard between our two houses when Don broached the matter.

After he told them of our plans and before either of the Linnstaedters could reply, Don told Celestine in a sharp, accusatory tone that he knew what she was thinking about the psychological implications of our frequent moves. Celestine was visibly stunned for a moment and then replied that this was untrue, that she had not made any sort of psychological observation about our moving. I too was shocked; we had enjoyed the change of environment in each home and I was accustomed to Don's ceaseless search for the "new" and for a place where "everything is different." I felt a little guilty about rejecting a home that was owned by friends, but in those years in Houston, if we a had lease at all, it was less binding than a lease today and it was easy for the owner to rent the property to another tenant.

We moved to Kipling Street in June of 1959. This was a two-story contemporary apartment designed by Burdette Keeland, an architect and professor of architecture at the University of Houston. Similar to a townhome in design, the apartment had a painted white brick exterior with polished red brick floors on the first level and a glass wall overlooking an enclosed garden. A wall mural was the only undesirable design feature, but

Don covered this with natural burlap, adding a wonderful texture to the living area. It was here that Don began to write more seriously than ever and where we formulated long-range plans for his writing full-time.

We no longer lived in the heart of what was then Houston's bohemian district, but we remained near museums and art galleries. Ours was a pleasant neighborhood just a few blocks from River Oaks, where many of the city's wealthiest families lived. We continued to take walks in the evenings, but the neighborhood was more commercial and the streets less inviting. We spent our time much as we had before, visiting the museums and new galleries that were opening, looking at architecture, buying books and records, and shopping for our home or for ourselves.

Don and I bought our first important painting that year, *Seance* by James Boynton. The painting was oil on canvas, an abstraction mostly in blue and black. Jack was on the faculty of the University of Houston and had already exhibited in a number of major museums. He had been chosen as one of a small group of young American artists for what was called the Brussels Exhibition. He and his wife Ann were now among our closest friends, and we occasionally had dinner together. They had two young daughters, so we usually went over to their house. Once we drove to Galveston and spent the day on the beach; Don did not enjoy traveling even a short distance, so this was an unusual event.

Ann and Jack had met when both were art students at Texas Christian University in Fort Worth. Ann gave up painting to be a wife and mother, but now she had begun to design and create original pieces of jewelry. Even though I knew their financial problems bothered her, I did not realize that she was emotionally disturbed as well. Don frequently saw Jack at the university and at Jack's studio and knew of Ann's difficulties; Ann had attempted suicide several times but no one told me. A few years later, she succeeded.[1]

During these months in 1959, Don was increasingly dissatisfied that he was not writing. When Maurice Natanson came to Houston for a lecture engagement sponsored by the Contemporary Arts Association, Don was reminded of the creative and intellectual world that was not available in Houston. *Forum* no longer held the promise that it had a year or so earlier, and so far no one had sought to interview him for an editing position in New York. Natanson urged him to act, but without a definite job offer, Don was unwilling to give up our lifestyle.

Finally, in the summer of 1959, his dissatisfaction with the university and his desire to write for a publication were such that he undertook self-analysis with a prominent Houston psychiatrist, Spencer Bayles. We seldom talked about his sessions in self-analysis with Dr. Bayles, but there is little doubt that they helped him to make significant changes in his life during the next few years. He underwent analysis for about a year and finally gave it up after he began to write in 1960. It was ironic that he turned to a psychiatrist after having dissuaded me from continuing with my psychoanalysis in 1956.

It was also during this period that we gave up our attempts to have a child. I had become discouraged over the loss of the second baby in December and decided to see a different gynecologist, Charles Bancroft. I now had ambivalent feelings about having a child, but I assumed that with Don's Catholic background, we would eventually have children. Dr. Bancroft recommended that Don and I undergo tests, but they revealed no problems and within a short time, I was again pregnant. After an early miscarriage, we decided to give up for the present.

It was apparent that Don detested having to undergo medical tests and seemed to feel that somehow it tainted the idea of having a child. I was struck by the depth of his need for "mystery" and spontaneity. It was becoming clear that Don's sensibilities made it difficult for him to confront the realities of being a father. Until now, we had sustained our "idyllic" world, and it was only years later that I saw how unrealistic I, as well as Don, had been. There was no way for us to have a child without the unpleasantness of pregnancy and childbirth and the fear of parenthood. But in the 1950s and even in the early 1960s, pregnancy was an event that a woman faced pretty much alone. I now had no desire whatsoever to become pregnant again.

A few months after this, Don read William Shirer's *The Rise and Fall of the Third Reich,* which was for most Americans the first full historical account of the systematic extermination of millions of people by the Nazis. Don was affected by the work to the extent that I became apprehensive that he might commit suicide. Although I knew that Catholics weren't supposed to commit suicide, Don had left the church and I could see and feel an abating of his exuberance for life. He seemed to now live with an intense consciousness of the world as evil. At one point, he said that he felt it would be wrong to have a child in such an evil world as ours. When we discussed this a few years later, Don told me that he believed that one had a responsibility to live out his life, whatever the circumstances.

In the spring of 1960, while Don was still editor of *Forum,* active in the Contemporary Arts Museum, and working on several essays, we talked again of Don's leaving the university in order to write. Don saw it as the need to confront the choice between a career with money and the lifestyle it could provide—"driving a Jaguar" was the way he characterized it—or a wholehearted commitment to writing.

By the end of 1959, I had started my own advertising agency and was continuing to teach at Dominican College as well, so that now I was earning the equivalent of two salaries. This meant that we could manage on my income. As it turned out, in spite of our income, we incurred more and more indebtedness during the next two years. But by the time he left the university in the fall of 1960, I wanted Don to have a chance to write and not be burdened with another job.

We had lived on Kipling Street for fifteen months, but Don said that he felt this beautiful apartment in which we were living was inappropriate for a serious writing career. He seemed to feel guilty that we were indulging ourselves by living in what was for us an expensive residence. Maurice Natanson had once alluded to Don's penchant for fast cars, a reference to his Austin-Healey, and another friend wrote from New York ridiculing Don's having purchased two Bertoia chairs. Although these comments offended Don and he talked of living more modestly, he nevertheless needed a beautiful place in which to live and work. And as it turned out, we sacrificed very little in the style in which we lived during the period in which Don wrote the stories for *Come Back, Dr. Caligari.*

I did not want to leave the apartment on Kipling Street, but after I finally gave in to moving again, we searched until we found the right house. We drove for hours in the evenings and on weekends, often at night. Don wanted to "see the interior and the lighting—we can learn more about the house at night." We looked for a home that was not only "different" but also well designed and functional. The house we found returned us to our old neighborhood, near the University of St. Thomas and not far from the museums and art galleries.

It was actually a duplex, with a small apartment in the rear for the owner's mother. The owner was a commercial artist and the small apartment opened into a yard adjacent to his office building. This one-story home, part of the Montrose and Westmoreland developments in the 1910s and 1920s, had high ceilings and a large attic. Located on the corner of Harold and Roseland Streets, the house had a sitting and sleeping porch enclosed by large screened windows with awnings. The porch became Don's study; it was located on the northwest corner of the house and looked out on the beautiful trees that lined the streets. There were large magnolias, Chinese elm, and oaks just outside his window. As a metropolis of the south more than the southwest, Houston is a city of trees. Even today, with skyscrapers sprouting in various parts of the huge city that sprawls twenty or thirty miles in every direction, one can look out from an airliner and see that trees remain a dominant part of the landscape.

All around us, homes were being converted into offices for architects, art galleries, advertising agencies, and other small businesses. Our house was at 819 Harold Street, one block from Montrose Boulevard, and only two blocks from our first apartment on Hawthorne Street. Next door to our home was a rooming house, making us aware of the presence of a few transients in our community. However, we felt neither threatened nor menaced by our neighbors or anyone on the streets. Houston was a large city and we locked our doors, but we felt safe and were not afraid of taking walks through the darkened neighborhood in the late evenings.

Don wanted to move to Harold Street immediately, but the interior required painting and I refused to leave our present home until that task was finished. We finally compromised on his completing the kitchen and bedroom before our move; with the help of his brother Pete and his friend Henry Buckley, Don had the house ready for us within a week or so. I was surprised at how easily he turned a dark, dismal, and neglected house into a lovely, cheerful, and spacious home. We had a white interior throughout, with a single ocher accent wall in the living room. We stayed here until October, 1962, when we gave it up to move to Manhattan; it was the longest we lived in one place.

We were living here when John F. Kennedy came to Houston to campaign for the presidency in the summer of 1960. We drove out Montrose Boulevard and parked our car just off Chelsea Street near Main Street. We stood alone on the grass and watched as he rode by on the back of the convertible and waved. I was surprised that he was quite handsome. The next time that Kennedy appeared in a motorcade in Houston was on Thursday, November 21, 1963, the day before he was assassinated during a motorcade in Dallas.

After we moved to Harold Street, I became unusually nervous. Not only was I still recovering from the emotional loss of the two little boys but I was also physically exhausted. Finally, Don telephoned my mother and asked her to take me on a holiday.

The next day, my mother and I left on a trip to South Texas and Mexico. She was a beautiful woman whose love for life I inherited. We spent the next few days driving through towns and villages along the Texas and Mexico border, mostly hunting rocks and touring cactus gardens. Then we drove back up to Baffin Bay, near Kingsville, to a small place that my mother owned, and she arranged for a fisherman to take us out to a private, isolated island in the Gulf of Mexico. We stayed in a cottage one of my uncles had built, and for several days we fished and walked along the beach. An older man lived on the island as caretaker; otherwise, we were alone. There were no telephones, nothing but the Gulf. We were gone long enough that when we returned I was calm and healthy again and had recovered my usual joy in life.

During our absence, I neither telephoned nor contacted Don. My mother called home once or twice, and one of my sisters told him when I would return. As we drove up to the front of our home, Don was waiting on the porch with his arms stretched out for me. We were happy to see each other and nothing else seemed important. The next morning we discussed children again, and this time I told Don that I also felt we should give up our attempts to have a child, at least for the present.

It was not long after this, in September, 1960, that Don left the university to pursue his writing. The previous four years, from 1956 to 1960, represented a period of extraordinary development for him; he created *Forum* and with it was zealous in exploring every possible source for new ideas and in making friends not only in the world of literature but in art and music as well.

FROM THE SUMMER OF 1956 through the summer of 1960, Don spent much of his professional life creating and producing the literary journal *Forum* for the University of Houston. From the moment he joined the university's public relations staff, Don had campaigned for a magazine that he could edit and over which he would have control. He desired desperately to become a part of the country's literary community, to be in contact with all the writers whose work he knew from the *New Yorker* and other magazines and journals. He knew he belonged in this world, and he believed that his chance to join it would come through working at the university and editing a magazine that combined the fine arts with scholarly essays and original short stories and poetry.

Just before our marriage, in the late summer of 1956, in spite of every imaginable obstacle—a scarcity of money, faculty indifference, and very little editorial talent other than his own—Don brought out the first issue of *Forum,* the new literary magazine at the University of Houston. By the spring of 1957, he was working on the second issue.

Don was certain of his own talents, his sensitivity to new ideas and to literature; he was confident he could create an important new journal. The University of Houston was largely known for the generosity of one of its benefactors, Hugh Roy Cullen, and not for its academic achievements. The Cullen endowment, however, was used for capital expenditures, not for operating expenses or for attracting faculty. To make matters worse, other potential benefactors were discouraged by the myth of Cullen's gifts. The alumni was not yet able to provide substantial support, and although the university was about to become part of the state system, it was still a private institution. There were no funds for the kind of magazine that Don imagined.

Nevertheless, by an unusual force of will, Don persuaded the president and vice president of development to provide minimal funds for a journal. Don was certain he could attract scholars of merit and even publish the work of important creative writers. Within a very short time, it was clear that this is what was taking place. *Forum* became the vehicle that opened the world of the literary "elite" to Don. Literally overnight, the new magazine gave him access to creative writers, scholars, artists, editors, and publishers—almost anyone that he chose to contact.

Editing a new publication was a dream that Don had even before he went to Korea; he now saw a chance to attain it and he meant to have it. He ignored obstacles that would have disheartened just about anyone else. His first move was to change the format of *Acta Diurna,* a small weekly faculty publication that I started at the university a few years earlier, to a standard magazine size. From there, it was just a matter of a few months before Don persuaded the University of Houston to go ahead with a scholarly journal. He argued that the journal could be produced with a very small budget, especially since it would be possible to use the university's existing printing plant.

Almost from the first, prominent members of the faculty at the University of Houston opposed Don's editorial philosophy. As editor, he not only sought articles covering almost every intellectual discipline, but he also wanted to publish original literary work and essays on the fine arts as well. For the faculty, a journal that combined several disciplines defied tradition, but the biggest heresy was that Don solicited authors outside of academia.

As editor of *Forum,* Don searched continually for contributors. In the small journals, he read all the new, experimental literature he could find, looking for new ideas among authors he knew or in whom he was interested. He read whatever he found compelling, including essays in philosophy, psychology, and political science.

The contents of the first issue fell short of what Don had envisioned but gave an indication of the kind of journal he wanted *Forum* to be. On the whole, contributions from the university's own faculty were disappointing; an article by Maurice Natanson was the one significant exception. In "Defining the Two Worlds of Man," Natanson, a phenomenologist, examined the "modes of approach to self-understanding," the scientific method and the existential approach. It was the first of several essays that he would contribute to *Forum,* and it gave readers insight into what might be expected in forthcoming issues.

Don also turned to Natanson for recommendations on authors as well as advice on the content and design of the journal. Natanson remained important to Don and his work throughout his life. Other articles in the first issue, all from faculty and staff of the University of Houston, were on history, music, art, television, photography, and engineering—a radical departure from traditional journals.

For the first three issues, Don continued to depend largely on University of Houston contributions, but by the spring of 1957, manuscripts began to come in from authors whose work he had solicited during the previous eighteen months. He was elated to have Walker Percy's "The Act of Naming" and James Collins's "Art and the Philosopher," and he used both essays in the summer, 1957, issue. Natanson had recommended Collins, and Don had discovered Percy in *Partisan Review*. In his quest for ideas and authors, Don read through journal after journal and then wrote to journal editors, to publishers, and to authors. He was looking for new ideas as well as new fiction. He discovered the essays of William H. Gass at this time, but it was only after he had written his own first stories that Don learned that Gass wrote fiction as well.

After reading Percy's "The Man on the Train" in *Partisan Review* in 1956, Don wrote to Percy On March 12, 1957, to ask for an essay for *Forum*. Using a letter that he had devised for most of his requests, Don wrote, "Your recent articles in *Partisan Review* and *Commonweal* . . . especially 'The Man on the Train,' represent the kind of thing in which we are particularly interested." Don also invited comments on *Forum* and thus a correspondence was established between them. Percy wrote on March 26, "What occurs to me is to send you a chapter from a forthcoming book, much of which has appeared or will appear in journals like *Sewanee Review, Thought,* etc. But it may be too long for you. . . . *Forum* is most attractive—and original (Rattle snakes and existentialism!). Liked articles on Kazan and consumer behavior. Would like to see more—to get a better feel of what you're trying to do."[1]

The "forthcoming book" that Percy mentioned was undoubtedly the collection of essays published in 1975, *The Message in the Bottle*. In a note to that book, Percy explained that the chapters were written over a period of twenty years. The *Forum* articles to which he referred were articles in the second issue of *Forum,* one on alienation in William Faulkner, another on venom research, and another on social motivation analysis, all written by University of Houston professors. A fourth was an essay that Don wrote on Elia Kazan.

When he received Percy's letter, Don was finishing the third issue of *Forum* and did not reply until May 20. Enclosing a copy of the magazine, Don wrote that he would like to have a contribution for the summer issue with a limit of five thousand words. Percy did not immediately reply, and Don wrote again on July 7 that there was still space available in the summer issue, which would be "closed out by the end of the month and appear sometime in August."

Percy wrote on July 10 that he was sending "Symbol and Sign," which would be "about 4000 words." Walker Percy was always generous and courteous in his correspondence, closing this letter with, "but don't hesitate to send it back." He sent the article on July 12 with an accompanying letter in which he writes that it was what he was "working on now . . . a subject which will interest both the scientifically minded and the literarily minded."

Under the title of "The Act of Naming," the article was published in the summer issue; in the 1975 collection of essays, *The Message in the Bottle,* Percy changed it to "The Mystery of Language." Percy wrote to Don on October 2, 1957, to say that he had just received *Forum* and that it was a "very good-looking job, striking format. I, for one, am proud to be a part of it. Thanks also for your skillful editing which helped my piece not a little." Then he continued that "it was a pleasant surprise to see the article by James Collins; he is that rare creature, a first-class philosopher who is also a first-class writer."

Don asked for another essay for 1958, but Percy wrote on August 4 that he was working on a book "and the chapters run about 10,000–15,000 [words]." Although he did not describe it further, Percy was alluding to the manuscript that became *The Moviegoer*. The only time that Percy mentioned payment for his work was in this letter: "Incidentally, how come a U. of Houston publication isn't paying about a dollar a word?" With writers that he especially wanted, Don was always concerned about the inability of *Forum* to pay. After he explained the journal's financial circumstances, Percy did not mention money again, even when he later sent Don a chapter from *The Moviegoer*.

The next essay that Percy sent to *Forum* was "Loss of the Creature," which appeared in the fall, 1958, issue of *Forum*. Then in June of l959, Don wrote to Percy again, enclosing a note that Dwight Macdonald, who was on the *New Yorker* staff, wrote on March 23. Don had requested an article from Macdonald and with his letter sent a copy of *Forum*, which included Percy's "Loss of the Creature." Macdonald praised the magazine but could not send anything special because of other commitments. He was also impressed with the paper by Percy and enclosed an article for Don to forward to Percy.

In June, 1959, Percy also wrote that "sometime this summer" he hoped to send another "Loss of —." And then on July 17, he wrote that he hoped in the fall to "get going on the kind of pieces you seem to like for *Forum*." Right now "I'm wrassling with a piece of fiction and not doing too well." He signed the letter, "Earl Long."

As soon as Don received this letter, he telephoned Percy to ask more about his "piece of fiction" and if Percy would let him have an excerpt for *Forum*. Percy did not give him an answer until December 4, 1959, when he wrote that his agent had his legible copy of the manuscript but that "as soon as I can, and am able, will send you 5000 words of the curious adventures of my ingenious young moviegoer."

When Don first learned that Percy was working on a novel, he suggested to Herman Gollob, now with Little, Brown and Company in Boston, that he contact Percy. But when Herman did, Percy replied that *The Moviegoer* was already under option to Knopf. At that point, after Don asked him about Knopf, Percy replied, "Yes, Knopf did option my book, paid me a small sum, then shot it back with the suggestion that I rewrite it. Since then I've been sitting here . . . of no mind to do anything. As soon as I come to a conclusion that (1) it needs rewriting or (2) does not, I rewrite it or not and give you any part you might want."[2]

Shortly after this, in spite of Knopf's option, Percy mailed chapter 2 of *The Moviegoer* to *Forum*, with a note saying, "Use any or all of it or more. Would appreciate any corrections and suggestions."

As soon as he read the manuscript, Don had it set in type for the summer issue of 1960. He had no doubt that in running Percy's fiction, he was achieving a victory. Don made several editing suggestions, all minor except for the concluding portion of the chapter. Don advised Percy that as a short story, the chapter should end with part 11, thus deleting all but a few sentences from the last twelve pages of the original manuscript of some forty pages. Percy's response was as generous as ever: "Glad you wish to use as much as you do. You are welcome to it. Your reaction to the last section will probably be of great value to me. There's my weakness and it may be fatal—this Platonizing." Later, for *The Moviegoer*, Percy wrote a new section 12 for chapter 2 that is quite different from the one submitted to *Forum*.[3]

Percy's literary agent, Elizabeth Otis of McIntosh and Otis, was dismayed when she heard that *Forum* was to have an advance chapter of the book. Percy telephoned Don to tell him of this development, and on June 21, 1960, Don wrote to her with the assurance that *Forum* did not expect to retain copyright of the published manuscript. Although she was clearly unhappy, Otis accepted this arrangement and asked that *Forum* send an assignment of copyright to Percy.

Percy clearly did not look forward to the prospect of further revisions of *The Moviegoer*, nor was he entirely satisfied with the finished manuscript. Don had forwarded several letters from readers who were interested in Percy's philosophical essays, including one from Nelle Haber at Simon and Schuster. On July 22, Percy thanked Don for the letters, then turned back to the novel: "They do not . . . dispel the melancholy gnawing that once having screwed it up in the end, it cannot be unscrewed."

At this time Don had written an early version of "The Hiding Man," which he sent to both Herman Gollob and Walker Percy while he was still at the university. Don was fearful that his story, which takes place inside a motion picture theater, might encroach on Percy's own tale of a moviegoer.

In a letter dated July 26, 1960, Percy was reassuring about this question and then went on to comment on what he called Don's "Catholicizing":

> As for your Hiding Man, you needn't have worried, of course. We're plowing different rows, I found it very funny but a bit nervous in its Catholicizing. It is gradually forcing itself upon me in the most painful way that it is almost impossible to Catholicize, pro or con, without falling on your face. It is a terrible something to have by the tail. My revision will largely consist of removing Catholic licks (and all other licks). Plato is killing us. Back to things. Zuruck an die Sache—that's my motto from here on (a lesson of the incarnation after all).[4]

The tenor of Don and Percy's correspondence was always friendly and generous. Although this was the only overt allusion to Catholicism in their correspondence, there is little doubt that Percy's Catholicism created an affinity between the two writers. Of course, Percy's philosophical interests, including his interest in language, were important to Don as well. Throughout his life, he referred to Percy as one of the writers he admired.

When Don advised Percy that he was leaving *Forum* to write full time but that he still hoped to find an editorial job in the East, Percy wrote that if he ever needed a letter "testifying to your editorial wizardry, I, having thrice benefitted, will go all out."

Forum allowed Don not only to read and even edit the work of a number of leading thinkers, it also produced several enduring friendships, especially those with Percy and Natanson. Don corresponded with prominent psychologists, including Henri F. Ellenberger and Joseph Lyons. Through Edmund Carpenter, editor of *Explorations* and a professor of anthropology at Adelphi University, Don learned of the work of Marshall McLuhan at the Center for Culture and Technology at the University of Toronto. McLuhan submitted as a manuscript a copy of a speech that he had made on his theory concerning the influence of electronic media on culture. It was entitled "The Medium Is the Message" and ran in

Forum in the summer of 1960, well before McLuhan's best-known work was published.

From the first, Don sought articles in philosophy and psychology, so that in every issue, there were at least one or two articles in these disciplines. Walker Percy's were among the more important contributions. Although he received little recognition for his essays in the 1950s, scholars have now recognized that by 1960 Percy's work had anticipated many of the later developments in the philosophy of language. Although these ideas were new to Don, he easily recognized that Percy's work was original. Even before the Percy essays, Don accepted an article by Edmund Pincoffs, a young professor of philosophy at the University of Houston, on the work of Ludwig Wittgenstein.

In psychology, Don turned to Richard I. Evans, another of the university's younger professors, for articles based on two important interviews conducted during the first years of *Forum*. One was an interview with Ernest Jones, who met Freud at the first analytical congress at Salzburg in April, 1908, and who later became Freud's eminent biographer. Evans traveled to Paris in the summer of 1957 for a filmed interview with Jones, then submitted it to *Forum* for publication. John W. Meaney, a professor in radio and television, accompanied Evans to film the interview. It turned out to be the last interview with Jones before his death in 1958.

Throughout the first year of *Forum*, Don worked on developing contacts—especially on the East Coast. He soon found that to print the major authors he desired, it would be necessary to turn to writers and their publishers for excerpts from forthcoming books, or in some instances, for reprints of previously published work. Beacon Press, a nonprofit press that had gained a reputation for publishing important but less commercial work, soon became one of his best sources for material, especially excerpts from forthcoming books. Negotiations with Thomas A. Bledsoe, director of Beacon Press, were sticky at first, inasmuch as writers and their publishers expected remuneration for use of their work. Don, of course, was working without any budget whatsoever for fees.

The first article that Don requested from Beacon was taken from Lewis A. Coser and Irving Howe's *The American Communist Party: A Critical History,* a major undertaking that was to be published early the following year and that the *New York Times* would call "the best single volume available on the subject today."

In June, 1957, at Natanson's suggestion, Don had written to Coser at Brandeis University, inviting him to write an article for *Forum*. Coser replied that he did not have time at the present but suggested that Don consider part of a chapter from *The History of the American Communist Party*, which he and Howe had written and which was to be published by Beacon Press.

Don liked the idea and replied that the article "might center about a portrait of The Communist with perhaps some material on the movement for background." After checking with Howe, Coser on August 1 sent Don two sections from the book, one called "The Nature and Ends of Stalinism" and the other, "The Party and Its Followers," and offered to write a short introduction. At the same time, he pointed out that Beacon would want to know what the magazine would pay.

But when Don wrote to Beacon Press, Bledsoe was dismayed to learn that *Forum* did not propose to pay for publishing rights. He sent Don a response on October 10, pointing out the irony that oil-rich Houston was too poor to pay reprint fees. Don had meanwhile corresponded with Irving Howe as well. Howe explained how much time the book had taken but promised that if they were unable to publish articles in a national magazine, then he would pressure Beacon to give the material to Don.

In reply to Bledsoe's letter concerning payment of a fee, Don wrote on October 14,

> Let me assure you that it is not because we are reluctant to
> trundle a few barrels of oil from vault to market that we are unable
> to offer you any substantial reprint fee for the Howe-Coser piece;
> sadly enough, neither vault nor oil exists. The University's wealth
> is a myth, and one that has severely damaged us. Such oil royalties
> as we have received have paid for our physical plant, and we have
> no endowment. We are not "oil-rich" but publicity-rich, and rich
> in publicity of the most unfortunate kind.
>
> Like Beacon, the University is a non-profit organization . . . we
> are quite simply unable to afford a respectable budget for the mag-
> azine and a decent honorarium for our authors.
>
> . . . still very much interested in running the section in question,
> and would be obliged if you would let me know when and if this
> becomes a possibility.

Meanwhile, in a letter to Natanson, Don related the incident, referring to Bledsoe's "very nasty letter," adding that he "took great pleasure in writing an equally nasty letter in reply, a pleasure which I can't often afford." Bledsoe, however, was not offended by Don's letter and expressed his sympathy. He went on to offer an excerpt of the book for *Forum*. A few months later, Beacon gave Don permission to go ahead with the article, and it was finally published in the May, 1958, issue of *Forum* as "Toward a Theory of Stalinism."

Don made a practice of sending copies of *Forum* to writers from whom he solicited articles so that from the first, most authors were pleased with both the unconventional content and the glossy magazine format. Determined to persuade authors that *Forum* provided an exciting format for publication, Don hoped that the sight of *Forum* would inspire them to submit work even though they would not be paid a fee.

For each of the first two issues of *Forum,* Don invited two of his friends, Pat Goeters and Henry Buckley, both architects, to design the covers. He even designed one cover himself for volume 2, number 2, in May, 1958, under the pseudonym of Saul Greenbloom. After that, cover designs came from Houston's fine artists and commercial artists, among them Robert Morris, Jim Culberson, and Bill Shields. The covers provided the journal with a contemporary look quite different from traditional scholarly quarterlies.

For each issue, Don brought galley proofs home for us to read at night; the articles were interesting, and I enjoyed reading them. He spent other evenings working on layouts and details of design as well. Don liked the overall design that he had developed but was never entirely satisfied with the page layouts. He brought the layouts home and with everything spread out on a rug, he spent hours moving type around. For Don, every element was part of the design, so that although he was usually preparing to go to press, he experimented with various type fonts and their placement throughout the evening. The next morning he would walk over to the university's press to help with headlines and other display type that was set by hand.

Throughout these years with *Forum,* Don reveled in the design and overall makeup of the journal. He wrote to designers of typography, requesting special fonts that he needed. He kept a file of clippings of miscellaneous art, mostly out-of-copyright art, that he could use as illustrations, a practice he had begun as a reporter at the *Post.* He had always been interested in typography as an element of page layout and design, but now he was experimenting with art incorporated into the text of the articles. It was not surprising that later Don continued this practice in writing fiction.

From issue to issue, Don changed page layouts, type fonts for the table of contents, and placement of page numbers and other elements of design. I found this particular effort tedious, but the magazine brought praise from all over the country, from its contributors and subscribers as well as from other scholars and artists to whom Don mailed the magazine, many of them commending the magazine for its departure from a traditional format.

By December, 1957, the tone of Don's relationship with Bledsoe had changed enough that Don felt sufficiently confident to send him a proposal for a new journal that Beacon might publish and that he, Don, might edit. Bledsoe had "assembled what is probably the most exciting group of writers at work today . . . a magazine which had these people as a sort of core of contributors could take a commanding place in the field almost immediately."

Don went on to propose a "*Beacon Review* devoted in part to excerpts from your upcoming books and in part to pieces from other sources":

> Your people [writers] are, certainly, widely disparate, but in a sense appear to belong together. In other words, the list as it stands might be the table of contents of a first-rate periodical, one totally unlike any other.
>
> My own interest . . . is simply that I would very much like, somewhere, to produce a magazine like this, and that at the moment none exists. In our journal here we have published some very good people (we have a piece coming up from your Leslie Fiedler, by the way) but it [is] rather too much like working in a vacuum.

When Don told Bledsoe that editing *Forum* was like "working in a vacuum," it was an astute description of Don's dilemma at that time. He had almost no one with whom he could talk, no resources, and an advisory board that was becoming more and more disapproving of his choice of manuscripts.

Nevertheless, around the country, he was establishing a network, and Beacon became part of it. In March, 1958, four months after he had written to Bledsoe proposing a magazine, Don received a reply from Edward Darling, who introduced himself as the new director of Beacon Press. Don's idea, Darling wrote,

> has a lot of merit; but right now we are negotiating with *The Hibbert Journal* and will become its American distributor. . . . Even so, I intend to discuss your basic idea with our Board of Directors. I don't think they will want to do anything about it for at least six months; and you should feel free to look elsewhere if you

wish. Just the same, this is not being placed in any circular file, such as a waste basket, because I think the idea has too many possibilities for that.

Don did not pursue the magazine prospect further with Darling but continued to correspond about publications for *Forum*. At this point, he had not yet received the okay on the Coser and Howe book and once again requested permission to use excerpts from it for an article. He wrote to Darling, "I can't suggest that publication of this material with us will send hundreds of people scurrying out to buy the book, but it might help, especially in this section of the country." Darling gave approval for publication of the piece in *Forum* and in the two years that followed, Don and Darling developed a friendly correspondence in which the latter recommended a number of authors and books that Don might consider for *Forum*.

On June 27, 1958, Darling asked about *Forum*'s article by Jean-Paul Sartre on Algeria, which he said "is driving me nuts":

> This also appears, either in this translation or another . . . in a
> book published by Braziller . . . entitled *The Question* written by
> Henri Alleg, the editor of the Algerian newspaper whose torture is
> described in part in the Sartre article. I have just finished reading
> the book, and while, in its way, it is just another detailed account
> of inhuman torture, there are things about it that give it a universal
> significance so that it stands as sort of an archetype of its kind; and
> of course the Sartre introduction, and I don't need to tell you, is
> pretty overwhelming.

The essay, entitled "Algeria," was the introduction to Alleg's book and Sartre's response to an account of torture by Alleg, a Frenchman who had survived the latest techniques of torture by French paratroops in Algiers after his arrest on June 12, 1957. Alleg, who was still in prison in Algeria, had resisted what was described as "inhuman torture" and had not "talked." Alleg's book, *The Question,* had been published by Editions de Minuit in early 1958, just a few weeks before Sartre's article was published in *L'Express*. The book was banned throughout France, but Malcolm McCorquodale, a Houstonian who represented the interests of Dominique and Jean de Menil, saw the essay in *L'Express* and proposed a translation for *Forum*.

In the article, Sartre recalls the torture of French people by Germans during World War II and explores the meaning of Frenchmen becoming torturers during the French-Algerian War. However, it would be four more years before General Charles de Gaulle negotiated a final peace with the Algerians and most colonials returned to their native countries.

Beacon wanted to reprint the article in the *Register,* a Unitarian church monthly that Beacon published. Don, of course, agreed and the article was published using *Forum's* translation.

After this, Darling sent lists of forthcoming books and advance galley proofs of books from which Don might extract articles. He quickly found an excerpt from William Carlos Williams's new book, *I Wanted to Write a Poem;* the article then appeared in the fall, 1958, issue of *Forum.*

Next, Don asked to see Walter Kaufmann's forthcoming book, *From Shakespeare to Existentialism: Studies in Poetry, Religion, and Philosophy,* from which he took excerpts for an article on Freud that appeared in the summer, 1959, issue of *Forum.* As he always did, Don made minor editorial revisions in his copy of the printed text, then had the manuscript typed and submitted to Beacon for approval. The changes were largely necessary to pull together excerpts from the book into a coherent article. By this time, in the late 1950s, Don's own reading background was such that he could quickly find in Kaufmann's book an article of significance for *Forum.*

In looking at the copy of the book in which Don made changes, I recalled how astute and sensitive he was to new work by established scholars—just as he was to new ideas from writers of whom he had never heard. Don's talent for recognizing new ideas and new writers when they were just emerging led to some of the most important work published by *Forum.* Walker Percy and Marshall McLuhan were among the contributors whose work was not widely known when Don first published them in *Forum.*

It was also from Beacon Press that Don obtained a copy of short stories by Bruce Brooks, a relatively unknown author whose story he wanted to publish in 1960. Don had read a story by Brooks entitled "Journey through the Skin" in *Accent* and "was greatly impressed by it." He then contacted Beacon Press in order to reach Brooks. However, the story that Don later received from Brooks was never published in *Forum.* By late 1959, Don's relationship with his editorial board was to become strained to the point that in November he attempted to resign from *Forum.*

But throughout 1958, Don had continued to work miracles, mostly through sheer will and the certainty that what he was doing was a good thing; by the end of the second year, his efforts to obtain the kind of manuscripts that he wanted were paying off. In the summer issue of 1958, he ran another interview by Evans, this time with Carl Gustav Jung. This interview was one of the last granted by Jung, who died in 1961. Another article was by Peter Yates, a West Coast music critic with whom Don became good friends, and there were photographs of paintings by Gerald McLaughlin, an essay on film by Parker Tyler (an editor of *Art News*), and an essay on architecture.

In this issue, the reader can see Don pursuing his theory of producing a magazine of "widely disparate" people who "in a sense appear to belong together." Joseph Lyons, a research psychologist when Don first contacted him, became one of Don's favorite contributors. Lyons was in the medical research laboratory at the Lexington, Kentucky, Veterans Administration Hospital when he submitted an article entitled "The Psychology of Angels." Within the next two years, *Forum* published three more essays by Lyons.

Don found the "angels" essay provocative and returned to it later in his fiction. In a short story entitled "On Angels," originally published in the *New Yorker* on August 9, 1969, Don incorporated quotes from Lyons's essay to develop one of the recurring themes of his fiction, the "search for a new principle."

Hugh Kenner, another writer and scholar whom Don admired, gave him "Sweeney and the Voice," an excerpt from *The Invisible Poet,* his forthcoming book on T. S. Eliot. It appeared in the spring, 1959, issue, and not long after that Kenner sent a longer article on Samuel Beckett entitled "The Rational Domain." This ran in the summer, 1960, issue of *Forum.*

Leslie Fiedler, who was teaching at Montana State University at that time, was one of the scholars from whom Don requested a contribution during the first year of *Forum.* Fiedler was initially interested in writing an essay on J. D. Salinger, but after two years of promising the article he proposed instead an essay from his book *Love and Death in the American Novel,* which was to be published in 1960. Entitled "The Secret Life of James Fenimore Cooper," the article ran in the summer, 1960, issue of *Forum.*

With each issue of the magazine and the praise it brought, Don's confidence in *Forum* and in his talents as an editor were strengthened. From the first, he was bold in asking for manuscripts. By looking for reprints as well as original work, Don was able to explore every conceivable source for contributions. Throughout this time, he used whatever tactic was necessary. He could not "browbeat" authors, but he could be persuasive in arguing on behalf of *Forum*. However, much of the time, it was still through the force of his own will that he got what he wanted.

In trying to get permission to print the translation of the essay on torture by French philosopher Jean-Paul Sartre, Don telephoned Sartre in Paris for his approval. When Farris Block, director of the news service and Don's supervisor, discovered that Don was making international telephone calls, he pointed out that the journal did not have the budget for this kind of expense. At this point, Don, in his cavalier fashion, replied "I'll pay for it." Accustomed to Don's intransigence at such times, Farris did not bother to argue further.

After more negotiations that required further calls to France as well as correspondence with the Paris office of *Time,* Don received permission to publish the Sartre piece. Because the French-Algerian War was a contemporary event, the essay was timely and Don was resolved to make *Forum* a journal of broad intellectual dimension. He would not permit anything as petty as the cost of transatlantic telephone calls to stand in his way. In fact, our personal telephone statement each month included several calls and telegrams to prospective contributors. Don simply called and charged it to our residence phone.

Even though the magazine was a shoestring operation from the first, the misconception that the University of Houston was wealthy from the gifts it had received from oilman Hugh Roy Cullen continued to discourage writers. When an author turned him down for this reason, Don would explain the circumstances and sometimes the writer relented and submitted the article anyway.

There were times when Don felt the magazine's position was untenable and he would not pursue his request any further. This occurred in Don's pursuit of an article from Alfred Kazin. He first wrote to Kazin on July 21, 1958, inviting him to send something to *Forum*. For Don, Kazin was one of the important critics of American literature. Kazin's *On Native Grounds,* published in 1942, had been an influential work in Don's own study of critical writing, and then more recently he had read and admired Kazin's *The Inmost Leaf,* published in 1955.

In his letter to Kazin, he explained that the "magazine is addressed not to scholars but to the educated general reader; the idea is to offer the kind and quality of thinking that a university, ideally, represents to a primarily non-academic audience." Don went on to say that "most of what we get in the realm of the humanities seems hopelessly dull—or else pale and new critical—and I am in hopes you might be persuaded to provide us with something that is not."

When Kazin finally answered in January of the following year, it was only to apologize for not having anything to send. However, in March, after learning that *Forum* did not pay contributors, he wrote that he appreciated Don's interest in his work but could not understand why the university did not pay authors. Like most people in this era, Kazin did not understand the financial problems of the university.

Don was frustrated and even a little angry at the plight in which he found himself—no money for authors. He wrote a lengthy, somewhat rueful reply:

> You are absolutely right but if I sent you this money I would have to cut exactly 16 pages out of the magazine. If I sent $300 each to three more contributors there would be no magazine. This perhaps would be no great loss but I must believe otherwise. The magazine is produced at absolute minimum cost. The University has an annual deficit of close to $600,000 a year. All of Cullen's money went into grandiose buildings with nothing left to keep the radiators burning. The magazine is printed in our own makeshift campus printing plant where the question of whether or not we should spend $15 for a new roller is gravely debated. The printers, about half of whom are students, are suitably underpaid. I set a good deal of the display type myself and do a number of other things which you probably wouldn't believe to save money. We bought the good paper in quantity at a distress sale. The handsome typefaces were begged by me from the manufacturers. If I send a telegram I have to pay for it out of my own pocket (I'm not a professor either, by the way). The faculty feels that it's too esoteric: what is all this Dada business anyhow? Because the magazine is produced here, all hands are pretty sure that it can't be much good.
>
> All of this is irrelevant. The answer to your question is that the printer *shouldn't* be paid when the writer is not. But the printer is invariably adamant whereas the writer is sometimes willing to be victimized. This difference between printers and writers is what makes possible marginal journals like our own, which have no real (economic) right to exist. Whether all this effort on the part of writers, printers, and editors is worthwhile—whether the maga-

zine itself is a good magazine, or is meaningful in any way—is another question. We are, of course, visited from time to time by the thought that we are merely deluding ourselves about the worth of the whole project.

I wasn't aware that you were not teaching; if I had been, I probably would have hesitated to ask you for a contribution. I hesitated as it was, the first time I wrote; I'm very conscious of the absence of that $300. But this is my problem, not yours.

Don took Kazin's rejection seriously, but at other times his reply to authors, especially those who were not dependent on writing income, was lighthearted and witty. On July 29, 1958, in reply to a complaint from Stanley Walker, a renowned author and newspaper editor, he wrote,

It is well known that your services are approximately priceless; and it was for this reason, and this reason only, that I was reluctant to offend you with the customary $43,000 honorarium.

Your cogent analysis of the matter has convinced me, however, that I have been overly scrupulous. I have therefore taken the liberty of donating this sum in your name to the local branch office of Sons and Daughters of I Will Arise, where it was received with tears and shouting.

As to your other point, we don't expect you to be helpful, friendly, courteous, kind, brave, clean and reverent. Just brilliant.

But after reconsidering Don's request to write on the state of journalism at that time, Walker turned him down, this time because he seemed to feel that writing on journalism would not do any good.

In the summer of 1959, Don began working on a project to bring together editors of journals from across the country for a national two-day conference to take place later that year. Don called it the "Conference of Editors of American Literary and Intellectual Journals" and first sought to convene the meeting in Houston. A similar gathering, "The Little Magazine in America," had taken place at Harvard University in 1956, and the editors to whom he wrote were enthusiastic about the prospect of another meeting.

After he was unable to get financial support from the University of Houston, Don set a new date and began to look elsewhere for funds. By this time, he had also decided to work on moving the conference east. He then submitted a proposal to the Ford Foundation for a grant, but on December 7, 1959, W. McNeil Lowry, director of the foundation, wrote to explain that there were no funds currently available for such an effort. Many of the editors and proposed speakers had assumed they would receive financial assistance if they participated in the conclave, so he could expect no assistance from other journals. Thus, with nowhere else to turn, Don reluctantly gave up the project.

Like most endeavors he undertook during these years, the proposed conference gave Don a reason to write to scholars and literary figures with whom he had not yet had a reason to correspond. By now, his name was becoming known in several realms of the literary world, even before he published the first of his short stories.

Through correspondence concerning the meeting, Don became friends with the poet Robert Bly, who was then editor of the journal *The Fifties*. He later invited Bly to Houston to read poetry for the Contemporary Arts Association. And Bly was one of the first writers that Don contacted when he later sought manuscripts for *Location* in New York.

In November of 1959, *Forum* experienced an editorial crisis over the subject of a short story. Don had from the first resisted what he felt was excessive interference by members of the editorial board. One frequent complaint was that the manuscripts he sought were "too esoteric." At one point he wrote a letter of resignation from his position as editor of *Forum*. He was persuaded not to resign, so for several more months he tried to resolve problems with the board. But when Don accepted a Bruce Brooks story in which homosexuality was a theme, it was immediately rejected by the chairman, John Allred, without submission to the full editorial board.

Outraged, Don wrote a letter to Allred. He argued that "not publishing this story (or the next one) is a certain way to kill *Forum*. The magazine is dead just as soon as we are governed by other people's anticipated reactions to what we print. We have killed it ourselves." He pointed out that

> Joyce, Pound, Eliot, Lawrence, Stein etc. etc. were all greeted with exactly this kind of outraged alarm when they first appeared. They were redeemed by time. Ought we to content ourselves with "safe" writers or writers for whom other people have already taken the risks? To argue that ours is a special situation is no argument. Our situation is exactly what we make of it.
>
> If you don't like the story, so be it. But a very reputable publishing firm (owned, incidentally, by the Unitarian Church) disagrees with you; I disagree [with] you, too. And in any case, I doubt that disliking the story justified attempting to arbitrarily upset our established reviewing procedure.

In response to Don's letter, Allred called a meeting of the board to clarify procedure when a single board member objected strongly to a particular manuscript. The policy that then existed was that a manuscript would be rejected if two board members vetoed it. But as a practice, the majority of the board did not read any one manuscript, making it possible for objectionable material to be printed.

The proposed meeting was held on March 23, 1960; in response to events of the meeting, the result of which was to give complete editorial control to the board, Don wrote a scathing letter of resignation on March 30. He wrote that "there is apparently a fundamental disagreement about what kind of a magazine *Forum* should be." He had "been attempting to publish a serious journal, comparable to other university-sponsored journals" and did not feel there was "sufficient support for this objective."

The journal must "display the highest standards of thought and writing, a reasonable freedom of expression, a willingness to experiment, and a degree of literary sophistication." He thought the board did not "share these goals" and "the last quality is notably absent" in some decisions.

Don was now preparing the summer issue of volume 4, the last *Forum* he would edit, and agreed to continue as editor for a while longer. He knew, though, that he should make new career plans and began searching for an editing job on the East Coast.

Throughout these years with *Forum,* Don had corresponded with Gollob, who always encouraged him in his writing as well as in his editing. After giving up on the University of Houston's fine arts department in 1956, Gollob had gone to California to study acting and to work on a master of fine arts degree at the Pasadena Playhouse. Before long, he was working for a leading talent agency for actors, MCA Artists. Then in January, 1958, he accepted a job as a literary agent with the William Morris Agency in New York.

Just after joining William Morris, Herman wrote to Don urging him to submit manuscripts that he would try to get published: "This is your big chance. The Lord has sent me here only to introduce you to the literary world. Dash off a few brilliant short stories and I'll try to peddle them for you."

Herman also mentioned a date he had had with Don's sister Joan, then working in New York. "I was amazed by Joan's resemblance to you—not just physical, but in the mannerisms, etc." And he told of running into Estes Jones, another acquaintance who had worked for the *Houston Chronicle* and who agreed with Herman that Don's column for the *Cougar* "was the best college column we'd ever read."

During 1959, Gollob recommended several writers for *Forum,* including Joanna M. Davis and Sue Levine. He also suggested that Don ask Charlie Blanchard from Little, Brown for permission to quote from a new Marcel Proust biography by G. D. Painter. This was to become the first volume of a two-volume biography of Proust, but when Don followed up on Gollob's suggestion, Little, Brown was unwilling to approve a reprint without payment.

While he was still at the university, Don sent Herman Gollob an early version of "The Hiding Man," the first of the new stories that he worked on, but the second to be published. Gollob was then with the William Morris Agency and had asked Don to send some work to see if he could place it. Don sent the manuscript, but Herman rejected it and wrote in a letter in late December, 1959 that, like Ebenezer Scrooge, Herman would be "wafted by the magic of Eastern Air Lines to his home in Houston on Christmas eve. There he will meet the friends of his innocent youth and realize how corrupt and narrow he's become through his activities in the world of commerce. In particular he will be haunted by the ghost of Barthelme, a young writer who slashed his wrists after receiving a brutal letter from Gollob dissecting a beautifully wrought short story."

Because Don threw away all typescripts of his work except the final version, there is no record of the version he sent to Herman. The "hiding man" or "underground man" theme was something in which he had been interested for several years.

Herman soon moved to Boston as an editor with Little, Brown, so that before long, Don started a campaign to persuade Herman to undertake a collection of Don's short stories.

After Don's first attempt to resign from *Forum,* we began to talk about his giving up everything else to write. Finally, on September 9, 1960, after the tenth issue of *Forum* was completed, Don wrote a brief letter of resignation from the University of Houston effective October 1.

Even then, Don desired a challenging editing job, and I feel sad for him each time I recall how much he wanted, almost desperately, to find such a position on the East Coast. He believed that once in New York, he could find time for writing fiction. But it was not until after he met Harold Rosenberg, the prominent *New Yorker* critic, that a suitable position in editing finally began to materialize.

During his five years with the university, Don designed and produced dozens of promotional graphics, work in which he had some interest but that was certainly not challenging to him. During his last year at the university, in the summer of 1960, he was invited to the University of Southern California to interview for a graphic arts position in the university's development program. We talked it over, and although I was not especially interested in living in Los Angeles, I felt he should go ahead with the interview. He then flew to Los Angeles, visited the campus, and was offered the job. An editorial position was his only real interest in employment, however, and he subsequently turned down the university's offer.

As it turned out, he was able to turn to writing at once and within a short time wrote the stories that would become *Come Back, Dr. Caligari.*

Don's work for *Forum* was finally over, and for the first time he was free to write without the burden of a salaried job. This new freedom enabled him to at last start writing the kind of fiction that he had imagined for the past four years.

At the university, Don had been faced with endless drudge work in editing and producing *Forum.* Much of his professional life was made up of correspondence, meetings, and numerous petty tasks necessary to the magazine and other work of the university news service. It must have been more deadening for him than anyone knew.

ON AN OCTOBER MORNING IN 1960, four years after he read *Waiting for Godot*, Don sat down at his desk in our Montrose-area home and began to write "The Darling Duckling at School." Later retitled "Me and Miss Mandible," this story was the first to be published of the brilliantly original stories that appeared in Don's first collection, *Come Back, Dr. Caligari*. Within a few weeks, the tale of an adult who found himself in an elementary school classroom was accepted by *Contact,* a West Coast literary journal, and appeared in the seventh issue, published in early 1961.

Now that Don was finally free to write, we set about arranging our schedules to accommodate the discipline of daily writing; mornings were set aside just for writing. A few weeks before leaving the university, Don had begun to work on weekends and in the evenings but so far had produced only essays and the first version of a short story. It was now necessary to have a more exact routine. Beginning with that first day, we planned everything so that he could work from around eight or nine in the morning to at least noon. This schedule included weekends and became a routine that we adhered to rigorously.

Don was twenty-nine years old when he first began to work on these stories in 1960; from this day in October until his death twenty-nine years later, he spent almost every morning at his typewriter. Working with two fingers on a manual Remington with a right-hand shift, Don slowly and carefully typed each story.

When Don began each day, he was meticulously dressed; he wore khaki or corduroy slacks with a button-down collar shirt and in cool weather, a dark gray pullover sweater. He wore suede oxfords, but was often in his stocking feet while he was in the house. He was always at his desk by the time I had prepared breakfast at eight-thirty or nine, so I took it out to him to avoid any interruption of his writing. Don did not like eggs, so most of the time we had bacon or ham with toast and fruit juice.

I worked at home during the hours that Don wrote. My advertising agency was growing but small enough to have my office at home. In the mornings, I worked on agency accounts and on lectures for my courses at Dominican College. My classes were in the afternoons and I scheduled meetings with clients in the afternoons as well. Although we had not planned it this way, we were able to talk about each story at any stage.

I used the dining room for an office, and sometimes Don would call from the porch to ask how to spell a word or what did I think the connotation was for a particular word in a certain context. I answered the telephone and tried not to let anyone talk to him before he had stopped writing for the day.

The house on Harold Street in which Don wrote the stories for *Come Back, Dr. Caligari* was just a block or two away from principal avenues covered with commerce and heavy traffic. Yet in the early-1900s residential neighborhood in which we lived people frequently strolled by, and occasionally someone on the sidewalk outside his window would comment on Don's typing. At that time of day, the neighborhood was quiet, and the sound of the typewriter carried into the street. Beautiful old mansions with wide lovely lawns, art galleries, artists' studios, and tastefully designed buildings that were offices for architects and advertising agencies occupied the area. Within a few years, the neighborhood would become considerably more commercial, with many of the remaining homes removed for apartment sites.

As he worked during the morning, Don often leaned back in his chair to look at the page and the words on it, at first reading silently and then testing the sound of a sentence or a word or a particular phrase he had just devised by reading it aloud. I could hear him reading a sentence over and over as he changed a word or phrase. If it did not sound "right" to him, then he would discard it and start over. At one point, he told me that when the great French novelist Gustave Flaubert was working, he would walk out into the woods and shout his words.

He sometimes paused to think and to smoke a cigarette. With his right foot resting on his left knee, he sat there smoking and looking through the screened window onto the street, silently musing over what he was writing.

Don smoked constantly. In the late 1950s and even through the 1960s no one was concerned with the health risks of smoking. In our home, there were ashtrays throughout the house. Don was extremely cautious about the danger of fire, and when he finished working each day, he carried the ashtray to the kitchen to be emptied.

Don's concern for perfection was such that he would revise a sentence again and again, and then even after a version of the story was ready, he made still more revisions. Before sending off a story, Don would have completed several versions. And once Don was satisfied with a story, he was adamant about not changing it.

In the process of writing, if Don changed just one word or two words, he pulled the entire page from the typewriter, tossed it into the wastebasket and started over. He used an eraser but mostly for typographical errors. Don wrote every story in this way, with the wastebasket filled with at least thirty to forty pages discarded at the end of the morning. For typing paper, he used the customary newsprint of journalism. Later, when he told his students in creative writing to write a story sentence by sentence, and to create the sentence word by word, he was describing his own method of creativity.

Several times each morning, Don would come into the dining room and ask me to read what he had finished—sometimes a complete story and sometimes just a single passage. He then waited for my comments. Before showing it to me, he tried to have it close to the way he wanted it, and he knew that I would bring to it the clarity or freshness of not having read it before. Or we would go into the living room and while I sat on the sofa, he walked slowly around the room, reading it with his beautifully modulated voice.

With these dramatic readings, he could not only emphasize the language properly but also be certain it was just right. After I had heard it and given my response, if he felt any uncertainty at all about even a brief phrase, he returned to his typewriter and worked until he was ready to read it again. This is the process we went through with each story. He had asked that I not read anything until he was ready for me to; I always honored this request and waited for the story to reach what Don felt was the right stage.

When he seemed to be stuck on a particular story, he would go out for a long stroll in our Montrose neighborhood. Large homes, a few mansions, some showing decay, were still interesting and beautiful to see. One small community, Courtlandt Place, was developed around 1905 and is now registered as a historical site. The years around 1960 were a transitional period for the area, making it possible for us to enjoy both the beauty and the complexity of a changing city. After twenty or thirty minutes, Don would return to his typewriter.

When Don quit at noon or one o'clock, whatever he had distilled from the day's work he was almost certain to revise further and read to me once more the following day. By the end of each morning, he might have one or two pages that he had finished or was still working on, but sometimes it was just a few sentences or nothing at all. He never tried to rush his writing and simply worked until he felt a story was right.

The morning mail also became a part of this ritual. As soon as he completed each story, Don mailed it to one of a number of journals that he routinely read and thought appropriate. About a week after he mailed out "The Darling Duckling at School," Don began watching from his desk for the letter carrier to arrive; when he saw him coming down the sidewalk, he would walk out to the front porch to take the mail and see if there were any letters of acceptance or returned manuscripts.

"The Darling Duckling" was soon accepted by *Contact*. When the galley proofs arrived, Don was pleased as he read it for the first time in type. When we saw the published version we agreed that the story took on a new character and seemed to be even better than before. Payment for the story was stock in the magazine, authorized by a letter from the attorney that read, "12 Shares of Class A Capital Stock of Angel Island Publications, Inc."

The journal had requested a photograph of Don that would appear on the back cover. For this I took several informal poses outside our house; in the one he chose to send, he is frowning slightly at the bright outdoor light.

As he was writing the story of the adult in an elementary school classroom, Don observed that he felt a bit like he was starting a new life, that he felt a little strange. Because the story is filled with autobiographical allusions, I assumed the situation was a metaphor for Don's own life.

"The Hiding Man" was accepted next and appeared in the 1961 spring-summer issue of *First Person* along with work by Federico García Lorca and Edward Dahlberg. As he did in his first story, Don created an allegorical world in which he could draw from his own experiences. In "The Hiding Man," the theater and motion picture probably represent the Catholic church and the Mass. The idea may have been suggested by an article that had appeared in *Time* magazine in which Marcel Camus is quoted as saying, "The cinema has replaced the church, and people seek the truth at movies instead of the Mass."

Don's stories gradually evolved from a combination of satire and an exploration of his own consciousness to stories that took in more of the world around him. One of his first stories was suggested by a couple who owned a dry cleaning establishment; Don felt considerable sympathy for the husband, who appeared to be dominated by his wife. In the story, the husband solved his problem by putting his wife into a huge drying vat.

Don sent the story out but I cannot recall where it was published, if at all. At the time, the wife frequently asked about Don's writing and I was afraid that she might eventually see this particular work. This story was one of the few in which it is easy to identify the models for the characters. "The Piano Player," written about a year later, reflects the increasing complexity of his work; it portrays a couple caught in a suburban horror but was undoubtedly suggested by more than one acquaintance or single event.

When "Florence Green Is 81" first appeared, several prominent Houston women believed the character of Florence was based on each of them. The story is mostly autobiographical, but it includes a composite of at least two women, including Don's own grandmother, who told him a funny anecdote about bathroom plumbing that he uses in the story, and Betty Bloxsom, a founding member of the CAA and an eccentric and wealthy patron of the arts.

These first stories were published by "little magazines," but after the first year Don began submitting stories to major publications. Within two years, "Florence Green Is 81" was accepted by *Harper's Bazaar.* Shortly after that, the *New Yorker* began publishing his work.

During this first period of writing, one of Don's favorite diversions was to stride through the house, quoting poetry or sometimes well-known lines by a philosopher. Fitzgerald's epigraph for *The Great Gatsby* was still his favorite. But now he quoted others as well, frequently T. S. Eliot's "The Love Song of J. Alfred Prufrock," and usually, such lines as he "should have been a pair of ragged claws," "I grow old . . . I grow old," and "shall wear the bottoms of my trousers rolled."

This soliloquy usually occurred when Don was on his way to the kitchen for another cup of coffee, or to the dining room to locate a book he needed. After these minutes of diversion, he would return to his desk. Often, as he walked by where I was working, he stopped for a moment, balancing a pencil on his nose to amuse me. Sometimes he leaned over to kiss me and then returned to his desk. I remember that during these first years of writing, he was irresistibly happy; he was at last writing and mailing out his first stories.

Like most of our generation, Don was indebted to T. S. Eliot and Ezra Pound as well as to the novelists of the 1920s. At the same time, he read everything that interested him, and often quoted such lines as Thomas Hobbes's "the life of man, solitary, poor, nasty, brutish, and short." He was consciously immersing himself in language and literature, so that the quotation from Hobbes—like much of what he read—would eventually find its way into one of his stories.

In "Down the Line with the Annual," which first appeared in the *New Yorker* in early 1964, Don used the Hobbes quotation at the end of a sentence: " . . . and transistor radios whose estimated battery life, like the life of man, is nasty, brutish and short." But when he collected this short satirical story for *Guilty Pleasures* in 1974, Don changed the analogy to " . . . like the life of man, is a feeble, flickering thing," clearly more fitting for his piece about contemporary life and an excess of products and consumption.

In these first stories, as Don developed an ironical persona to serve as narrator for his work, he distanced himself from the immediate world in which we lived. This perspective enabled him to create a sharp contrast to our way of life, while at the same time providing him with a way to explore his own consciousness, his "dissatisfaction" with the world, and his desire to go someplace "where everything is different."

As he developed his own style of fiction, he used incisive wit and carefully wrought irony along with absurd situations and complex metaphors. But occasionally Don revealed a personal self through a lyrical or non-ironical passage that might occur anywhere in the story but frequently appeared in the concluding lines.

These passages or asides at times appear unintentional, as if Don unwittingly revealed a personal response that he meant to conceal. But as I watched Don work every day, I knew that each word, each development within a sentence was consciously shaped. It was as if in each story Don created for the reader a dramatic microcosm of himself, a young man who in public — especially among strangers — was witty and ironic, and who in private was kind and sensitive.

At this time, of course, Don did not realize that literary fame would come from short stories. What mattered was that he was at last realizing what he had been trying to do for at least ten years: to write fiction that he believed was worth publishing. And the kind of writing that he felt was "right" was antirealistic fiction in the ironical mode of Samuel Beckett.

The short dramas of Beckett and others seemed to free him from the constraints of lengthy fiction, but he still wanted to write a novel. He had abandoned the novel that he had worked on in the early 1950s and had not yet started another. As it turned out, the short story was ideal; he could experiment and revise each work to perfection.

From Beckett and other European writers that he had read since 1956, Don learned that his way of viewing the world could be fictionalized. He had experienced liberation in reading *Godot* four years earlier, but it was not until late 1958 that he talked of creating a "new" fiction. The "cool sound" for which he searched during the Korean War would now be a style of his own or a new form that would be different from anything that anyone else was doing. He wanted his story to take place where "everything is different," in another dimension, a place outside of time, but he could not yet think of how to do this.

We first talked about this on a late afternoon in the fall of 1958. We were sitting in the backyard of the house that we rented from the Linnstaedters when Don started to talk about what he wanted to achieve. We discussed plot devices, vehicles for situating his story outside of ordinary time and place. Recalling Walker Percy's essay "The Man on the Train," we discussed the possibility of a train. But actually situating a character on a train would have been trite for Don, and he quickly dismissed this idea; what he needed was a place or dimension of time that would give him more freedom to experiment. Later, he felt that the form itself would provide this freedom.

In the Modernist world that Don knew, "form and content" or "form and meaning" were inseparable. In "A Note on Elia Kazan," an essay that Don wrote for the January, 1957, issue of *Forum*, Don used what he called the "theatre of Elia Kazan" to write about the difficulties that writers face in the use of language to establish meaning in the contemporary world of science and sociology. He concluded that the "form of these dramas *is* their meaning; an interplay of silences, it speaks in accents that are eventually unmistakable." In the Elia Kazan theater, "wordlessness and frustration seem overwhelming images of helplessness, a universal lostness in the face of an existence that is complex and unforgiving."

As other avant-garde dramatists experimented with new forms to overcome the difficulties of the traditional use of language, Don felt that he too must break away from old forms. He had to find his own way of using language. Above all, whatever he wrote had to be "new" and must take place in the present, not in the past. I remember with striking clarity that when we first discussed how he could create another dimension of time and place, Don said, "What I write has to be in the present. I cannot understand how anyone can be interested in the past." He meant, of course, the historical past, of an individual or of a community. When I sometimes related family stories that I recalled from childhood, he was intrigued and said they were material for a good gothic novel. But such stories were of no interest to him for his own work.

When he spoke of "another dimension of time and place," he was suggesting a break from a traditional use of historical time. Through the years, Don often achieved meaning in his stories through the narrator's recognition of the value and significance of the present. Very early, this became a recurring theme in his work. In "Overnight to Many Distant Cities," published in the *New Yorker* in 1982, Don ended the story with the narrator having lunch "with the Holy Ghost" in Barcelona. They agree that it is a "wonderful city" and the narrator recalls that "in an ecstasy of admiration for what is we ate our simple soup." This excerpt also illustrates what I call the lyrical in Don's work, when the tone shifts from the ironical to the lyrical.

Within two years of our discussion in 1958, and within a few days of leaving the University of Houston, Don at last began to realize what he had so far only imagined.

Don had been a writer since he was a child, but in 1960, he had not yet produced anything that he could call a "literary achievement." While editing *Forum*, he found time for essays and book reviews. But he was dissatisfied that he had not yet written fiction that would satisfy his own criteria. He had discarded or put aside whatever he had written in Korea and in most of the years since then. In his single file folder of completed typescripts, he kept mostly copies of the essays that he had recently written. These included several manuscripts for *Forum*, including letters to the editor as well as a short story entitled "Pages from the Annual Report."

Under the pseudonym of David Reiner, whom he identified as living in New York City and "at work on a novel," Don published "Pages from the Annual Report" in the fall, 1959, issue of *Forum*. Although listed by bibliographers as an essay, "Pages from the Annual Report" is a work of fiction and is filled with absurdities and echoes of Kafka. If one reads the story closely, it is possible to recognize Don's voice and to hear it as a precursor of his *Come Back, Dr. Caligari* stories, but the tale is long and Don wrote it with few revisions. He needed a work of fiction to complete this issue of *Forum*, and suffering from what he thought was unjustified interference by the journal's editorial board, he wrote a story that satirized the role of his department in university bureaucracy. Don developed the story from a television script that he had written earlier that same year. The script was for a skit that was part of a series of impromptu live television shows that Pat Goeters was then producing for the University of Houston station KUHT.

But "Pages from the Annual Report" does not reveal the creative genius and control over language that is apparent in the first *Come Back, Dr. Caligari* stories. This difference is significant because once he was committed to writing fiction as his raison d'être, he then worked on everything with an intensity that must have been greater than at any previous time. I don't believe he could have achieved what he did any other way.

Don continued to write essays and book reviews, but most of his writing after leaving the university was fiction. About a year earlier, he had written a review of H. L. Hunt's *Alpaca,* which appeared in *The Reporter* on April 14, 1960, under the headline, "Mr. Hunt's Woolly Utopia." A Dallas billionaire, Hunt created his own version of utopia in a brief novel published by the H. L. Hunt Press. When Don saw the book at a bookstore, he was curious and bought a copy. Amused by it, he proposed a satirical review to *The Reporter.* Hunt's imaginary "Alpaca," described by Don as a "tiny, vaguely Southern American republic," would have a constitution in which voters who paid the most tax would get the most votes. It is at the end of the review that one hears the voice that Don would use in his fiction: "Perhaps he is only interested in re-establishing the views, somewhat tarnished in recent times, that money is something more than bonds and banknotes—it is manna, a mark of wisdom and a sign of grace."

Soon after this review appeared, he wrote an essay titled "The Case of the Vanishing Product," an article on contemporary advertising based on the *Thirty-Ninth Annual of Advertising and Editorial Art and Design.* He first attempted to sell it to *The Reporter* and was unsuccessful, but *Harper's* magazine bought it for the October, l961, issue. During this period, he also contributed a piece to the *Texas Observer* and wrote book reviews for the *Houston Post.*

Don wrote advertising copy for my clients as well. He used humor as much as possible, especially for radio commercials. Although he wrote copy quickly, he did not enjoy writing such material, especially anything in which humor was inappropriate. For print media advertising, he was much more interested in art and design than in copy. I worked with several commercial artists, but Don designed most of the ads during the first year of my agency. He liked choosing typefaces and creating clean, distinctive layouts with single headlines and one or two blocks of copy, a simple but effective format that usually worked.

But Don was more interested in the graphics of advertising than in how effective it might be for the client; sometimes he would insist that I submit an ad that I knew could not work. Shortly after I founded my agency and was preparing a campaign for the developer of a residential community for middle-income families, Don designed an ad for newspapers using a photograph that I had taken of the interior of our apartment. The layout was striking, but the interiors of the homes that were to be advertised were in no way similar to the scene in the photograph. Don could see neither the necessity of being realistic nor of pleasing clients; it was only after this particular client rejected the ad that I could persuade Don to design another.

Writing any kind of promotional copy presented little challenge to Don, and he later wrote catalog and promotional pieces for the Contemporary Arts Association and then for *Location* magazine. In 1960, however, his concern was almost solely with the fiction he had begun to write.

As Don wrote his first stories, trying to do something that no other writer had yet attempted, I did not find his work strange. Nor was it puzzling. The most interesting and experimental fiction in the late 1950s, including John Barth's *The Floating Opera* and *The End of the Road,* were breaking away from earlier forms, even those of the Modernists. The antihero was already established through the work of Barth, Saul Bellow, J. P. Donleavy, and others. John Hawkes and later Joseph Heller were among the new writers who used surrealism and other devices to create unreal, sometimes nightmarish worlds. Beckett and other European dramatists had introduced other possibilities. The idea of creating fantasies or incongruous situations, of combining the real with the unreal, was emerging as a new way of interpreting the world.

In the literature of the post–World War II period, and with the continuing dominance of New Criticism, the story as an object mattered; it was a work of art that the writer created. And the most powerful influence of all continued to be what the Modernists, especially Pound and Eliot, had given us: the necessity of creating something "new."

A reader did not ask what a story or a poem meant, nor did one necessarily expect to understand the logic of it. Its theme or the meaning might be implicit in the story, and it was enough that the reader could intuitively understand a literary work and realize its significance for that time. What you talked about was "form and content." This phrase seems hackneyed today, out-of-date and overworked. But it was real then, and what is more important, it was at the heart of Don's creativity.

When I began teaching a course on the short story at Dominican College, I discussed some of my lectures with Don, and he offered to write out some of his thoughts on creative writing. Although he wrote these notes for young college students, they provide a deceptively clear statement of his own approach to writing fiction:

> Form and content are not new. In a work of literature form and
> content are so beautifully welded together that it is difficult to

separate them. . . . Form may be said to be the arrangement of parts so that a preconceived effect is successfully achieved. In a successful work of literature, *Form* is used to state or establish *Meaning*. . . . [the] task of the writer in general is to give form to the raw material of experience—to say what it means.

Don's reaction to the fiction of J. D. Salinger illustrates both a dominant influence of the postwar world and Don's rejection of it. Don was a typical younger writer in that he admired Salinger immensely and was among those in the 1950s who searched the *New Yorker* every week hoping for one of Salinger's stories to appear. Just after "Seymour, An Introduction" was published in the summer of 1957, we were at a party at which everyone began to discuss the Salinger story. Several people were deeply moved by the scene in which Seymour's father, Les, asked him "if he remembered the time Joe Jackson had given him, Seymour, a ride on the handlebars of his bicycle, all over the stage, around and around." Seymour "replied gravely and at once, and in the special way he always answered questions from Les—as if they were the questions, above all others, he preferred to be asked in his life. He said he wasn't sure he had ever got off Joe Jackson's beautiful bicycle. And aside from its enormous sentimental value to my father personally, this answer, in a great many ways, was true, true, true."

Don, in contrast to others in the group, thought this scene was much too sentimental. I was startled by the certainty of his conviction that the scene was wrong, and I recall clearly that it was at that moment that I became aware of how completely he resisted the sentimental in his own writing. Salinger nevertheless retained a kind of legendary quality for Don, somewhat like that of F. Scott Fitzgerald and Ernest Hemingway. And I did not find it surprising that later I could hear echoes of Salinger in some of the lyrical moments in Don's own stories, including his "true, true, true."

Don and other younger writers tended to idolize Fitzgerald, whose tragic life had ended almost two decades earlier, but like most talented authors of his generation, Don preferred the more ironic style of Hemingway for his own work. An ironic tone was especially preferable to the sentimentality and nostalgia that seemed to be one of the characteristics emerging in early post–World War II American literature.

As he talked of Hermingway's fiction, Don described specific scenes that he had found unusually powerful. On first reading *The Sun Also Rises,* he was deeply moved and almost shocked at discovering the relationship between Brett and Jake at the end of chapter 3. And he especially admired the devastating irony at the end of the novel when Jake tells Brett that "it's pretty to think" that they could have had "such a damned good time together."

In spite of his great admiration for Hemingway, Don knew that it was imperative to find his own style. It had to somehow reflect the new world in which we found ourselves.

Later, when asked about his "spiritual ancestors" in a 1981 *Paris Review* interview, Don cited such pairs as "Perelman and Hemingway. Kierkegaard and Sabatini. Kafka and Kleist. . . . Rabelais and Zane Grey," along with Feodor Dostoevsky and his *Notes from Underground.*[1] Don acknowledged other influences as well, including films, art, and music. He linked Rafael Sabatini to Errol Flynn and the film *Captain Blood,* recognizing his indebtedness to the films of the 1940s and 1950s. Don's reading was such that his influences, if not always what he termed his "spiritual ancestors," eventually took in much of the major literature of the Western world in the nineteenth and twentieth centuries. Although Don mentioned only Beckett and Kleist in the *Paris Review* interview, as a matter of fact he was reading all the leading European dramatists before and during the three or four years in which he actually worked out his style.

W<small>HEN</small> D<small>ON</small> <small>BEGAN WRITING THE</small> *Come Back, Dr. Caligari* stories, he worked in even greater isolation than when he edited *Forum*. There was no other writer with whom he could talk about his work, at either the University of Houston or at the *Houston Post*. There was simply no one at all.

George Christian was at the *Post*, but he knew little more than that Don was writing; they did not discuss the stories themselves. Joe Maranto was no longer in Houston. Pat Goeters, with whom he shared an interest in art and architecture more than in literature, had established his own architectural firm. And Bob Morris was in Connecticut.

Don occasionally wrote or called Herman Gollob, now in Boston with Little, Brown, to talk over an idea. In fact, he began almost immediately to harangue Herman into convincing Little, Brown that they should publish a collection of his work.

Most of Don's other friends were artists or architects. After writing all morning, Don usually spent the afternoon at the Contemporary Arts Museum. Jack Boynton and Jim Love were among those interested in the fact that he was writing, but they did not talk about his work.

So I was the only person he talked to about what he was writing, both during the creation of the story and after he had completed it. The innovations that he brought to his writing were such that after reading a story I usually found it difficult to tell him precisely what concerned me. But if I stumbled over a phrase or an incident as I read it over and over, I pointed this out. He would then return to the typewriter and work until he felt the story was flawless.

As Don read his work aloud each day, the role I played was one of a delicate balance, that of his only critic as well as his sole audience. Occasionally, I preferred an earlier draft over the final one. I became inwardly frustrated, even exasperated, and wanted to tell him that he was "writing it away," because it seemed that in his rewriting, the form would take over and he would revise it to a stage in which the power of the story was lessened. At such times, the story seemed to become more of an object, completely freed of all subjectivity and emotion. Of course, once Don was satisfied with what he had written, I never told him that I felt he had taken something important out of a work. I knew that my comment would not have helped; he was his own final critic and was adamant about making changes. And even when I objected to a change that Don made in a story, I inevitably found the new version to be such that the original no longer mattered.

As he worked out on the porch in the morning, getting a story to "sound right" as well as "read right," I could hear him reading for dramatic effect, then after revising—even just one word—reading it again, and so on. His work was not only intense, it was plainly difficult. Although what he wrote was inevitably funny, he seldom laughed as he wrote. This was a serious process, and by reading it aloud, he could hear the humor, but more important, he could hear the effect of the language, its drama, and its poetry.

One day when he was working on "The Joker's Greatest Triumph" and had read the story to me for perhaps the fourth time that morning, editing it to a shorter and shorter version each time, I protested that he had removed something important and was losing what he had already created. Nevertheless, he went on revising it for at least another day, giving up one wonderful line after another. This story was one of those that bothered me as Don read each new draft, but he had none of the earlier versions with which I could later compare it.

As it turned out, the final version was superb. Don's story of the Joker's unmasking of Batman was not only comic and original, but as a very early story it accomplished some of the things that Don was trying to do in broadening his new form. In it, the focus shifted from his own inner self or stream of consciousness to parody and satire of the contemporary world.

Don wrote this story in the spring of 1961, and although he sent "The Joker's Greatest Triumph" to several journals, the story was turned down, so it was not published until Don's collection *Come Back, Dr. Caligari* appeared. Don did not keep a list of what he sent or to whom, so there is no record of the publications that rejected this or any other story during that period.

In watching Don write, I was reminded continually of Samuel Beckett and the evolution of his plays. The restraint, the essence of language, the reaching beyond language—whatever it was—Don was trying to do it too. I thought of his writing as an effort to get at the essence of the story through the essence of language. At times, I felt the form he was creating had begun to take over and assume control of his work.

I remembered these intense hours when years later in "The Genius," a story filled with autobiographical observations, Don wrote, "I think that this thing, my work, has made me, in a sense, what I am. The work possesses a consciousness which shapes that of the worker. The work flatters the worker. . . . The gaiety that once existed between the worker and the work has evaporated. A fine situation! Don't you think?" [1]

This passage keenly describes the way in which a relationship seemed to develop between Don and the story on which he worked. I felt certain that when he sat down at the typewriter, Don had little more than a glimmer of what the story might be about. I believe, too, that he never knew how it would end. Instead, once he started, the story itself seemed to take him there. Most of the time, he just sat at his desk until something finally occurred to him. Then as he wrote the story, it would develop, change, and grow until it finally reached a satisfactory whole.

When he reached the concluding sentence, he often imbued it with special significance; Don would return to a central theme, a theme frequently overlooked by the reader until Don offered this final insight. Very early, he began to include an incident that gave meaning or value to the world. Sometimes it would be just a brief observation about an incident in the story or an observation that in itself had value, such as Don's definition of the "aim of literature" in "Florence Green Is 81": "'The aim of literature,' Baskerville replied grandly, 'is the creation of a strange object covered with fur which breaks your heart.'"

As Don's method of devising a structure for each story evolved and because his stories were filled with personal references, reminiscences, social observations, fantasies, or whatever he found appropriate, the significance of the conclusion was discernible but elusive. But by the time he wrote "Kierkegaard Unfair to Schlegel," which was published in the October 12, 1968, *New Yorker*, the structure that Don had devised for each story had become essential to the meaning of the tale. In "Kierkegaard," the structure or the dialectic leads to the story's extraordinary conclusion, a moving and ironical turn in which "irony" itself is defeated in the final exchange between A and Q.

At the University of Houston in the 1980s, Don talked about theories of creativity with a friend and colleague, Samuel Southwell. One day, he told Southwell that Anton Ehrenzweig's *The Hidden Order of Art: A Study in the Psychology of Artistic Imagination* is "the only thing I know of that makes sense of creativity to me." [2]

Ehrenzweig was a psychoanalyst whose book *The Hidden Order of Art* was published shortly after his death in 1967. His theory of creativity helps to illuminate Don's method of working and why he was able to find what Ehrenzweig described as a "hidden order" in the "deceptive chaos in art's vast substructure." Ehrenzweig wrote that creativity "requires a diffuse, scattered kind of attention that contradicts our normal logical habits of thinking." And that he did not think that a reader who wants to proceed on a single track will understand the complexity of art and creativity in general anyway."[3] Don must have recognized in Ehrenzweig's work his own experience of creativity; it appears to have enabled him to understand why his work made sense to him but often seemed chaotic and fragmented to readers.

In "Florence Green Is 81," which he wrote in the spring of 1961, Don brings together numerous allusions, many of them probably emerging from his subconscious as he wrote. As his narrator says, "I am free associating, brilliantly, brilliantly, to put you into the problem." But he struggled with the story for several months, writing and revising, to arrive at its final shape.

By the time he wrote "The Genius" in 1971, Don had probably read Ehrenzweig, making him fully aware of the kind of observation that he was making about himself in the passage quoted above.

I was not surprised then when Don later said that he found in Ehrenzweig's work an explanation of creativity. In the early 1960s, before Ehrenzweig's book was published, it was not difficult to see that Don took what occurred to him or interested him and then sat at his desk and mused about it until something further developed. I could easily accept the idea that you did not know what you were going to write until you began to put it on paper. The richness and complexity of Don's life provided him with material for his resourceful mind and imagination. As he responded to people and events around him, sometimes expressing contradictory emotions, he also drew on the resources of his reading as well as his rich background in music and art.

In the early 1950s, Hemingway and Fitzgerald were the authors that most young writers admired and imitated. The Modernists had taught readers to appreciate the surface complexity of literature, but Ehrenzweig was describing the complex process of combining the conscious and the unconscious.

We were accustomed to reading such work as that with which Ehrenzweig seems to have been concerned, especially plays from the avant-garde work of the late 1940s through the early 1960s, including the European Theatre of the Absurd—Samuel Beckett, Jean Genet, Eugene Ionesco, Arthur Adamov, and Harold Pinter. With the antihero, descended from Dostoevsky's *Notes from Underground,* and the allegories of Franz Kafka and George Orwell, experimental fiction was becoming even more removed from traditional realism. The antirealistic, nightmarish novels of the American writer John Hawkes, *The Cannibal* and *The Lime Twig,* were published in 1949 and 1961.

Because I read most of the literature that Don was then reading, especially the new drama and new fiction, I was conscious of the forces of both the powerful Modernist tradition and the new Absurd coming together to shape Don's style. His earlier reading in the novel had covered classics — British, French, Russian, as well as American, including modern works of the late nineteenth and early twentieth centuries. He had, of course, read James Joyce's novels as well as those of Virginia Woolf, but he also knew earlier novels such as Laurence Sterne's *Tristram Shandy.*

And he read all the new British novels, including the work of Iris Murdoch, Muriel Spark, and Kingsley Amis. There was always an ironic, darkly humorous, and sometimes mysterious aspect to novels by these British authors not found in the American literature of the post–World War II era.

In the *Tulane Drama Review,* edited by Robert W. Corrigan, with whom Don corresponded regarding *Forum,* Don read new plays and excerpts from new work, chiefly European, as well as such essays as Martin Esslin's "Theatre of the Absurd." Both Edward Albee and Arthur Kopit were American dramatists whose work Don read around the time he began to write in 1960. Also, we saw Jack Gelber's *The Connection,* an innovative play about drugs, when it was first produced in Houston in 1959.

The absurd world of Joseph Heller's *Catch-22,* published in 1961, and the frightening, surrealistic world of Anthony Burgess's *A Clockwork Orange,* published in 1962, were being written into existence at the same time as Don's first work. Thomas Pynchon was also writing *V.,* his first major novel of the absurd. Among others whose work Don knew was Jorge Luis Borges, whom he first encountered in small journals in the late 1950s. He discovered Günter Grass and other young German authors in the *Evergreen Review* in late 1961. And he found the 1958 English translation of *I'm Not Stiller,* Max Frisch's tragicomic novel, while browsing for new European work at Brown's Bookstore in Houston.

Thus, as Don sat at his desk each day, he could draw on his unconscious, his enormous store of literary images and language, even his own fantasies, and then confront each idea as it took shape in front of him.

Much later, in a 1981 interview with the *Paris Review,* Don told his interviewers that "all the magic comes from the unconscious." Don also knew that many of his readers felt there was too little emotion in his stories, and he told the *Paris Review* that "jokes short-circuit emotion" and that he prized "a kind of low-key emotional touch that speaks volumes."[4]

When I read these observations that Don had made about himself, I was intrigued that he had described what I knew but what I felt few critics had yet recognized. In the early years of his work, he achieved this "low-key emotional touch" by countering the irony and satire of his observations about life with feelings that are clearly there, if not sharply defined. For Don, the possibilities, whatever they might be, offered hope, and the value of art provided meaning. I believe that at times, the dissatisfaction or even sadness in his life could be countered only by yearning to be somewhere else. Along with the "low-key emotional" touch, he offered the notion of possibility that lay in being some place other than the present place.

In "Kierkegaard Unfair to Schlegel," Don took a philosophical idea and worked through its logical argument, but in the story's conclusion he undercut reasoning with emotion that may have emerged from below the surface of consciousness. In this story, the speaker is in a conversation with himself. In it he gradually examines the writer's use of irony and its implications for the writer himself as well as for his work. The story's conclusion could have emerged only from the complex use of irony that preceded the ending and yet is an emotional departure from the careful reasoning that seems to direct the story. The exchange between "Q" and "A" at the end, in which Q tells A the story of Pasteur and Madame Boucicault, not only gives us a glimpse into the mystery of human encounter but also introduces into the story the kind of emotion that irony was intended to defeat but could not undercut.

"Kierkegaard Unfair to Schlegel" also echoes Walker Percy. In the essay "The Man on the Train," Percy wrote that a "man riding a train may incarnate alienation (the commuter) or rotation (i.e., the English variety): 'I was taking a long- delayed holiday. In the same compartment and directly opposite me, I noticed a young woman.'"[5] Don opens "Kierkegaard" this way: "I use the girl on the train a lot. I'm on a train, a European train with compartments. A young girl enters and sits opposite me."

Driven by the need to create perfect stories, Don was able to chisel and sculpt away hour by hour on a single story, but once he felt a story was finished he did not want to change it. For *Come Back, Dr. Caligari,* Don made minor changes as he selected published stories for the collection, but these revisions were minor. Later, he seems to have accepted suggestions and editorial revisions from editors at the the *New Yorker,* but most of the time he insisted that his stories were right the way they were. When Roger Angell, an editor of the *New Yorker*, telephoned Don about a story in which Don had used the word "butter" 132 times, he explained that there was a space problem and they had to cut ten lines somewhere. Did Don have any ideas on what might be cut? Don replied that "the word butter must appear 132 times, you can cut out any other butter after that."[6]

In the early 1960s, the idea of writing and revising until a story turned into a work of art was the tradition in which Don worked, but the need that Don felt for perfection was unquestionably more intense because of his father's influence. Dissatisfaction with what he had already done or the need for an ideal creation that seemed almost impossible was a trait that he had seen in his father. Donald Barthelme, Sr., with a reputation for being a talented, innovative architect as well as a professor of architecture, was a demanding and harsh critic of his own work and was portrayed by his son as never satisfied with his achievements in architecture.

According to Pat Goeters, Don and his father were "alike, neither was ever satisfied." Don, however, was usually pleased with what he had finished writing. Having decided on an ironic perspective and willing to give up character development and traditional plot, setting, and time, Don focused on the ideal "form" for each story. This drive to perfect each story led him not only to a new form in fiction but to ceaseless experimentation within the boundaries of this form. When Samuel Southwell observed that he found the form of every Donald Barthelme story original, something no one else had ever done, Don replied that just as Picasso had to create a new form for each painting, he found that each story required its own form.

Don's dissatisfaction came less from his work than with his life and the world around him. This dissatisfaction became a theme or a motif in Don's stories. In "Florence Green Is 81," which Don started in early 1961, Florence gives voice to this theme. At a dinner party, the elderly woman says, "*I want to go somewhere where everything is different.* A simple, perfect idea." Written before "Kierkegaard Unfair to Schlegel," this story was one of Don's first to reflect the influence of Walker Percy's essay on alienation.

Don's attitude toward literature was consistent. He was a purist about the books that were in our library; if he did not admire a work, then he simply did not buy it, and if he owned a book that he did not want, he gave it away. He read numerous books that he did not want to own. When we married and combined our libraries, Don wanted to remove several of my books by American authors; he rejected my copies of John Steinbeck's

Cannery Row and *The Wayward Bus,* along with work that might be thought of as "regional," such as Ross Lockridge's *Raintree County.* Nor did he want Thornton Wilder's *Heaven's My Destination* or *The Ides of March.* We kept my Thomas Wolfe novels even though he did not seem especially interested in Wolfe. He did not, of course, question such authors as the nineteenth-century Russian novelists or Greek and Roman classics that I owned. Herman Gollob later pointed out that my experience with Don was a story of "the definitive Don"; his rejection of certain books from our library was characteristic of the way he lived his life.

Within a decade or so after 1945, Jean Genet had written *The Balcony* and other experimental plays, Eugene Ionesco had written several plays in the absurd style, including *The Bald Soprano, The Lesson,* and *The Chairs.* Fernando Arrabal had written *The Automobile Graveyard,* and Alain Robbe-Grillet had written *The Voyeur.* In 1960, just after beginning his writing routine, Don read Arrabal's play, first available in translation in an Evergreen edition. He constantly searched for new translations of earlier work, and one day in 1961 he bought Eric Bentley's collection of Bertolt Brecht plays. Don found this and others mostly at Brown's Bookstore, where at least once a week he browsed through new Grove Press editions.

From drama, he seems to have learned to abstract the essence of his story and to present it in whatever form appropriate. In the Theatre of the Absurd, absurd situations and characters, complex metaphors, and the elimination of customary forms were being used to portray contemporary anxiety and despair. From this new drama, Don learned ways of experimenting with metaphorical language. He learned to develop distancing with the radical metaphor, to create absurd situations, and to use the fantastic and sometimes the surrealistic in his stories. He later observed that he avoided "saying anything directly," that the writer "discovers that in being simple, honest, and straightforward, nothing much happens."[7]

IN EARLY 1960, while still on the staff of the University of Houston and at the urging of his friend Pat Goeters, Don joined the board of the Contemporary Arts Association and began working closely with a group of architects and artists to expand the role of the young Contemporary Arts Museum.

Don knew most of the board members and was eager to join with them in an intense arts program that would thrust the young, struggling museum into the foreground of the arts. It was here, rather than with a circle of writers, that Don shared in the excitement of the new ideas of postmodernism.

In the late 1950s the museum was a fledgling institution that occupied a contemporary glass-and-steel building on the grounds of the Prudential Insurance Company, a site on Fannin Street near the intersection of Holcombe Boulevard. It was moved there from an earlier site closer to downtown Houston on property owned by the Detering family. After the organization had to give up its one-dollar-a-year lease on that site, and after it failed to gain permission to move to a site in Hermann Park, the museum was invited to move to the Prudential property. Today, the CAM is in a much larger, modernistic building at Montrose Boulevard and Bissonnet Street, across from the Museum of Fine Arts. The land it then occupied on Fannin Street has been incorporated into Houston's giant medical center.

In the early 1950s, philanthropists and art patrons Jean and Dominique de Menil brought Dr. Jermayne McAgy to Houston to direct the museum. She was a prominent art historian, renowned for her knowledge of Precolumbian Art and other primitive sculpture. A few years later, when the Menils became interested in establishing an art department and gallery at the University of St. Thomas, Dr. McAgy left the CAA to chair the St. Thomas program. She was there until she unexpectedly died of diabetes in 1963.

With the loss of its director and a major source of funding, the Contemporary Arts Museum and its board of directors turned to new kinds of exhibitions and programming. They recruited artist Robert Morris as director, and it was during Bob's tenure that Don joined the board. Just after that, Morris resigned from both the museum and the University of

Houston to return to his home state of Connecticut and join the faculty of the University of Bridgeport.

In October of 1960, the museum announced a program that would give the same emphasis to film, theater, music, and architecture as it had previously given to sculpture and painting. To carry out these plans, each board member agreed to assume responsibility for a single show.

Keen to bring in a series of lecturers, architects arranged for Richard Buckminster Fuller, known for his revolutionary approach to the enclosure of space, to visit the museum and for Pat Goeters and his students to build a geodesic dome to demonstrate one of Fuller's designs.

Another visitor was Harley Parker, a cultural anthropologist associated with the University of Toronto and the Royal Ontario Museum, who gave lectures at the CAM on the significance of the new electronic media. The work of both Dr. Parker and Marshall McLuhan was also published in *Forum*.

As a board member, Don agreed to plan and install what he called "New American Artifacts," an exhibition privately referred to as "The Ugly Show." Described as "devoted to cultural artifacts of ambivalent status," it was controversial in that it made ironical observations about the debris accumulated in contemporary life. Displayed in the context of an art museum, the show focused on objects that were ugly and often useless but that made up a great part of the decor of most homes. Plastic flags and a set of brass knuckles that Don bought at a pawnshop were among the pieces shown. The exhibit was popular in spite of disapproval from former CAM board members who challenged the validity of the show as a museum exhibition.

That fall Don also took over the CAA program for drama, and in December, 1960, he managed to secure a commitment from the New York producers of Edward Albee's *The Zoo Story* and Samuel Beckett's *Krapp's Last Tape* to bring the cast to Houston for a production in early 1961. With the Off-Broadway cast from the Cricket Theatre, where it made its New York debut, the double bill was performed on January 30 and 31 on the stage of the Ezekiel Cullen Auditorium at the University of Houston.

Don was then able to produce a series of low-budget programs using local talent. Tom Toner, an actor with the Alley Theatre, gave a reading of Dostoevsky's *Notes from Underground*, which Don believed relevant for the contemporary world. And then in March, Mack McCormick's *Hang Down Your Head*, a play based on the folk song about the final, desperate hours of Tom Dooley's life, was given a reading by folk singer Pete Rose. McCormick, already known for his work in folklore and folk music, also arranged for Lightnin' Hopkins to perform for the museum. Hopkins was an internationally known blues singer who began recording in 1946 but whose records had stopped selling; in the late 1950s, McCormick rediscovered him in the Dowling Street dance halls on the east side of downtown Houston.

The museum struggled without a professional director during these months, but finally in the spring of 1961, Don was invited to become director on a part-time basis. Don relished the challenge of it; this position would give him an opportunity to invite to the museum several of the writers, critics, and scholars with whom he had corresponded while he was editing *Forum* at the University of Houston.

Don was eager to accept the job with the understanding that it would be part-time and only in the afternoons. We then began a schedule in which he wrote for at least four, sometimes five hours, after which he turned his attention to the museum. It was an ideal schedule for Don, and he later called his museum position "the best job I ever had."

Harold Rosenberg, art critic for both the *New Yorker* and *Art News* and a member of the elite circle of Abstract Expressionist painters and critics that included Willem de Kooning, Franz Kline, and Hans Hofmann, was among the first that Don invited to lecture in 1961. Don knew Rosenberg from reading his work in the *New Yorker* and more recently from reading *The Tradition of the New*. Also, he had corresponded with Rosenberg on behalf of *Forum*.

Rosenberg came to Houston in May, 1961, for a lecture and a series of discussions with museum members. During his visit, we became friends, and he and Don spent a lot of time together. I found Harold easy and comfortable to be around, and he seemed to enjoy his visit with us. He was not only intellectually exciting; he was a gracious visitor as well. Although he was a tall, large man who limped on a stiff right leg, we heard no complaints from him; he rode around town with us in our small Hillman Sunbeam, with his leg that wouldn't bend and with his head touching the convertible top.

In the early summer, Elaine de Kooning, the wife of Willem de Kooning and a friend of Harold Rosenberg, came to the Contemporary Arts Museum to give a two-week short course in painting. Congenial and a good teacher, she became friends with Don and with the artists active in museum affairs.

In May, 1961, after Don had written at least six stories and four or five had been accepted or published, he sent an application to the annual New York City Writers Conference that was to be held in July at Wagner College on Staten Island. The conference was open to only forty-five students, fifteen in fiction, fifteen in drama, and fifteen in poetry. As part of his application, Don sent a biography along with a copy of "The Big Broadcast of 1938," which he had already sold to *New World Writing,* as well as a copy of "Me and Miss Mandible," his first published story. He was immediately accepted, and we began to make plans for the trip. We had decided to turn it into a holiday and on July 9 departed for New York City.

We flew into Newark and from there took the shuttle to the East Side terminal in Manhattan. We then took a cab to our hotel, which was located at Grand Central Station. Although it was convenient and adequate for our visit, the hotel and its setting were bleak. We knew very little of New York hotels and it was a good location for the trains. Also, Joe Maranto's office at Mobil Oil was just a few blocks from the terminal.

We spent the weekend in Manhattan, visiting art museums and looking for art galleries that were open. Walking in New York was a treat, so we walked wherever we could. On Sunday, we took the Fifth Avenue bus up to Central Park and the Metropolitan Museum and then spent the afternoon stopping in galleries on the way back.

On Monday morning, we took the ferry to Staten Island and then caught a taxicab to Wagner College. At the college, we stayed in a student dormitory and ate in a student dining hall. Don had chosen this conference because three of the country's leading writers would teach the classes: Saul Bellow in fiction, Edward Albee in drama, and Robert Lowell in poetry. Although I would not attend the morning classes, I looked forward to the school and to meeting the three writers. The classes were to begin on July 11 and to last ten days. Most of the students had already published, and all had submitted manuscripts with their applications.

The three classes met every day, and students met in individual conferences with their instructors as well. In the afternoons, the students from the three classes gathered in an informal lounge area for discussions or to hear guest speakers, in publishing or in writing and in theater production. This was Don's first intimate contact with other accomplished writers and the first important critical acknowledgment he received.

In the fiction class, "The Big Broadcast" and Don's reading of it clearly intrigued other students, but Bellow was much less enthusiastic about what Don was doing than the younger people were. I believe he was interested enough but perhaps thought that Don's fictional world was too restricted. He told Don that his world was clearly not entirely negative, that there was a positive side of it that he was disregarding. As he pointedly alluded to our marriage, Bellow said that it was apparent that life was not all bad for Don and that he should include all aspects of his life in what he wrote. In other words, Don's stories should offer a balanced perspective of life.

Don admired Bellow and his work and saw him as the major American novelist of our time, but he was uncomfortable in trying to justify his work. Because I knew that he needed Bellow's acceptance of and even praise for what he was doing, I believed that Bellow became one more voice of authority who was disapproving. Don had developed an ironical stance from which to tell his stories, and he wanted to talk about that. He had, after all, been thinking about the form for his stories and the narrative style he would use since the summer of 1956, when he read Beckett's *Waiting for Godot* for the first time.

I have no doubt that Don now began to recognize how acute the differences were between his own writing and the fiction of our leading literary figures. He admired the originality of Bellow's antiheroes, the tone of contemporary desperation of his characters, and the wonderful originality of *Henderson the Rain King*. Nevertheless, Don had moved into his own realm of creativity, and this was the realm he needed to discuss. Fellow students in the class recognized this originality and became immediate admirers, so that during these ten days it was with them that he exchanged ideas.

Throughout the conference, Don was often uncomfortable in the role of student. Since his teen years, he had been at the center of any creative group in which he took part. But now, we were on Staten Island with three internationally recognized writers, each of whom many critics regarded as the preeminent writer of his genre in American literature.

I saw how difficult the experience was for Don when we were walking across the campus one day and Bellow stopped to talk to us. He again mentioned that there were obviously good things in Don's life that he ought to include in his work, so that his writing would encompass the whole world. Don was friendly, but concerning the approach that he should take to his work he did not reply to Bellow's advice; instead, he just responded by nodding pleasantly.

I saw Don as more insecure with the three authors than I thought he would be. His insecurity, however, seemed to come more from his desire to have his talent recognized than from any doubt about what he was attempting to write. He knew that he was already an accomplished writer and wanted to be taken more seriously.

General sessions, with all faculty and students taking part, were held in the afternoons. Don participated very little, but the topics raised few questions or problems with which Don was concerned. At one session on realism in fiction, the panel discussed the need for accuracy, for authenticity of place and scene. Bellow, whose comic novel, *Henderson the Rain King,* was published two years earlier, was challenged on the fact that he had never been to Africa even though the setting for the novel is in Africa. With fiction moving in the direction of antirealism and the absurd, I thought the novel was a contribution to this tendency and was puzzled that anyone would question it.

Albee was the writer with whom Don might have had greater rapport, but he was concerned only with the students in drama. *The Zoo Story,* like Beckett's *Waiting for Godot,* was far more relevant to Don's writing than Bellow's work, and I think that during those days at the conference Don fully understood this. However, even though Don was excited about having produced Albee's play for the Contemporary Arts Association, he appeared uncomfortable that Albee was the "writer" and he was the "pupil." Albee had not read any of Don's stories and knew nothing of what Don was attempting to do. Don spoke with him just once briefly and that conversation concerned the Houston production of *The Zoo Story.*

Younger than either Bellow or Lowell, Albee had only recently achieved the kind of international recognition that the other two men already knew. Generous with the time he gave to his students, Albee spent evenings as well as weekends talking to them and seemed to appreciate the interest and commitment that brought them to Staten Island. I recall that at one of the general sessions, he spoke admiringly of the fact that a student in the drama class had traveled cross country by bus in order to come to the school.

Bellow, who was pleasant and kind in conversation, was informal in class and told the students of his marriages and the alimony that he paid each of his former wives. But outside of class he was more reserved and often returned to Manhattan in the evening and then on weekends.

It was at Wagner College that Don first became acquainted with other serious creative writers of his own age; these contacts were very important to him. He met Arno Karlen, whose work he had earlier published in *Forum* and who recommended Don to his own literary agent, Sterling Lord. Lord was among the guest speakers during one of the evening programs, and two years later, his agency became interested in Don's writing and began to represent him in 1963. It was through Lord that Don first sold a story to the *New Yorker* in 1963.

Don met several young women writers whom he liked; one I recall was Sarah Dabney, a graduate student and member of the faculty at Smith

College. I found Sarah attractive and interesting; we were both teaching at women's colleges, she at a major eastern college and I at a small Catholic women's college. We both taught undergraduate classes in contemporary literature, and in comparing our reading lists I found that they were almost identical. She was genuinely surprised that a college in Texas was teaching the same "new" authors, especially those of the Theatre of the Absurd.

Ed McClanahan, another student, was then teaching English at Oregon State University and told a story about the model for one of Bernard Malamud's characters in *A New Life,* a professor who was known for searching out the sources of plagiarism in freshman writing.

While we were there, I took the ferry to Manhattan at least twice, taking a taxi from the south end of the island to midtown, where I could visit the Museum of Modern Art, the Guggenheim, or the Metropolitan. The real problem was learning how to locate the right taxicab company to pick me up on Staten Island. In any event, I usually attended the general sessions of the conference in the afternoons and evenings. As I listened to the panels and speakers, I gained insight into the New York literary world. Although not completely closed to people outside of Manhattan, it was a world in which there was a genuine conviction that if you mattered as a writer, then you lived in New York. Don wanted to find an editing position on the East Coast, but now I could see that he had to be there for his writing as well. He could write and experiment with the same material in Houston, but living in Manhattan itself was certain to open up major publications to him.

During the writing conference, I found Robert Lowell the most interesting. Speaking slowly, his low voice seemingly filled with anguish, Lowell had a movingly sad look. I commented to Don that I thought Lowell should not have been there—it appeared too difficult for him. However, as I saw him at other readings in later years, I came to believe that readings were probably important to him.

I had a glimpse of another side of Lowell one evening when we saw him alone with one of the women students at the conference. I recall the incident because he and the girl were laughing at something that must have just happened or something that one of them had said. He seemed much happier at that moment with whatever he was sharing with her than as the serious, somber poet sitting in front of an audience, talking about his work.

Even though he did not receive much encouragement from Saul Bellow, by the end of he conference Don was more confident than ever, buoyed by having been in the company of three such important American authors and by the support that the younger writers had given him.

Don used the experience of the writing class to portray Baskerville in "Florence Green Is 81," a story he wrote a few months later and published in *Harper's Bazaar* in 1963. At one point, he wrote, "Baskerville was stoned by the massed faculty of the Famous Writers School upon presentation of his first lesson: He was accused of formalism." The "Famous Writers School," a reference to a writing school often advertised in magazines, appears to comment on the culture of postwar America, but Don is referring to his own experience on Staten Island as well. "Florence Green" is richly autobiographical, filled with personal thoughts, feelings, as well as observations about the contemporary world, apart from the New York City Writers Conference. In this one story, he recalls reading about the extermination of Jews in the Holocaust, the Greenbrier Resort we visited in 1962, his experience with *Forum,* and even his fourth grade class in Houston.

In the characters of both the narrator, Baskerville, and in Florence, Don explores themes that he would later develop further: the necessity of finding a way to live in the world and "dissatisfaction" with himself and with the world around him. In the voice of Baskerville, he imagines the philosopher Edmund Husserl telling him, "But you have not grasped the living reality, the essence!" to which Baskerville replies, "Nor will I, ever." At this point, "J. D. Ratcliff," described as "his examiner," says, "Baskerville, you blank round, discursiveness is not literature." In Baskerville's answer and in defense of what he wanted to do in his own fiction, Don wrote the lines that he often quoted in later years: "The aim of literature . . . is the creation of a strange object covered with fur which breaks your heart."

Near the end of "Florence," Don speaks for himself: "*I want to go somewhere where everything is different.* A simple, perfect idea. The old babe demands nothing less than total otherness." The narrator's observation that Florence "demands nothing less than total otherness" is intense, but low-key in its emotion.

From Staten Island, we returned to Manhattan and took a train to Boston to visit with Herman Gollob and his new wife, Barbara Kowal. They had married in April and were living on Centre Street in Newton Corner. Barbara graduated from Barnard College in 1959 and now recently had returned from the University of Gutenberg, where she earned a master of arts in German literature. She had given up career plans for the present but later undertook translations of German into English.

While we were there, Herman talked to Don about a magazine editing job on the East Coast and also read Don's story, "The Big Broadcast of 1938." For the past year, Don had urged Herman to sell Little, Brown on publishing a collection of his short stories, and now they talked about it again.

This was our first trip to Boston, so Don and I spent the morning after our arrival walking around Beacon Hill, down Commonwealth Avenue, and through other streets in older parts of the city. From Boston, we traveled down to Madison, Connecticut, to visit Bob and Gitta Morris and their two daughters. Bob was from New England and had disliked living in Texas; he reveled in showing us the picturesque towns, country drives, and historical homes of New England. Gitta, the daughter of a University of Texas professor, had been a journalist in Houston and was now a freelance writer.

We spent an afternoon at the "private beach" for which they had a membership. This members-only piece of coastline apparently was the only kind of oceanfront bathing beach available to residents of Connecticut, a strange experience for two Texans who had always lived on or near the Gulf Coast with public beaches stretching for miles.

We returned to Manhattan and spent another day in the city. We tried to telephone Harold Rosenberg at his apartment but failed to reach him. We then met Joe Maranto for lunch; he commuted daily from Connecticut and was in New York for his job with Mobil Oil Company only on weekdays. In the afternoon, we shopped at Saks Fifth Avenue and Brooks Brothers, visited another art gallery, and then flew home to Houston the following day.

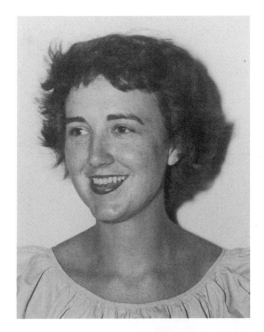

Helen
as a student
at the University
of Houston.
From author's
collection

Don's parents
with Joan and
Don at the Texas
State Fair in 1936.
They are on the
steps of the State
Building which
the elder Barthelme
designed.
From author's
collection

Don and Joan
in Galveston
in early 1930s.
Photo by Donald
Barthelme, Sr.,
from author's
collection

Joan and Don
with brother
Peter.
Photo by Donald
Barthelme, Sr.,
from author's
collection

From left to right: Don, Harry Vitemb, and Pat
Goeters behind Joe and Maggie Maranto after their
wedding. Courtesy Joe Maranto

Don and George
Christian at the
Houston Post in
the early 1950s.
From author's
collection

Don at
Barthelme
family home
for Christmas
of 1958.
Photo by Donald
Barthelme, Sr.,
from author's
collection

Helen at
Barthelme
family home
for Christmas
of 1958.
Photo by Donald
Barthelme, Sr.,
from author's
collection

Helen and
Frederick
(Rick) at
Christmas
in 1957.
Photo by Donald
Barthelme, Sr.,
from author's
collection

Don on trip to Tokyo during his assignment to Korea at the end of the Korean War. From author's collection

Don and friends in Korea, with what he described as the "dirty hills of Korea" in the background. From author's collection

Sutchai Thangpew, Don's close friend in Korea.
A member of the Thai Royal Battalion, Sutchai hoped
to one day become prime minister of Thailand.
From author's collection

Helen and Odell Moore leaving their offices to see
advertising client in 1964.
Photo by Maurice Miller, from author's collection

Don with his drums at the Barthelme family home.
Photo by Donald Barthelme, Sr., from author's
collection

Helen opening package at Barthelme home on
Christmas Eve, 1961.
Photo by Donald Barthelme, Sr.,
from author's collection

Above
Family portrait in 1962. Don's mother is seated in front, with (left to right) Peter, Steven, Lillian, Joan, Helen, and Don. Photo by Donald Barthelme, Sr., from author's collection

Helen presenting an award on behalf of Theta Sigma Phi to Carroll Camden, Rice University professor and scholar of Elizabethan literature.
From author's collection

At the Barthelme home opening gifts at Christmas, 1959. Rick and his mother are on left; Joan has just opened a gift with Steve, Pete, Helen, and Don talking. Photo by Donald Barthelme, Sr., from author's collection

Helen at the Jewish Community Center in Houston, 1962. Photo by Maurice Miller, from author's collection

Don as director of the Contemporary Arts Museum. Courtesy *Houston Chronicle*

Don and his three brothers: Peter and Rick standing, with the youngest Steven in front. Photo by Donald Barthelme, Sr., from author's collection

Helen with art directors Tom Felder, left, and
Kieran Kilday, at advertising meeting in 1971.
Author's collection

Above
Helen and Don
at the Barthelme
home in 1961.
Photo by Donald
Barthelme, Sr.,
from author's
collection

Don and Joan at
family home.
Photo by Donald
Barthelme, Sr.,
from author's
collection

Don during a visit at his parents in the 1980s.
Photo by Donald Barthelme, Sr., from author's
collection

AFTER WE WERE BACK IN HOUSTON, Don rigorously followed his writing schedule every morning, turning his attention to the museum in the afternoon. For me, there was always work to be done at the agency, so everything was pretty much the same.

Don was especially happy. The freedom that he now had at the CAA in introducing the "new" to Houston audiences was a challenge that he liked. And his work in all the "arts" provided even greater motivation for him to write.

Although no one at the museum—including artists, staff, board members, and patrons—read any of his short stories, his writing was clearly enriched by what the museum was undertaking—avant-garde theater and new trends in painting, as well as readings in poetry and lectures in philosophy, architecture, and anthropology. He was excited about the entire effort, but above all, about what was taking place in the theater.

In midsummer, the CAA presented Fernando Arrabal's *The Automobile Graveyard* in the museum's gallery. The museum's presentation was the first time that the play had been produced in the United States and one of the first productions outside of Europe. Arrabal's play is a two-act tragicomedy that provoked controversy when it first appeared in Paris in 1959. That debut was just two years earlier, but Arrabal was already recognized as one of the foremost dramatists in the tradition of the new European drama that included Beckett, Genet, and Ionesco.

Ned Bobkoff, a young director originally from Brooklyn who had come to Houston fifteen years earlier, directed the production. The play attracted full houses for nine performances, but Don was frustrated continually by Bobkoff and his demands in the staging of the production. After it was over, Don attempted to discourage Ned from working on a second production that was already scheduled. Nevertheless, in February, 1962, Bobkoff directed stagings of Edward Albee's *The American Dream* and Jules Feiffer's *Crawling Arnold*. And although he did not feel any better about working with Ned, Don was happy about both productions.

By now, the new drama seemed appropriate for the world of the early 1960s as we perceived it. Albee's *The American Dream* was described as a "comic nightmare and a fantasy of the highest order"; Feiffer's play was a satire about a thirty-five-year-old businessman who suddenly reverts to childhood and who describes his bomb shelter as the only one that had been written up in *Good Housekeeping* magazine. The cold war was still under way, and although bomb shelters were being constructed by people across the country, the whole idea had a surrealistic aspect that made it good material for the Theatre of the Absurd.

Throughout this time, Houston's senior critic, Hubert Roussel, for whom Don had worked and who was still amusements editor of the *Houston Post,* remained at a safe and disapproving distance from the CAA's efforts. After seeing *The American Dream,* he wrote in the February 2 *Houston Post* that the play was a "structural katzenjammer which makes its points 20 times over with lamentably amateur enthusiasm and winds up as a greatly pretentious bore."

Roussel's reaction to Albee's plays was typical of what Don could have expected if he had shown his stories to many of the journalists he knew. But at least the CAA, with its sizable number of enthusiastic artists, architects, and patrons, provided a cultural environment that was encouraging and supportive of new ideas in the arts.

Other theaters in Houston now began to offer experimental drama, so Don believed that the CAA could give up this responsibility after the season concluded. The Playhouse Theatre started a series of Monday night productions that included experimental work; one of these was a Bobkoff-directed production of Jack Gelber's *The Connection,* a play dealing with the topic of drugs and an early experiment in actor-audience interaction.

The Playhouse also staged Ionesco's *The Lesson,* Beckett's *Krapp's Last Tape,* and Jean Genet's *Deathwatch.* In Houston, the only other avant-garde drama was an earlier staging by the Alley Theatre of Beckett's *Waiting for Godot.*

Although Don was continually confronted by fiscal concerns at the CAA, he pressed the board almost unmercifully for money. He had acquired from his father an extraordinary ability to challenge another person, to oppose someone else's will with his own. Colleagues, members of the board, creative artists — anyone with whom he negotiated — had difficulty in resisting the strength of Don's convictions. With *Forum,* it had been university administrators, members of the faculty, and even authors and publishers from whom he sought manuscripts. At the museum the board of directors was uncertain how the organization would pay its bills, yet Don made decisions based on what he thought was best for the museum and then fought with board members to underwrite the activities.

CAA activities were usually planned over a two-year period, so that during Don's tenure with the museum, first as a board member and then as director, the CAA planned and undertook four separate festivals in the arts: drama, music, poetry, and film, along with a year-round schedule of exhibitions of paintings and sculpture. With the series of dramatic events already under way, a series of "new music" performances began in the fall of 1961. Don was excited by this; he had collected the recordings of the Modern Jazz Quartet and other groups since the late 1940s. Opportunities to hear famous jazz musicians play in Houston were rare, almost non-existent. The John Coltrane Quartet, Miles Davis, and other groups were performing mostly in New York, so Don worked fervently to arrange for the Coltrane ensemble to give a modern jazz concert in Houston on September 10.

The day before the scheduled Coltrane concert, Hurricane Carla had begun to menace the Gulf Coast. Hurricanes often threatened the region but seldom reached Houston with more than heavy rains and strong winds. No one knew when or if the storm would arrive, and Don argued with Coltrane's agent that there was enough time for the group to give the concert and leave Houston before there was any danger. But the musicians opted to use the cancellation clause in their contract, declining to perform but collecting the fee anyway.

As it turned out, although Coltrane could have performed and departed before the storm, Carla became one of the century's most destructive hurricanes. In fact, it was this news story that gave Dan Rather, then a television news reporter in Houston, his big break into the national news media.

Another musical event, one of much greater significance but of less interest to many people, was also scheduled for September. Composer Elliott Carter, unknown to most Americans, had recently won the Pulitzer Prize for music; his presence in Houston was expected to be a memorable occasion. Don had managed to arrange for a distinguished string ensemble from Urbana, Illinois, to perform Carter's "First String Walden Quartet." Also on the program was Charles Rosen, a prominent young concert pianist and friend of the composer. For the event, Rosen played the composer's "Piano Sonata," which had already been recorded for Columbia Records.

But the evening was a disaster. Only fifty or so people came to hear the renowned composer and his music. Neither of the music editors of the two major metropolitan daily newspapers attended the event nor did they send anyone to cover the story. Don was both embarrassed and angry. He had believed that in Houston there was a sophisticated music audience.

After all, within the past few years both Leopold Stokowski and Sir John Barbirolli had each been director-in-residence of the Houston Symphony Orchestra. But now he felt that he had naively misjudged the public's interest in new music.

Don later described the evening as "one of the loneliest evenings of a rather cloistered life." He had negotiated the fees with both Carter and the quartet and was especially pleased that Carter had arranged for Rosen to come with payment of expenses only. Carter was gracious and seemed not to be offended by the lack of interest in his work. But this was perhaps the worst such evening for Don at the CAM. I knew that it evoked memories of his trials with *Forum*.

On September 30, the arrival of Peter Yates, a high-spirited and enthusiastic musicologist from the West Coast, revived Don's confidence about his efforts to bring "new music" to Houston. Through an extensive correspondence concerning *Forum,* he had established a friendship with Yates and had now invited him to be both speaker and moderator for a program on experimental music, including new electronic work.

The program consisted of a work composed by a digital computer at the University of Illinois and played by the New Art String Quartet—a group made up of members of the Houston Symphony Orchestra. David Wuliger, Houston Symphony tympanist, played two pieces for kettle drums by Elliott Carter. There were other works new to Houston audiences, one by composer Harry Partch that used "cloud chambers," which were large glass vessels that emitted unusual tones when struck. The Partch work, "Revelation in the Courthouse Park," set Euripides' tragedy *The Bacchae* in the Midwest. This work employed a forty-three-tone scale that permitted singing, chanting, and speaking to pitches. There were also scores by Edgard Varese and Charles Ives.

This program and others in the series were presented at the University of St. Thomas in Jones Hall, a new Modernist structure designed by Philip Johnson. The audience was a respectable size and provided Don with some reassurance that he had not wholly misjudged the community's interest in music. The last event for the music series was an orchestral jazz concert directed by Johnny Richards, a West Coast jazz composer whom Yates had recommended.

A festival of poets in November included Robert Bly, Kenneth Koch, and W. D. Snodgrass reading from their work. Snodgrass's collection *Heart's Needle* had won the Pulitzer Prize the year before. Koch had published *Ko, or A Season on Earth* and was teaching at Columbia University and the New School for Social Research. Bly was known both for his poetry and as editor of the literary journal *The Sixties*.

Don was in high spirits when we had such visitors, and he was comfortable as their host. He was relaxed and witty, a striking contrast to the unease he seemed to have felt with Saul Bellow and Edward Albee at the writing conference in July.

Snodgrass read on November 10, and Bly and Koch read during the following week. Another board member entertained Snodgrass, and we entertained Bly and Koch; Don liked Bly's work but was drawn to Koch, whose humor was closer to his own.

After Kenneth's arrival, when Don saw that there was enough time on the first afternoon for the poet to talk to a group of students, he called me at Dominican College to arrange for an informal reading. I searched the campus and finally managed to muster about thirty undergraduates. When Don and his guest arrived on campus, I had to admit that we did not have a single copy of either of Koch's books, *Poems* or *Ko, or A Season on Earth*. Nor did Don or Kenneth bring with them anything that he could read. We were a small college of fewer than a thousand students, so I was not embarrassed that our library did not yet include Kenneth's work.

Kenneth could see that Don had arranged the reading at the last minute and was amused by the situation. As he considered our predicament, Don was cavalier in resolving it; in fact, he thoroughly enjoyed the situation. After I made the introductions, Don turned to Kenneth and simply asked him to speak. He felt that Kenneth, who had a Ph.D. from Columbia, could lecture without copies of his poetry. Without hesitation, Kenneth talked about contemporary poetry and the writing of poetry, recalling lines from individual poems to illustrate his points. After that, the two of them left to spend a couple of hours together before we were to meet for dinner.

That evening, we took both Koch and Robert Bly to dinner at our favorite French restaurant, La Louisiane, a beautiful old restaurant situated on Main Street across from the Shamrock Hilton Hotel. It was decorated with romantic paintings of nymphs and satyrs romping through forests. Because they were painted in the 1920s, the nymphs wore short "flapper" haircuts. The paintings had been shipped from Europe, and when they arrived some did not fit the walls. The owner had them cut so that they would fit and turn the corners of the room. Owned by a New Orleans family, this restaurant had a small menu of expensive but exceptional dishes, most of them prepared from family recipes.

After the readings the next evening, Howard Barnstone, a member of the CAA's board of directors and a Houston architect, and his wife Gertrude, now a prominent artist, gave a party for the two poets. And then the third evening, we again had dinner with Koch and Bly, this time at Ye Olde College Inn, a renowned Houston restaurant located on Main Street across from Rice University.

Both guests seemed to enjoy the evening, but I was shocked when the check came and Don announced to the two visitors that it was their "turn to pick up the check." The two men had offered to pay at La Louisiane the first evening, but we had insisted that they were our guests. Nothing had been said about our not paying this evening as well. They were startled, but after joking about getting stuck with the bill at the "most expensive restaurant in Houston," the two poets good-naturedly paid the bill.

Later, when I spoke to Don about this, he replied that the CAA was paying them enough that he thought they could share the costs. Although Don and I were personally paying for most of the entertaining that we did, I felt we had taken advantage of Koch and Bly and should have paid that evening's check as well. Don and Kenneth seemed to get along so well that the latter probably regarded it with humor. But I doubt that Bly thought it was funny.

I found both men interesting, but unlike Don, I felt a greater affinity for Bly. Kenneth and Don had immediate rapport, so that neither was intimidated by the wit and ironical humor of the other. Kenneth seemed to have a great deal of fun, almost like a kid. Robert Bly was serious, older, and told us that he was soon to be a father. He had wanted to spend his last evening in Houston at the hotel, writing letters and working, but had graciously accepted our invitation. Later, when we drove back to the elegant Warwick Hotel where they were staying, both poets leaned over to kiss me lightly as they said goodnight. I was pleased, and as we drove away, Don remarked that "now you have something you can tell our grandchildren, the night when you were kissed by two famous poets." Don's remark was sincere and without irony and typical of the way in which he often said something both tender and unexpected.

While the two poets were in Houston, Bly's demeanor and actions were serious and dignified, whereas Koch, who spent a lot of time with a young woman poet, was more lighthearted about his visit and his own actions. In fact, by the time they departed, an embarrassed Bly observed that "at home" in New York, Koch would not have "behaved that way."

Throughout these months, while Don continued to write and work at the museum, my own schedule was filled with managing my advertising agency along with teaching at Dominican College. Months earlier, my sister, Odell Pauline Moore, had become my business partner and we changed the name of our firm from Helen Barthelme Advertising to Barthelme and Moore Advertising. Odell had studied economics and worked in city government as well as in business, so she had a much more pragmatic view of business than I had.

We now needed more room for our agency, so this year we moved to a building that Pat Goeters owned and in which he had offices for his architectural firm. This was 5 Chelsea Place, just off Montrose Boulevard near the Museum of Fine Arts and not far from our home on Harold Street.

In the early summer, Don's younger brother Peter was married to Lillian Foote in a ceremony at St. Michael's Church with Don as the best man. Pete and Lillian had known each other since elementary school, their parents had carpooled, and they lived near each other. Her father was Stephen Foote, a prominent physician whose offices were on Chelsea Place across the street from the building in which our agency was now located.

Peter had graduated from St. Thomas High School in 1957, then enrolled at Cornell University to study architecture but found the weather there too cold. After that he enrolled in the University of North Carolina but soon returned to Houston and began working. Before long, he enrolled at the University of Houston, studied philosophy, and then graduated with a double major in English and psychology in 1963.

After graduating, Peter began to write advertising copy for our agency. With a special sense of humor and extraordinary talent, he was soon creating campaigns for most of the accounts. And in the years that followed, he worked for Aylin Advertising Agency, was on the staff and board of Goodwin, Dannenbaum, Littman, and Wingfield, and then founded his own agency in 1975. A typical Barthelme, he gave his firm an unconventional name, Old Crow Ink, Inc. The company continues to be active today.

ONE DAY IN THE EARLY SPRING OF 1962, I was in the office of Sister
Mary Antoinette, O.P., president of Dominican College, to discuss strat-
egy for establishing a comprehensive fund-raising program. We both recognized the need for someone to plan and direct an overall development
effort. She knew of Don's and my own activities at the Contemporary Arts
Museum and the association's efforts to raise funds. Impressed by Don's
accomplishments there, she asked if I thought he would consider such a
position at Dominican College.

I did not want Don to give up his writing schedule and told her that if
he was interested, he would be available only in the afternoons. Unde-
terred by this, she wanted me to talk to him, so when I picked up Don at
the museum that evening, I related the conversation to him. Don was interested but stipulated a considerable increase in salary over what the
CAA paid.

Sister Antoinette agreed to his conditions, and after meeting with her,
Don promised to consider the offer but told her that he could not give her
a decision before the fall. She suggested that meanwhile we both attend
the annual meeting of the American College Public Relations Association
at the Greenbrier Resort in West Virginia. Scheduled for July, the conference would give Don a chance to meet development people from other
colleges and universities.

Don was eager to accept, but not because of his interest in Dominican
College. We had already thought of flying to New York in the summer
but could not see how we could possibly finance the trip. Now we could
take a train from West Virginia to Manhattan, making it possible to pay for
the trip.

Our finances were severely strained by our increased expenses, in part
from our trip to New York the previous summer and in part from the cost
of entertaining for the museum. Don continued to write checks whether
we had funds or not. I was drawing extra money from my advertising
agency and was growing increasingly alarmed about our company's debt.
And even with the extra money I was borrowing from the agency, it had
become difficult just to pay our personal bills. But Don wanted desperately to find a magazine editing job in Manhattan and was eager to see

Harold Rosenberg again to discuss a job that Harold had mentioned when he was in Houston. Besides, I was just as eager as he to combine a trip to New York with the meeting at Greenbrier.

Unlike Don, however, I looked forward to the conference. So in the latter part of July, we traveled from Houston to White Sulphur Springs, West Virginia. Once the meeting was under way, Don attended only the opening session. He rented a typewriter, and throughout these days he spent every morning in our room working on "Florence Green Is 81." Like all the bedroom suites at the Greenbrier, ours was spacious and had been individually decorated. Don sat at his typewriter looking out over an extraordinary view of the grounds.

Don was not at all interested in taking part in the conference nor did he care to meet people from other universities. I attended meetings each day but found his absence disquieting; some of the people at the conference were my own professional acquaintances who usually asked about him, but there was nothing to be done. I knew that what mattered to Don was to write and to pursue a job in New York.

Apart from the conference, we enjoyed the resort itself. In the late afternoons, we rode bicycles or walked around the grounds. And then each evening, we ate in one of the formal dining rooms. Everything about the Greenbrier was luxurious.

In our walks over the grounds, we saw that one wing of the resort was closed for a remodeling project. I realized later that it must have been the site of the secret underground headquarters for Congress in the event of nuclear war, a secret that was finally disclosed to the public in 1992. In the 1950s and into the 1960s, the fear of nuclear war—especially an attack from the Soviet Union—was such that all kinds of underground bomb shelters were constructed throughout the country. I had learned from students at Dominican College that in public schools they had drilled for such an attack. John F. Kennedy was now president and would soon be in a historic confrontation with the Soviet Union over its military installations in Cuba.

After we arrived in Manhattan about a week later, Harold invited us to meet him at the brownstone in which he lived on East 10th Street. The apartment was a place he used for an office and residence whenever he was in the city, mostly during the week. We were waiting on the steps of the building when he arrived. Harold's first words to me were generous and those of someone who saw the world in terms of a New Yorker: "How good you look against a New York background."

Inside the apartment, the big rooms were dark and cluttered. Much of the clutter was artwork scattered throughout every room. The first room had a dining table and paintings everywhere—stacked on the table, in chairs, and leaning against the walls. In the bed/sitting room, there was a Murphy bed that was still down. Harold hastily straightened the bedcovers to give an appearance of orderliness, a touching gesture from a man for whom housekeeping appeared to be so alien. As he prepared drinks, I looked around the apartment trying to imagine living there. It was not inviting; it was dark, almost oppressive. I did not yet understand that it was just a place for Harold to stay in Manhattan as well as an office for the Longview Foundation. I had a lot to learn about life in Manhattan.

At first, we talked about current art exhibits that Harold thought we should see in Manhattan. But more important for Don, while we were there Harold told us more about the proposed magazine that he had already mentioned to Don, a magazine that would soon need an editor.

Harold, art critic of the *New Yorker,* and Thomas B. Hess, formerly an editor at *Art News,* were planning to publish a journal that would be similar to *Forum* and would be sponsored by the Longview Foundation with which Harold was associated. When he was in Houston, Harold had told Don that an editorial job might be available on the magazine; however, we had heard nothing further. Now Harold asked if Don would be interested in becoming the managing editor.

Don was, of course, interested, but Harold told us little more than this while we were in New York. He wanted my assurance that moving to New York was what I wanted to do as well, and then he added that as soon as plans were more concrete he would contact Don. Although he was restrained in showing how he felt, Don was elated. Ever since the New York Writers Conference the previous summer, he had become more eager than ever to find an editing job on the East Coast. What we did not realize was how quickly a concrete offer would come from Harold and Hess.

After an hour or so, we parted; Harold had a dinner appointment and we were on our way to dinner and the theater.

While we were in New York that summer, Elaine de Kooning invited us to her studio in the Village. Her studio, a huge open loft that served as both her studio and her home, was up a long flight of stairs. The doorbell to her studio was at street level, and Elaine made a practice of looking out the window at the street below to see who was there before opening the door. She would not admit even her friends unless she was expecting them.

The art studio itself occupied the front of the loft and overlooked the street; at the other end was a partitioned area with a bedroom, kitchen, and bathroom. The kitchen was equipped with a commercial serving bar. She had paintings, books, clippings, and other things hanging or pasted on the walls around the entire floor.

Elaine was cheerful and generous, but I found her a little intense as a hostess. She entertained a lot, and that evening we met a number of her friends, including several younger artists who seemed to be around most of the time. Elaine showed us some of her completed portraits along with works in progress. These were large paintings, perhaps five or six feet in height, hanging or stacked against one wall. In each portrait, she had painted the figure of the subject without a face; from the figure, the subject was easily recognized, but I found it strange to look at portraits without faces. They were not abstract; details of the figures were realistic so that the blank faces made them resemble unfinished paintings.

Uncertain of our future, we returned to Houston a day or so later. During the weeks of August and early September, Don discussed both the CAA and Dominican College with his parents and they both urged him to accept the position with the college. At this point, he did not discuss New York as a real option. He did not mention it to Pat Goeters or anyone else at the museum. Don faced difficult choices; he was happy at the museum, and I did not believe that he could be satisfied in college development. There was no doubt that he was considering the appointment only because it put him in a negotiating position with the CAA.

After Don told Pat of his offer from Dominican College and asked that his museum salary be increased 100 percent, Pat as chairman discussed it with others members of the board. They were reluctant, but Pat insisted and the board finally conceded. They also agreed that he could keep his mornings free for writing. This negotiation occurred during the first week after our return from New York.

And then almost immediately, in early September, Harold called to offer Don the job with the new *Location* magazine in New York and to ask if he could assume the work by the first of October. Don accepted with almost no hesitation. This meant that we had a very short time in which to radically alter our lives.

Pat Goeters, unaware of Don's prospects for an editing job in Manhattan, was infuriated when Don told him. He felt betrayed by his closest friend.

At first, we thought that we could both move to New York at the end of September. But then as we tried to make plans it became apparent that we faced severe financial problems. We could not afford to move. Don did not want to ask his father for assistance, but he had resolved to accept the job.

I had other concerns as well. I had just begun a new fall term at Dominican College, but what was more important, I became uneasy about walking away from my responsibilities, especially financial, at the advertising agency.

Our business had grown steadily, and it would now be impossible for Odell to manage alone. We talked about bringing in another partner but knew that this option would take some time. The overriding problem, moreover, was financial. I would be walking away from a company that was in debt almost exclusively from my excessive withdrawals. Each time that I tried to discuss the problem with Don, his reply was that I should not worry, that "we would take care of it." Don could have turned to his father for help if I had pressed him to do so, but his father wanted him to accept the position with Dominican College and would undoubtedly have lectured him on fiscal responsibility.

At this point, I suggested that I remain in Houston for a few months to try and pay off the agency's debt, and in doing so, I could finish the academic semester at Dominican College as well. Don was reluctant to agree at first, but he was so eager to be in New York that he agreed to my plan. And I don't believe that he ever understood the seriousness of our financial plight.

During the next few weeks, Don continued to write and to work at the museum. Although Pat and other members of the board of the CAA were angry, nothing could dampen Don's high spirits. He would at last be an editor in Manhattan.

The two previous years as director of the museum were rich for Don. He had made a singular contribution to Houston's cultural life and, albeit unknown to most people, was at the same time becoming one of the most innovative writers of the twentieth century. When he recalled his work at the museum a few years later, it was with a touching sense of loss. He called it "the best job" he had ever had. I don't think he felt as good about himself and his work again until he returned to the University of Houston to teach in the 1980s.

On one of the last Sundays of September, we drove to Galveston to see Don's grandmother and to tell her of our plans and take her to lunch. We ate at John's Seafood Restaurant just past the causeway from the mainland. She emphatically disapproved of our plans to live apart for a few months and admonished me to change my mind. She told me that she had never been separated from her husband Bart except when he made the trip with Don's father to Mexico City.

During the brief time left before Don's move, we spent almost every evening with friends and family. George and Mary Christian invited us to their home for a final farewell dinner. George was the only friend in Houston who understood that Don felt compelled to be in New York. He was still second in command to Hubert Roussel, amusements editor of the *Houston Post,* but could see no alternative. The number of large daily newspapers in the United States continued to decline rather than to grow, and consequently, there were few such positions around the country. Mary, a former staff member of the *Post,* was now freelancing while she raised their children.

Pat and Bill Colville gave a party for us a few days before Don's departure. They lived in Montrose just a few blocks from our house, and most of the guests were artists, architects, and other friends from the museum. Don had continued to compartmentalize the people he knew; I don't think it occurred to him to include George and Mary or other literary or newspaper friends in the social life of the art community.

We drove out to Cypress just northwest of Houston on another day to see the new house that was being completed for my sister Margo Vandruff and her husband Roy. Pat Goeters had designed the modernist house, which was surrounded by woods. Like most younger architects in Houston, Pat had studied with the elder Barthelme, and so the house reflected the influence of the modernists as well as Frank Lloyd Wright and, at the same time, bore some resemblance to the Barthelme family home.

As we walked through the house and grounds, Don turned to me and asked if I was sure that I would rather that we go to New York "than stay here and build a home like this." I was startled but told him that I was certain. Although Don would have delighted in such a home, should I have urged him to remain in Houston, he would have been more disappointed and dissatisfied than at any other time in his life.

We made plans for me to stay with my mother until I moved to New York. The house on Harold Street had a large attic in which we stored a lot of our possessions, and we then sublet the house to Don's brother Pete and his wife Lillian.

On the Sunday of Don's departure, we had lunch with his family and then I drove him to the airport for his flight to New York. No one wanted Don to leave, but throughout most of our visit that day, his mother and father were encouraging about what he was undertaking and what they believed he might expect in New York. And then, the elder Barthelme bluntly advised Don to "be prepared for failure." Although I was shocked by these words and have always been puzzled by this harsh warning and the unhappy prognosis that it implied for Don's future as an editor, Don did not appear to be disheartened as he said goodbye to his parents.

Later that afternoon, Don flew from Houston's Municipal Airport to Manhattan. There he rented a room in a midtown hotel and the following day met with Harold Rosenberg and Thomas Hess.

AFTER DON HAD ARRIVED IN NEW YORK and checked into a midtown hotel on the West Side, he called to give me his telephone number and address. After that, he telephoned every other day. I was miserable over our separation and I could hear Don's loneliness as well, but for a while at least, the telephone conversations made it bearable.

The new magazine, to be called *Location,* had offices at 16 East 23rd Street. Its emphasis was to be on the contemporary, in art as well as in literature and criticism—a combination that was new but similar to that of *Forum.* Conceived as a quarterly, the journal was a project of the Longview Foundation.[1]

At his new office, Don kept to the same schedule as before; he wrote in the mornings and then edited the magazine in the afternoons.

New York fascinated Don; although he was lonely, he saw friends, often Joe Maranto, who shared with him a love of modern jazz. Joe's office at Mobil Oil was close to Grand Central Station, which made it easy for him to meet Don after five in the evenings. Joe introduced him to clubs where he could hear such figures as Miles Davis and Sonny Rollins, as well as numerous other talented musicians.

He began working on *Location* at once. For the first issue, Don solicited contributions from writers whom he knew, especially those who had contributed to *Forum.* The poets Kenneth Koch and Robert Bly were among the first, and both accepted his invitation to submit manuscripts.

But his work with *Location* was also disillusioning almost at once. He was disappointed to learn that he would have to share decision making with both Harold and Hess.

Meanwhile, Don lost little time in contacting the Sterling Lord Agency in Manhattan, so that by January, Lord had become his agent and soon placed "L'Lapse," a parody of a Michelangelo Antonioni film, in the March 2, 1963, issue of the *New Yorker.* Meanwhile, *Harper's Bazaar* had accepted "Florence Green Is 81" for the April issue.

Our strained finances continued to be a problem, both for me and for Don. Don had arrived in Manhattan with sufficient cash to pay all his expenses for at least a month—even while he lived in a hotel. In less than a week, however, he asked that I wire additional cash. After that, it was every two or three days, so that within a short time I had sent him a considerable sum and had to finally explain that we simply could not continue spending this much money.

At that point Don called his father for financial help. He was spending every evening enjoying New York, especially the music of entertainers he had known only through their recordings. The restaurants were expensive as well. He needed much more income than he earned from *Location.*

In any event, we just could not manage it. What I did not know was that the abrupt change of lifestyle, from one in which we both worked almost every evening to one in which his work ended around five, would ultimately have more serious consequences for his health. As Don later described the world in which he found himself, "there was too much booze."

Meanwhile, Odell and I continued to acquire new clients and soon had more work than the two of us could handle. During these first years of our agency, in the 1950s and the 1960s, the population in greater Houston reached one million, so that real estate development and construction became one of the mainstays of our business. Even after most of our other business was made up of industrial accounts, real estate was an important part of it. In this early period, we also represented several local retail and service businesses.

Earlier in 1962, we added a downtown restaurant and private club to our client list. The owners constructed a building across the street from the new Sheraton Lincoln Hotel on Polk Avenue. In a city in which only beer and wine could legally be served in restaurants, private clubs were essential. Our client, Captain John Theocharidis, had already established two prominent restaurants in Houston. A native of Greece and a colorful sea captain during World War II, he had made a fortune in shipping during and after the war and was now retired.

We were soon working late into the night to meet all the deadlines. We were not in a financial position to recruit additional professional staff, but we managed with freelance writers and artists. We recruited our sister Margo Vandruff to take over direct mail promotions and to help in running the office.

Pete Barthelme, now married and completing his work at the University of Houston, had joined our staff in 1961 as a writer, but he quickly assumed the role of creative director. Pete had an impressive talent for creating campaigns as well as for writing. He was not only talented and possessed the Barthelme wit but also seemed to enjoy such writing, unlike Don, who felt that the writing of advertising copy would corrupt or even destroy a writer's creativity. In these early years, Pete was able to take

Don's place in writing for our agency; later, however, he joined the staffs of two of Houston's leading advertising agencies and eventually founded his own firm.

By late October, my separation from Don was becoming intolerable. On October 12, our sixth wedding anniversary, Don sent a telegram: "On this worst of anniversaries love and hope for many better." Finally, I talked to my sister and she agreed that I should go ahead and move to New York and she would try to manage our business without me. Besides, I could at least commute occasionally to Houston.

Don was elated when I gave him the news, and he set out to search for an apartment. The flat he found was in the new Mayfair Fifth Building at Fifth Avenue and 15th Street. The address was 96 Fifth Avenue, about six blocks from Washington Square. He wrote that he had "walked around for days" looking at

> lovely old picturesque dirty apartment buildings in filthy and fine neighborhoods, bits of old Village, up to 36th Street (Murray Hill district) and as far up as the sixties where the rents are really high but everything is double-picturesque. On the Lower East Side the rents are lower but the place is filled with bums (an estimated 45,000) whereas on the Upper East Side the rents are higher but the place is filled with . . . [homosexuals] . . . (an estimated 100,000). On the West Side the place is filled with Puerto Ricans and Americans who will, it is said, cut your throat for a nickel.[2]

The area he chose was filled with all of these. He described the apartment itself and gave me a list of the furniture we would need. He also sent a sketch of the floor plan. It was very small, with a sleeping alcove that Don described as "like the dining room part of a living room–dining combination rather than a bedroom." There was also a "handsome parquet floor." The building had "a 24-hour doorman and the neighborhood is quite good." Our rent would be $163 with a sublet clause that allowed us to sublet after one year. He wrote at the end, "Sweetheart, I look forward eagerly to your goddamn arrival." This note was followed by instructions to get help from his brothers, a reminder that he would call me on Thursday, and then he signed it with "every kind of love."

For the next two weeks, I worked long hours at the office and then packed in the evenings. I chose books and records to move, packed the kitchen, moved more things to the attic, and finally arranged for the younger Barthelme brothers to help move everything else to my mother's home. Exhausted, I was unable to go to New York on Thursday to hear a major poetry reading at the Poetry Center as he wanted. Instead, I managed to leave on Saturday morning. My sister drove me to the airport, and we parted with all kinds of last-minute plans for clients. I really had no idea how we would get our agency through this crisis, and I told her I would fly back for a short visit as soon as possible. I knew that I was leaving Odell with a serious indebtedness, but I departed anyway.

On Saturday afternoon I arrived at the Newark airport, and Don was waiting just inside the arrival gate. We took the airport bus into Manhattan and then a taxi to our apartment. The flat was described as two and a half rooms, but in reality it was an efficiency. As our furniture had not yet arrived, Don managed to provide a few minimal furnishings so that we could live there for a couple of days.

Directly across from us on 15th Street there was a garment manufacturing shop. We could look into a room crowded with sewing machines, racks of clothes, and the workers — all women — bent over them. It was exactly as we had seen in motion pictures.

After lunch, Don took me over to the *Location* office at 16 East 23rd Street. The entrance lobby was dreary and empty; the only person around on Saturday afternoon was an elevator operator. Upstairs, the journal was housed in drab offices looking out over Broadway. It was dark and dismal, with little more than a desk, a few chairs, file cabinets, and a typewriter. I did not know how Don, who had always been so conscious of the design around him, was able to work there. The files for the new journal were in one of the cabinets, but Don continued to carry his own manuscripts with him in a single file folder that he took to and from the apartment each day. As Don had already told me, he was adhering to his familiar schedule of writing in the mornings and editing the magazine in the afternoons.

On Sunday evening, we walked to Kenneth Koch's apartment in the West Village for Don to discuss the manuscript that Kenneth promised for the first issue of *Location*. We arrived late, around nine, and stayed for two hours or so while they discussed what to use from Kenneth's new work and the number of pages that Don needed.

Kenneth was cheerful and witty, as he had been in Houston, but here at home where he was engrossed in his work, I saw a more serious dimension of his personality.

We met Kenneth's wife, who was working on her dissertation in the kitchen, where she had set up a table and typewriter for her work. Before we left, we briefly discussed my plans in New York, and after learning of my intention to enroll in graduate school, Kenneth promised to help me obtain a part-time teaching position at the New School for Social Research.

The apartment in which Kenneth and his wife lived was extremely depressing; it was in an older building that needed remodeling. The paint was flaking and peeling everywhere, and there were water stains on the wallpaper and other signs of decay. When I saw the bathroom, I immediately thought of *Baby Doll,* a 1950s film with Karl Malden. The film became famous in part for a notorious scene in which Carroll Baker is bathing in an old enamel tub in a run-down farmhouse.

In the southwestern states, most of the existing homes in the 1960s had been built after World War II; the older houses dated mostly to the 1920s. I soon learned that buildings such as the one in which Kenneth lived were more typical in New York than the kind of high-rise in which we had just leased an apartment. Nevertheless, I was extremely uncomfortable and relieved when we left the building. Don said he thought Kenneth's apartment could be comfortable as a home, but I could not take his comment seriously.

On Sunday, we resumed a routine similar to the one we had in Houston. After breakfast, he walked to his office while I took care of the apartment. I immediately began walking around the area to locate the grocery store, cleaners, and whatever else we needed. Don then came home for lunch and returned to the office afterward.

In the afternoon, I walked to midtown and then uptown, usually down Fifth Avenue toward the museums, sometimes all the way from 15th Street to the Metropolitan Museum of Art in the Eighties. In the late afternoon, I returned to the apartment to prepare dinner.

Our furniture did not arrive for a couple of days, so on Monday and Tuesday in the first week of November there was no reason to remain at home. Among the new books that I read that week was Joseph Heller's *Catch-22.* Other than Don's stories, Heller's novel was the first of what critics were soon labeling "absurdist" or "antirealistic" fiction.

We spent Monday evening with Joe Maranto, who met us after leaving his office at Mobil Oil. We had dinner at a spaghetti house where we saw Dwight Macdonald, whose *Against the American Grain* was among the current popular texts on American culture. After dinner, we went first to the Village Gate, where we heard Miles Davis, and then to another bar, where we heard Sonny Rollins. Around midnight I was too exhausted to continue so we took a cab back to our apartment.

It had been an exciting evening, but when we reached our apartment, I saw that Don was unhappy at giving up the evening so early. For the very first time, I became unreasonably angry with him and we were soon having an explosive and devastating argument.

Don told me that the first few weeks of our separation had been agonizing, but that now he had begun to enjoy the freedom of being alone. He thought we should live apart a while longer. In fact, he now wanted to "live alone and date other girls." I was shattered by this admission, even though I too had begun to enjoy the freedom of being without the daily responsibility of marriage. I told him that I "understood" and had certainly found other men attractive but that I could not fathom giving up our marriage. I knew that Don should be in New York and I felt I had helped to make it possible for him to be there, but not only was I physically exhausted, I had been and still was under great stress concerning our financial condition and the debts we had in Houston. That evening, I had little tolerance and understanding of the stresses that he still faced in this new life. By the end of the evening, I had decided that I should just return to Houston.

The next morning, we agreed to wait a few weeks before deciding anything definite. We arranged a daily schedule and made plans for the day. Don had made an appointment for us to have lunch at the Museum of Modern Art with Jack Kroll, with whom he had become friends during the past few weeks. Jack was nice, intelligent, and, according to Don, a good writer. But he seemed a bit lost. Don told me that Jack's friends wanted to help him, but it was not clear what he wanted. Jack was already an established critic but had not yet joined the staff of *Newsweek*.

That day in Manhattan was a brilliant November day, and I remember that I found Jack very nice but sometimes difficult to follow in his stream of erudite conversation—allusions to people, events, and ideas that were then part of the New York scene. Before we parted, we invited Jack to come to dinner for "fried chicken" at our apartment the following week. This was Don's idea; it was one of his favorite meals but one that I seldom cooked.

We saw Elaine de Kooning several times during these first weeks. We met her one evening for dinner at an Italian restaurant in the Village. Friends from Houston, Bettiruth and Adolph Susholtz, were with us. It was a small, shabby basement restaurant that had excellent food and that for Elaine resonated with memories of Willem [Bill] de Kooning and other Abstract Expressionist artists.

She invited us to a party about a week after I arrived. The guests included Bill, to whom she was still legally married. He was extremely appealing, and it was apparent why he had a reputation for being attractive to women. Gray haired and very handsome, he was easy to talk to. He came to the United States long before World War II and told me a story about returning home to Europe for a visit after the war. Whenever he had found himself homesick for the United States, he would go to see American westerns, especially films directed by John Ford.

Elaine drank heavily, in contrast to Bill de Kooning, who had given up alcohol and seemed not to fit into the frantic atmosphere of her studio. That evening, Elaine and the others were talking about the artist Franz Kline, who had died on May 13.

Harold Rosenberg was there as well; he was one of this small circle of artists and critics who wielded considerable influence in New York's world of Abstract Expressionism. I learned later that when Elaine attempted to help Guy Johnson find a gallery in New York, Harold and Tom Hess had discouraged the effort. She had met Guy at the Contemporary Arts Museum in Houston and liked his work. He was now on the faculty of Bridgeport University in Connecticut, but his work was probably too realistic—largely social commentary and in this sense not of interest to Rosenberg and Hess. Abstract Expressionism still ruled the art scene. Don later told me that, as it turned out, Guy was able to find a gallery on his own.

One evening, Elaine invited us to her home and studio for a history of art lecture with slides from the Metropolitan Museum of Art. She wanted to rehearse it for a university presentation that she was to give, but the lecture was surprisingly prosaic. After the lecture, she showed her portraits again. One was a commissioned painting that was to be an official portrait of the new president, John F. Kennedy. Elaine had spent weeks photographing the president at his home in Palm Beach and was now using these pictures along with some sketches for her portrait. She showed us the photographs and slides that she had taken, informal scenes of Kennedy from a number of angles. As she had done in other portraits, Elaine painted him as a recognizable seated figure, yet without a face. My reaction to the painting was similar to those she showed us earlier; it was disconcerting to see a portrait of Kennedy without a face. Don later told me that her painting of the president was turned down as the official portrait, but it now hangs in a gallery at one of the Smithsonian centers.

During these few weeks in Manhattan, Don was more passionate than ever but unyielding in asking for a separation. He thought that the life we had shared was "too pretty," that the "real world is not like that." And then almost brutally, he added that he "hated the idea of having a child."

I did not feel that our marriage had been as "pretty" as he suggested.

Also, I had known that Don was repelled by the physical realities of pregnancy, a reaction I certainly shared. That day, I began to understand for the first time the enormity of the commitment Don had made to our life together and how difficult it must have been at times for him to "take care of me" in the way that he thought he should. I had fallen in love with Don and married him at least partly because he so clearly wanted a happy and pleasant relationship as well as a passionate one. We had spoken harshly to each other only two or perhaps three times during our marriage; if this had not been true, I doubt that I would have wanted to be married to him.

My perspective was naive and unrealistic. As we continued to talk over the next few weeks, I began to grasp Don's dilemma. He wanted us to continue to love each other, but he was unable to continue in the role of "Prince Charming," one of the names he would use to characterize himself in *Snow White*.

Don no longer wanted to sustain our almost idyllic relationship of more than six years together. This was more than implicit in what he said. "Taking care of me," as he called it, seemed to demand of him a pretense of happiness that he now felt was false. When I asked him about the "endearing phone calls" that he had made throughout our weeks apart, he threw his arms around me and, hugging me tightly, said they were sincere and "they *were* endearing." Throughout these days, he would often unexpectedly put his arms around me as if he did not want to let go no matter what he said.

At first, it was impossible for me to believe that he wanted to be anywhere without me. But it was soon clear that Don did not want to give up our marriage but wanted to change the conditions of it. I don't know that anything would ultimately have been satisfactory for us, but for several weeks, we lived with the same routine, undecided about our future.

AFTER ARRIVING IN NEW YORK, I realized immediately that Don was now drinking excessively. In Manhattan, there were endless reasons for drinking, among them the jazz clubs, where he could indulge his passion for music, especially modern jazz. Don spent as many evenings as possible in one of the Village-area clubs where the most talented artists performed. He occasionally worked with an author on a manuscript in the evening, but there seemed to be at least one or two social affairs to which he was invited each week, including those at Elaine's home. Even though he continued his morning schedule of writing, few evenings were needed for *Location,* which meant that he no longer worked at night as he and I both had done in Houston. Nevertheless, I could not have imagined that alcoholism would eventually become a serious problem.

I looked forward to enrolling in graduate school at either New York University or the New School for Social Research. As both institutions were nearby, I walked first to the New School and then to NYU to pick up catalogs and application forms. Don wanted me to submit my applications for graduate school, but at the same time he urged me to look for a job. Although I had in some sense abandoned the agency, I could not ignore my responsibility. Don, however, was heedless of financial concerns that either of us had in Houston. The debts were his as well as mine, but I had learned that he would do nothing until he found it necessary to turn to his father for help, and I did not want him to have to do that. It was futile for me to attempt to talk to him about it; I could only work with my sister from New York and then return to Houston whenever necessary. I was, however, adamant about not being interested in an advertising or public relations job in Manhattan.

In the 1960s, New York offered numerous possibilities in these areas, many of them listed in the *New York Times.* Each morning at breakfast, Don pointed out positions listed in the classified section of the *Times.* I was dismayed and then finally annoyed that he would urge this upon me day after day, but I remained resolute in my refusal to search for a job. He should at least have understood how I felt about this.

The irony of our discussions about my work was that I was in touch almost daily with Odell at our agency in Houston, and two or three times a week I used Don's office to write copy. It soon became clear, however, that what Don wanted was for me to stay in New York but to have an income independent of his. Such an arrangement would free him of concern for my financial well-being.

In just three years, I had been successful in founding and developing a small advertising agency, and I did not want to be an employee of some-one else's company, not even a large firm. Besides, I found much of the world of advertising distasteful and hated the notion of working on an ac-count over which I had no control. But above all, I had looked forward to New York and to the academic life available there, and I was sure that I could teach part-time at a university. I felt betrayed as Don urged me to look for a job that I did not want.

When I started the agency in Houston, I was governed by an overrid-ing desire for independence that made being someone else's employee not only unattractive but intolerable. It did not seem extraordinary to me at the time, but my sister and I were unique in that we were women who were successful advertising agency owners. Advertising was among the few professions open to women; in fact, a top administrative or management position was not even a possibility in almost any other business. But even in this profession, a woman was expected to be an employee, at best a man-agement executive, eventually a partner. She was not likely to be the owner of the firm.

My attitude undoubtedly reflected the independence and autonomy sought not only by our mother and her mother, but by generations of my ancestors, some of whom arrived in the Massachusetts Bay Colony in the seventeenth century, others in the eighteenth century. They were mostly farmers, among them our great-grandparents, who left the East and came south to Texas just after the War between the States. Our mother was a beautiful girl of whom her family expected only marriage and family, but she had the independent spirit of both her parents and this she be-queathed to me and to my sisters.

By 1962, I had already been on the faculty of both the University of Houston and Dominican College and knew that teaching was ideal for me, but I needed a Ph.D. to pursue a traditional teaching position. I did not care that most women in the university world had little chance of becom-ing full professors, especially in literature. It was even difficult for a woman to join the faculty of a major university. As in other professions, it was a blatant act of discrimination that most women accepted.

Manhattan was nevertheless an adventure every day. Walking around it was an exhilarating experience. We could walk everywhere—to restaurants, theaters, museums, art galleries, and even produce markets, grocery stores, and the laundry. Even though our future together was still undecided, we spent hours looking at furnishings for our apartment. There were so many shops, however, that the search for new or exciting designs was exhausting and made the effort less an aesthetic experience than we had known before. About a year later, in early 1964, Don's story, "Down the Line with the Annual," satirized the overwhelming choice of household goods and the information and advice given in the *Consumer Bulletin Annual.* Don used a brief quote from the story as an epigraph for the story.[1]

Around the middle of November, I took the train out to Stamford to spend the day with Maggie Maranto and their two children. Once the commuter train was past the blighted neighborhoods of New York's outer boroughs, the scenery was picturesque, with the roadways and villages and towns free of the pervasive billboard signs to which we were accustomed in much of Texas. The countryside was lush and the affluent homes well tended. In Stamford, Maggie took me on a driving tour and then we had lunch at her home. Later that afternoon, I returned to Manhattan.

At Thanksgiving, we accepted an invitation to visit Don's aunt, who lived in Bucks County, Pennsylvania. Don's sister Joan was then working and living in Washington, D.C., so she joined us for the weekend. The aunt's restored farmhouse, built in the eighteenth century, had large, high-ceilinged rooms, with a tall staircase and landing, and even though it was much older, it reminded me of the one my paternal grandparents had built in Kleberg County, Texas, near the King Ranch, at the beginning of the twentieth century.

The following week, we returned to New York, with nothing yet resolved about our marriage.

We were invited to several parties during these weeks in November and December, among them one on Riverside Drive in an older apartment building with an elevator. The hostess was the owner of an art gallery, someone Don met through Elaine. From the street, the building was depressing and promised a shoddy interior, and the dark lobby and shabby hallways fulfilled the promise. But the interior of the gallery owner's apartment was handsome and beautifully decorated. The evening gave me my first glimpse of the elegant interiors that one finds in the older structures of New York.

Throughout this time, New York was fascinating. The holiday decorations had been installed and the town was breathtakingly beautiful. In spite of my anguish, I was eager to explore as much of the heart of

Manhattan as possible. I visited museums and galleries, went to afternoon movies, and shopped with great relish. I was beginning to feel quite comfortable, but before long Don made it impossible for me to stay.

Near the end of November, as I resisted searching for a job, Don said that if I decided to remain in New York, I could stay in this apartment and he would look for another for himself. I had seen Don use this kind of coercion to obtain what he wanted with other people, but never before had he used it to impose his will on me. For us to have separate apartments, I would have no choice but to obtain a professional position in New York. Don knew this but was adamant. I was equally unyielding about not searching for a job that I did not want.

After a few days more, I was discouraged enough to give up and return to Houston in early December. I was numb with grief but unwilling to stay in Manhattan under the conditions that Don demanded.

Back in Houston, with no home of my own, I moved in with my mother temporarily. It was a miserable experience, but I immediately resumed work at the agency and made plans to return to my classes at Dominican College.

During the next week or so, Don and I talked over the telephone almost daily. Even though he was following his schedule of writing, I could tell that he too was miserable and told him that I had decided to return on December 19. However, his response made it impossible for me to do this. He wrote a letter in which he said that "the fact is that I want to live alone and have wanted to for a long time. . . . I can give you what you want only by pretending that I feel otherwise than I do feel. . . . it is better to hate myself than to hate you, and I am afraid, if a reunion is forced rather than natural, it would come to that." Finally, he concluded that we would "have to remain apart for now, being miserable in our separate ways: everything feels so temporary to me I don't know what's happening."

He was discouraged about his stories and told me that "no other stories have been sold, or for that matter written." Don had, in fact, become a client of the Sterling Lord Agency, and his work would soon begin to appear in major publications rather than in "little" magazines.

Manuscripts were coming in for *Location,* but Don was concerned about an article that Jack Kroll had promised: "I finally got Jack Kroll on the phone by calling him at 3:30 AM. He assured me that the article was in the mail; of course it wasn't, and hasn't appeared. It appears that there is a good likelihood of his being sent to jail for nonpayment of alimony. What a mess he's in."

Jack was the first new friend Don had found in New York, and he mentioned him frequently.

He also wrote that Kenneth Koch "came over the other night and declared that everything is going to hell all around him," which, he added, "seems to be true." Another evening, Kenneth took him to the Columbia University faculty club, where he met Dwight Macdonald.

Don had also asked Robert Bly, who was then living in Manhattan, for a contribution to *Location*. Bly was friendly and "asked me over to his house for a couple of drinks, and I went yesterday. They have a pleasant small apartment on West 11th." At Bly's house, he also met "Louis Simpson, middlingly-famous poet." Bly submitted his contribution for the magazine but became angry with Don's proposed changes and retracted the article. Don wrote that

> Bly reacted so violently to the rather violent editing job I did on his
> thing that our relations deteriorated rapidly from an impasse to a
> shambles, with the result that he picked up his marbles and went
> home. He told me that he'd shown the edited version to his friends
> Louis Simpson and John Logan (both Poets), who agreed with
> him that it was the worst single job of editing a manuscript seen in
> the Western World since the invention of movable type. Luckily,
> Harold didn't agree.[2]

Concerning the first issue of *Location,* Don wrote that the

> magazine is now an uneasy collection of good things which don't
> seem to cohere in any meaningful synthesis. Maybe they will with a
> little more tinkering and shifting about. Best things we have now
> are four brief chapters from Koch's novel, my story called "For I'm
> the Boy Whose Only Joy Is Loving You" which Rosenberg and
> Hess insist we use in the first number,[3] and a strange piece from
> the Canadian anthropologist Marshall McLuhan. . . . I'm sup-
> posed to go out to South Hampton next week and spend two days
> with Larry Rivers working on layouts.[4]

Don did not like the Rivers layout, but there was nothing he could do; he was finding that Rosenberg and Hess would make most of the decisions dealing with art and design.

In Houston, I spent Christmas with my sister Margo Vandruff at her new home that Goeters had designed. Don and I talked on Christmas Eve, and he sounded okay. He was relishing a special Christmas gift from his parents: packaged meals for the holidays. But then he wrote to his parents that I seemed "fairly cheerful if not deliriously happy." This was not true, but I had decided to go ahead with my life, at least for the present.

In spite of what he said about not writing, Don sold "Florence Green Is 81" to *Harper's Bazaar* for three hundred dollars. Even when he was not working on a new story, Don was still following the routine he had started in Houston, revising manuscripts and sending them out; in Houston, he had written most of the stories for *Come Back, Dr. Caligari* and was able to work on these in December and January. By the middle of January, he had manuscripts at *Esquire, Noble Savage, Contact, Paris Review,* and *Evergreen Review.* And within a few weeks, he had produced several additional stories.

In January, I decided to return to New York without telling Don that I was coming. I knew that if I attempted to talk to him about it, he would find a way to stop me. Thus, near the end of the month, I arrived at our apartment early in the morning without calling first. As I had anticipated, Don was surprised yet extremely happy to see me. I would not have been shocked if he had not spent the night at the apartment; instead, a girl was there with him. When he told me this, I discreetly waited downstairs until he had escorted her out.

We were glad to see each other, and he was so clearly happy with my arrival that I was not angry at first. In fact, we hugged, laughed, and talked for several minutes. About the girl, Don said simply that "she was not anyone that mattered." Before long, he became as passionate as ever. But suddenly, it was impossible for me to respond to his gestures of love. I was affectionate but at that moment felt nothing more.

While I was there, we went to several parties, including one at Elaine's. When I mentioned how many parties there were in art circles, Don's reply was that "no one else works as hard as we did." I recalled this exchange much later after he returned to the University of Houston in 1981 and how happy he appeared to be with the increased responsibilities of his professorship at the university.

I was in New York in January just a short time when Don once again proposed that I stay in the Fifth Avenue apartment and that he move to another. I decided there was nothing for me to do but give up for the present and return to Houston, where I moved in with my mother on what I intended to be a temporary basis. However, I stayed there through the first months of 1963, resuming my work at the agency and at Dominican College, and within a short time I started a new social life without Don.

In New York, Don not only followed his writing schedule every morning but began a campaign to get his first collection of stories published through his friend Herman Gollob. In Houston, Don had pressed Herman to publish such a collection. He now wrote to Herman in Boston that if Herman "were a really courageous book publisher," he would publish Don's stories. "They're brilliant, they're better than anyone else's," Don wrote, "so why don't you have a little courage." Gollob later described Don's letters as "swaggering almost, but ingratiating as well as engaging." This was "part of Don's posture, not much of a posture actually, but I never saw Don suffer much about the quality of his work."[5]

After moving to Manhattan, Don continued in his attempt to browbeat Herman into publishing his work. Finally, Herman came down to Manhattan from Boston and they talked about the possibility of a book. Don was confident that he already had enough for a first collection, and finally Gollob promised to pursue it with his editorial board.

"Florence Green Is 81," "To London and Rome," "The Joker's Greatest Triumph," and "Up, Aloft in the Air," were among the stories Don proposed for the collection. Another was a new one that he worked on in December; he first gave it the title of "Carl" but then changed it to "Margins," the name under which it appeared in the *New Yorker* in the February, 1964, issue.

When he was working on "Carl," Don wrote to his father, to whom he had sent dialogue from the story, that it "further extends the line of attack originally announced in my stories 'The Joker's Greatest Triumph' and 'The Ohio Quadrilogy.'" Although Don's own experiences continued to provide ideas for what he wrote, the stories were now more satirical, especially in his portrayal of contemporary life. In "Margins," he again used allegory, as he had in his very first published work, to provide a portrait of the artist-writer.

Another story he would submit was "Up, Aloft in the Air," a four-part story that he originally wrote in Houston under the title of "The Ohio Quadrilogy." By the end of 1962, he had also completed a final version of "For I'm the Boy Whose Only Joy Is Loving You," a "fragment" of which was first published in the *Houston Post* in January, 1962; the entire story appeared in the first number of *Location*. "To London and Rome," which he wrote in the fall of 1962, was rejected by *Evergreen Review* but later published in *Genesis West 2* in the fall of 1963.

"The Piano Player," initially written in the fall of 1962 but later revised in New York, was published in the August 31, 1963, issue of the *New Yorker*.

As the first issue of *Location* neared completion in 1963, Don continued to be unhappy about it. He described the title as "most ungraceful, flat and pedestrian." And the cover that Larry Rivers had done "is awful" but "Tom and Harold like it." Nor did Don like "a fifteen-page poem by Kenneth Burke" that he called "fantastically poor," but he was outvoted. He pointed out that this is "the first time I haven't been sole proprietor, and it's difficult to adjust to the committee system, especially when the other members are formidable thinkers."

The *New Yorker* soon gave Don a "First Reading" contract, which meant that Don received what was for him a premium payment for every story they accepted—$750. Besides "L'Lapse," a ten-page parody of one of Antonioni's films, the *New Yorker* accepted three additional stories in 1963: "The Piano Player," "Marie, Marie, Hold on Tight," and "A Shower of Gold."

Don's Antonioni parody was translated into Italian by Niccolo Tucci, a writer for the *New Yorker,* and sent to Antonioni. When he first learned of the translation from Roger Angell at the *New Yorker,* Don joked that the director might "sue him in Italian."

In the first version of "The Ohio Quadrilogy," which Don wrote in Houston, he had used the name of Helen for Buck's "wife in Texas." I objected to my name appearing in his stories; he seemed surprised that I would disapprove but changed the name to Herodiade, and after that whenever he made references to a character whom I might have suggested, he gave her a name starting with the letter "H." One name he used frequently was Hilda.

Four more of his first stories were included in the collection for Herman. They were "The Darling Duckling at School" (a title that was changed to "Me and Miss Mandible" when the story appeared in the collection), "The Hiding Man," "The Big Broadcast of 1938," and "The Viennese Opera Ball." They had appeared in *Contact 7, Contact 20, First Person 1,* and in *New World Writing.*

In the spring of 1963, I decided to look for a new apartment in Houston. I had been living with my mother but now wanted to establish my own household again. Inasmuch as I had shipped our furnishings to New York, I asked Don to send some of our things back to Houston. He was aghast that I wanted to do this. "What about when you return to New York?" he asked. I was puzzled and frustrated, but when I asked if he were ready for me to come back, his answer was "not yet." And so within a few days, the moving truck arrived and I established my own home once again.

Meanwhile, Don looked for a different apartment that would cost less than the one on Fifth Avenue. One of his new friends soon found a rent-controlled flat at 115 West 11th Street in the Village. These apartments were difficult to obtain, and most tenants stayed in them for years. It became Don's permanent address in Manhattan.

Before long, Herman successfully persuaded Little, Brown to take a chance with Don. His presentation to the editorial board was on the significance and originality of Don's fiction. To accomplish this, Herman wrote and sang a song with lines from "A Shower of Gold" for the lyrics. Although Don had written an earlier version of this story in Houston, he revised and completed it while visiting the Gollobs at their home on Martha's Vineyard during the summer of 1963; from the room where he worked, he could look out at the ocean. "A Shower of Gold" rounded out the collection that became *Come Back, Dr. Caligari.*

After the editorial board approved Herman's proposal, *Come Back, Dr. Caligari* was scheduled for release in early 1964. Meanwhile, in December, 1963, "A Shower of Gold" appeared for the first time in the December issue of the *New Yorker.*

In "A Shower of Gold" Don not only commented on the world he was then experiencing in New York but also incorporated philosophical influences of the day. Since the late 1940s, Don had read work by Husserl, Kierkegaard, Heidegger, and Pascal, along with such influential writers as Sartre and Albert Camus. In the story the character Peterson experiences a series of fantastic absurdities but argues that "possibilities nevertheless proliferate," an optimistic notion that persists in much of Don's fictions, even in *The King,* which he worked on in the spring of 1989, not long before his death.

The first issue of *Location* appeared in May, 1963. It had ninety-eight pages, and although the content was somewhat different from what Don had envisioned, he was satisfied enough. He thought it impossible to produce a quarterly as Rosenberg and Hess had planned. He continued to be disappointed that they participated in all the editing decisions. In fact, the contents of *Location* resembled an issue of *Forum.* Kenneth Koch, Saul Bellow, Robert Rauschenberg, Marshall McLuhan, David Levy, Saul Steinberg, and Peter Yates were among the contributors. Interviews with artists, photographs of the work of painters and sculptors, poetry, fiction, and articles on philosophy and technology were all part of the magazine.

Just before Christmas, Don came home for two weeks. *Holiday Magazine* had given him an assignment to write an article on Houston, a writing task he detested and ultimately did not complete. But he had already accepted payment for the article, and it gave him an excuse to return home.

For two weeks, we saw each other almost every evening and part of each day. We ate at some of our favorite restaurants, but Don wanted to avoid the places that had been part of our weekly ritual since 1956. I could see that he was cautious and unwilling to risk anything that might threaten his self-control.

In 1963, I made new friends and became interested in activities that were a change from my former life with Don. I bought an Austin-Healey sports car and attended sports car races, and along with a young biology professor who was a colleague at Dominican College, I learned to fly a Cessna 150. We usually went out to Collier Airport in northwest Houston once or twice each week to take lessons. It was frightening and exciting; I was introduced to a world of risk takers who knew nothing or very little of writing or any other art.

I invited Don to go to the airfield with me, but he was nervous about watching me do something that he considered so dangerous. Don feared flying even in a passenger jet. After I described the small Cessna 150 that we used for a training plane and talked about the pilots who were instructors, he asked if the pilots "were tall and blond and wore long white scarves."

Upon arriving at my apartment on the first day of his vacation, Don had with him a copy of the June issue of *Cavalier*. In it was a short story that he had written the previous December and submitted to *Playboy*. But "killing my hopes of a warm winter," the story was turned down. He then submitted it under a pseudonym to a *Playboy*-styled magazine, *Cavalier*. *Cavalier* accepted the story, but Don said it "paid not nearly so well."

The story was "The Ontological Basis of Two," and it appeared under the name of Michael Houston, a pseudonym he had used for *Forum*. A parody of B. F. Skinner's *Walden Two*, it is an ironical tale of a girl—Peridot Concord—who was "raised in a glass box by a Harvard professor." He says of Peridot that because she "inhabited the box until her fourth year, she is now "as healthy and natural as a shrub." Although she is free of the inhibitions of appearing nude that beset the narrator and everyone else, four years spent in the box have also left her "*lacking in basic carnality.*"

Although a humorous satirical tale, the story shows that Don could easily write a more traditional narrative. Nevertheless, like his other stories, it is filled with allusions to cultural clichés, including books and fashionable clothes, and contains such descriptions as "Madison Avenue eyes" and "Guggenheim-applicant feeling."

Don had applied that year for a Guggenheim fellowship that would enable him to work and travel abroad for a few months. Although he said nothing of it to me at the time, he was taking the advice of Lynn Nesbitt, whom he first met when she was a receptionist at Sterling Lord in late 1962 and who was now his agent. She told him that he should travel because he "had not been anywhere."[6] Presumably, this meant that he could enrich his work from travel abroad, particularly travel in Europe.

When it was time for Don to return to New York, we talked about the future. Don wanted to continue living alone but had not given up on a later reconciliation. As we walked to his car, I looked up at him and saw that tears were streaming down his face. It was the first and only time that I saw him cry. But for me, the worst was past; I had grieved for an entire year and could no longer feel the sorrow that he appeared to feel at this moment. It was too late to recover what I believed he had so carelessly thrown away. My pride and my own expectations of our marriage made it impossible for me to propose any kind of compromise. We said goodbye that night, and I did not see him again for a long time.

In January of 1964, two Houston newspaper columnists received advance copies of *Come Back, Dr. Caligari;* both knew Don but neither had known of Don's work while he was in Houston.

George Fuermann, columnist for the *Houston Post,* recalled Don as a former staff member of the *Post* and was shocked that he knew so little of Don. Fuermann reviewed the stories on January 26; like many reviewers of this first collection, he wrote admiringly of Don's talent but found it difficult to take the stories seriously. Don had "written a book whose fortune would break his heart if he were sane." The stories were "absurd exercises in well-tempered nonsense."

Since he previously knew nothing of what Don had been trying to write, the columnist observed that he read the stories "with the feeling that they must have been written by some other Donald Barthelme, someone unknown to me. What a come-down to find that I know more about Chiang Kai-shek than about a former colleague!"

Bill Roberts, another columnist for the *Post,* wrote that Don's book of short stories "is getting the fanciest promotional treatment in years from Little, Brown: A red-boxed letter, containing three of the stories."

Whether they liked his work or not, most critics were astonished by it. Among the reviewers who saw that Don's writing might open up new possibilities for literature was Granville Hicks, who wrote in the *Saturday Review* on April 4, 1964, that "Barthelme's kind of controlled craziness may be showing literature a new path to follow."

In the *New York Times,* R. V. Cassill observed that Don had "mastered many of Joyce's comic devices—though his debt to *Mad* magazine is almost as considerable." Like many reviewers, he appeared not to see—except for the allusion to *Mad Magazine*—the ironic stance that was central to Don's writing. In fact, he apparently saw little in the way of innovation and concluded that ultimately "the literary allusions and adaptations amount to something analogous to name-dropping." In contrast, a review in the *New Republic* carried an enthusiastic headline reading "Come Back, Mr. Barthelme."

Meanwhile, Don completed the second issue of *Location,* which, because of money problems, was to be the final one. But he had now received a Guggenheim Fellowship and in the fall would be traveling to Denmark, where he expected to write his first novel. He had already discussed his plans with Herman, whom he expected to publish it. They had talked about developing it from "A Shower of Gold," the final story that Don wrote for the *Dr. Caligari* collection.

Even though Don and I never talked about his work being autobiographical, "A Shower of Gold" seemed to provide an ideal beginning for an autobiographical novel. The story is made up of his observations about life in New York and the challenges of surviving there as an artist. He brings in all kinds of cultural, literary, and intellectual forces, among them some of the philosophers whose work he had read or in whom he was especially interested, including Kierkegaard, Sartre, Nietzsche, and Pascal. And the conclusion is a fitting description of Don's own life: "My mother was a royal virgin . . . and my father a shower of gold. My childhood was pastoral and energetic and rich in experiences which developed my character. As a young man I was noble in reason and, infinite in faculty, in form express and admirable."

When Don reached Copenhagen in September, he wrote that "the town is very beautiful and oldworld-ish with cobblestones instead of good sound asphalt and no buildings taller than six stories." He rented a "small but pleasant flat for five weeks at the end of which I'll have to get out and hustle up another." The ballet in Copenhagen was only fifty-two cents "for a seat in the last row of the top balcony," but cigarettes were seventy-five cents and Scotch "ten dollars a bottle." [1]

Before long, he decided there just wasn't enough material in "A Shower of Gold" from which to develop a novel and began to look for another idea. He wrote that he was "still groping for a handle" on it but that now he had "a fair idea of what I ought to be doing, if not precisely how to do it. The truth of the matter is that I haven't been doing as much Serious Thinking as I should be doing, but I hope to remedy that shortly. But first I have to stop and write a new story as I'm getting to the point where I'll need some money."

At the ballet, he saw *Cavalleria Rusticana* and a Balanchine production. He also told of an eighty-year-old man who sat next to him and who "spoke to me about the wickedness of old New York, thumping me in the ribs from time to time. He had lived there as a boy, heh heh." He went to "an old church and sat in the royal box. And the organist was practicing. And then into the graveyard next to the church. Here lies Anna Pederson, a good woman. I threw a mushroom on the grave. Bach streaming from the church windows. I felt like Old Werther."

He was expecting a visit from a Danish poet and his wife whom he had known in New York, where she worked for *Newsweek*. Don complained that since she was pregnant, he would have "to do the noble thing" and give up his bed. His friend lived "on the other coast" and was planning to translate *Dr. Caligari* into Danish.

In December, Don wrote that he would return home after the first of the year. And on December 24 we sent each other a Christmas telegram, but he stayed on past the winter without any further mention of coming home. Instead, he wrote and suggested that we should go ahead and get a divorce. By this time, I was not really surprised but angry. I would not consider a divorce, and so we went on toward the summer.

After the first of the year, Don had gone to London, where he found the "tone and style of the place gray." Although he visited museums, theaters, the Houses of Parliament, the London Bridge, and a long list of other famous sights, he found it "gray and dismal." He also described "hordes of Indians and Frenchmen and Italians cruising the streets in cheap overcoats and too much hair and nothing-to-do (a lumpen-proletariat if ever there was one; what hope, what felicity for these troops?) and a general air of having settled for much, much less than any minimal idea of human possibility known to me or thee — cities are deadly, the Japanese in Tokyo in 1953 looked more human than this."

Early in 1965, Don's mother was gravely ill and in a coma for two days at the hospital in Houston. Don was in London at the time but upon returning to Copenhagen wrote her an entertaining letter, telling of the "landlord" who had "soft-footed in and taken my 60-watt Lightbulb. Cunning Landlord. He thinks I will not Notice, But I have counted the Watts and having a very good Grammar School Education by the Nuns, I Noticed that a few Watts were Gone. But I fixed Him." He also went to the zoo, where the "biggest Giraffes" he had ever seen were wearing "Neck Sweaters." The "zoo like the rest of Denmark was not Heated Properly."

He described a bar where he heard "people talking in a Strange Language. After a time it came to me that they were speaking English. And I said to myself what a beautiful language! I would like to hear more of it." His mother was a stern advocate of speaking and writing proper English—I believe she taught him more about writing than anyone else. In his letter, he added that there is "no other Intelligence of moment except that I have thrown away a lot of bad Prose that I made myself. And that I am still Endeavoring to Complete a new Work with which to Finance my future Life, if any."

Although I knew nothing of it, Don was now living with a girl named

Birgit. Regarding his new social life, he had written to both me and his parents of an incident in which he had a date with a "beautiful blonde Communist." She had taken him to "a café where there were a great number of depressed-looking young men sitting around being depressed," and then later he "made the mistake of chuckling about some aspect or other of the Hungarian Revolution." To his comment the girl had said "You are a fool. Get oudt uf my room." In writing to his parents he had added that since then he had "met a girl named Birgit who seems a little less doctrinaire." He also wrote that he would send pictures of Birgit as they had requested. But I don't think at this point that they had plans to marry.

Don's writing continued to appear in print. He had written earlier that a new story, "The Indian Uprising," should appear immediately; it was published in the March 6 issue of the *New Yorker*. In the late spring, he wrote to his parents that he had three new stories of which "the *New Yorker* has bought two and a half." A story that would become "The Game" and ran July 31 "is about two Army officers in an underground missile control room." The "half-bought" story was about a "young man who busts onto the world like a rocket ready to take over and rockets to obscurity."

According to Don, "Game" evidently stirred considerable interest among the military. He said that "GAME had knocked them all for a loop in the Pentagon," but "not because it was true." He later told me that although the story caused a small furor, he heard nothing further about it.

Among the stories that Don mentioned to his parents during this period was what he called an "architectural" story that he ultimately threw away "because it wasn't any good." Don said that there was a good line in it about a conference of three famous architects: "an old German one with a black cloak and Stokowski hair, a terribly young one sitting on the floor in his yellow tweed suit, and the rogue, who refused to attend but could be heard trumpeting in the corridors outside." The "rogue architect" was undoubtedly a reference to his father, who, I have no doubt, recognized himself in the story.

Another story, "Can We Talk," which Don had described as "very tiny and brilliant," was published in *Art and Literature* in 1965. Made up of reminiscences of friends with jarring, unexpected images that follow one another, the story is told by a narrator making direct remarks to a girl, thus providing a narrative thread for the story. The story ends with, "After you sent me home you came down in your elevator to be kissed. You knew I would be waiting." As he did throughout much of his work, Don provided meaning through the "possibility" that existed in the girl.

In the middle of the summer, he received a letter dated July 15 that

Little, Brown had forwarded from Boston University. Howard B. Gotlieb, chief of reference and special collections, invited him to deposit his manuscript and correspondence files at a "magnificent new library on our Charles River Campus." The university hoped "to collect the papers of outstanding contemporary literary figures." Don declined the offer and sent the letter with notes he had typed in all the margins, including the top and bottom, to his family. In one of the notes, he wrote "i am really immensely flattered even though i know he's circulating the younger generation. as purdy says, there are two things we can't get enough of, praise and encouragement." He also noted that *Harper's Bazaar* had bought "The Affront" for three hundred dollars, which was "not much."

On June 10, Don wrote to me and once again asked for a divorce. Previously, I told him that I would get a divorce when I chose to and not before. But now, he gave me a reason about which I could do nothing. He told me he had met a girl in Copenhagen named Birgit who "had a rather tragic history" and whom he wished to marry; she was pregnant and could not travel with him to New York unless they were husband and wife. He was afraid the child would be born before they could leave Copenhagen. If I did not grant the divorce, not only would the child be illegitimate but he would be like the Flying Dutchman who had to "keep moving from country to country." My refusal would keep him "floating in space" for the rest of his life.

He had as yet "told the family nothing, in the hope that the whole thing could be regularized before I broke the news."[2] He asked that I file as quickly as possible since "the immigration business is . . . suitably Kafkaesque and hideous." In the States, he would "probably live in Maine, a place near Liberty—the lease is up on the apartment [in Manhattan] and my hair is falling out at an ever-accelerating rate and I haven't written a word of the novel that's supposed to be delivered in September. But none of these things is faintly as important as the problem of the divorce has suddenly become." In conclusion, he wrote that he hoped we were all "prospering, as much as one can prosper in this evil world." Later, Don would refer often to "this evil world."

I had just received Don's letter telling me of Birgit's pregnancy and asking for a divorce, when Frederick Barthelme stopped by my office at 5 Chelsea Place to borrow my Austin-Healey. He had wrecked his father's Corvette and could no longer be covered by insurance, so he occasionally came by to borrow my sports car. I enjoyed seeing Rick and talking to him. He was interested in literature as well as in art, and his conversation was both serious and witty. Rick was now twenty-two and studying architec-

ture at the University of Houston. He was interested in the "new" literature of postmodernism, including the work of John Barth, whose *Giles
Goat-Boy* was published about this time. He also was one of the new
younger artists in Houston, interested in pop art and what would soon be
called "minimalism."

On this particular day, I was reading Don's letter when Rick appeared
at my office door. When I showed him the letter, he responded with the
wit and comic sense of all the Barthelmes, laughing at the triteness of the
Flying Dutchman comparison.

I did not think it was at all funny. Rick could not understand the depth
of my sadness. Besides, I had never confided in him as I had in his older
brother, Pete, and my lifestyle probably seemed appealing. He was aware
that I was dating a lot and probably assumed that I was no longer in love
with Don.

I talked to Rick about whether I should inform his mother of Don's letter before I did anything further. But he knew as I did that she would be
distressed by the news, and he did not want me to tell her. I felt that Don
probably wrote the letter with both sadness and frustration. The "Flying
Dutchman" cliché was one of his typical self-directed jokes. I believed that
he must have been in love with Birgit, but I do not believe that he wanted
to be married again at that time.

I considered his letter for about a week, and then I talked it over with
my sister Odell, whose response was one of intense anger toward Don. Finally, I decided to go ahead with the divorce and wrote to tell him so. I
knew that it should be possible for the judge to grant a divorce in sixty
days. I concluded my letter by telling him that what we were about to
do was "wrong, wrong, wrong" and that "one cannot end love with a
divorce."

He wrote on July 5 asking that I go ahead with the divorce "without
paying the lawyer's fees . . . for the time is growing short." I did not know
at this time that the baby was due in October. He said he would send some
money in a short time and then added that he had been borrowing money
since January "to buy bread and booze." He thanked me for my "magna-
nimity in this meaty matter." I did not feel magnanimous, but I had no
alternative.

Earlier in the year, Don had written to Herman Gollob to tell him of
his predicament. Herman, who was waiting for Don to send a manuscript
for the new novel, promptly replied that Don should not get a divorce in
order to marry Birgit—in spite of her pregnancy. But Don could not be
moved.

Although Don did not want me to tell his parents of the divorce, I finally decided to call his mother. I wanted to talk to her about it, but there was another reason that I could not ignore. Houston was still a small enough city that as soon as my attorney filed the divorce suit, a notice would appear in the daily newspapers, the *Houston Post* and the *Houston Chronicle,* as a court record. And to have Don's mother read about our pending divorce in this way would have been unforgivably cruel. When I telephoned to tell her of our plans without explaining about Birgit, she said simply, "I don't think you have to do this." Rather than explain anything more, I said that she would understand after she heard from Don.

After Don told them of our pending divorce and his plans to marry Birgit, his parents, especially his mother, expressed such disapproval that Don angrily retaliated by reducing marriage to a "domestic arrangement": "I am sorry that I did not treat the announcement of new domestic arrangements seriously enough," he wrote, "or that I somehow did it in the wrong way, or that I am somehow wrong, wrong, wrong, probably fundamentally. You have to remember that for me levity is a mode of seriousness, my only mode of seriousness."

After his parents failed to urge him to come home, Don wrote to them that he could not decide where to live and was "thinking of coming home to Texas where it [the baby] can be had in a WARM, CHEERFUL, LOVING atmosphere . . . rather than a cold New York atmosphere. This a cue/cuties." Don named all the people who were in New York that he missed by living abroad, but he said he missed his family in Texas more. Nevertheless, Don and his new family did not go home to Houston until the following year.

At this time, he also told of two new stories that would appear in the *New Yorker,* including "Snap Snap."[3] For these, he would be paid twenty-four hundred dollars, a sum that he expected to cover transatlantic travel expenses to New York, where he had renewed the lease on the West 11th Street apartment. In spite of his optimism about his finances, however, Don finally asked his father to send him the money "so that he could bring Birgit back to the States."[4]

Don had written to his father earlier about designing a home for them, but now he supposed "a house is out of the question, really." He had an offer in New York to fill in "for the book editor of *Newsweek* for eight weeks, but the pay is low, low and I think I could do better sitting at home staring at the typewriter."

After receiving notice that I had filed for divorce, Don was able to arrange for their departure from Copenhagen even though they were not yet married. Birgit was almost nine months pregnant, and Don was anxious to be married in the United States. They were taking a flight on Icelandic Airlines, and Don was more nervous than usual about flying.

As soon as they arrived in the States, Don telephoned to tell me where he was. They had gone immediately to the home of Robert and Gitta Morris in Connecticut, and it was from there that he called. He was ecstatic to be back. He wanted to talk further about what had happened with Birgit and to explain why he had insisted upon a divorce. He said that he wanted the child to have his name when it was born. "Otherwise," he added, "I will have to adopt it later and it would always be an adopted child. Nor did I want to have to go to Mexico for a divorce." He had considered every possibility, even a divorce in Mexico. I listened but simply could not discuss what for me was still a painful experience, so our conversation turned to everything else.

Don was eager to know what each of his friends was doing, whom I had seen, and what was happening at the museum, at my office, and in the lives of our friends and families. We both were reluctant to end our conversation, but when we at last said goodbye, I felt very sad, for Don as well as for myself.

Don had arranged with Herman Gollob, who was now with Atheneum in New York, for an immediate, private wedding ceremony in New Jersey. Herman and Barbara were to be the only attendants. The ceremony was performed by a priest who had assumed that the Gollobs were the bride and groom. When he was told that the bride was Birgit, he was displeased that the marriage was being performed so late, but he went ahead with the ceremony anyway.

Don and Birgit then found a temporary apartment where they could stay until Don's apartment at 113 West 11th was available. Their daughter Anne was born in Manhattan in October.

IN THE SPRING TERM OF 1965, while Don was in Europe, I became a graduate student at the University of Texas in Austin, the first step toward earning a Ph.D. in American literature. Each Saturday morning, I drove 165 miles from my apartment in Houston to the campus for a nine o'clock class. In taking one course, I could determine just how much I wanted to pursue a Ph.D. program at Texas and, after that, could enroll for additional classes in September.

By the end of the term, I had decided to go ahead with more courses and enrolled for a Tuesday-Thursday schedule, arriving in Austin late Monday or early Tuesday and returning to Houston Thursday or Friday. I saw advertising clients on a regular basis, but now the agency was largely in the hands of my sister. She managed all the accounts, we talked daily, and whenever necessary I took a flight to Houston for special meetings.

But as I returned home one Friday afternoon in March of 1966, I was in an automobile accident that was serious enough to delay my studies. Driving my Austin-Healey, I had just reached the outskirts of Austin when I was struck by a Triumph sports car driven by a student from Texas A&M University. The oncoming vehicle swerved onto my side of the road, and we collided head-on. The other driver and his passenger survived, and I managed to complete the semester at the university; however, my injuries were serious enough that I decided to stay in Houston the following year.

Don was then living in Manhattan with Birgit and their baby daughter, but the last time we were in touch was upon his arrival in the States the previous year. His family and friends often mentioned him, but I had no reason to contact him until the summer of 1966 when, returning home from a trip to Boston, I was forced by an airline strike to stay overnight in Manhattan. When I telephoned his apartment, Don was startled to hear my voice, but after a moment he recovered his equanimity and we talked for a long time. I asked about his work, but he was more interested in telling me of his role as "father of the child."

"I do everything for my daughter—bathe and dress her, feed her, everything," he said. Stressing each word, Don repeated "everything" several times. He was learning to cook as well. And then after the first few minutes, he began to tell me of Birgit's emotional condition and how it had manifested itself in both Copenhagen and now in New York. He told me that before they met, "something" had happened to her in Denmark. He was vague, referring to an incident that had affected her life. He insisted upon telling me this, but I simply could not ask what he was talking about, so I never knew what the "something" was.

Before they were married, Don was aware that Birgit was probably already suffering from a crippling disease, likely Huntington's disease, from which her mother had died and which was genetically passed on to one of every two daughters. Birgit, who witnessed her mother's suffering in the hospital, was now tentatively diagnosed as having the disease. Symptoms usually appeared by the age of forty, but Birgit's behavior, presumably caused by the disease, had been a problem for Don almost from the first. He cited as an example that "she may suddenly step into the street to cross in front of a truck."

Notwithstanding these family responsibilities, Don managed to continue a morning writing schedule and was trying to complete his first novel, *Snow White*. As we talked, we were both warm and kind to each other. In fact, I later realized that I had talked to him with the same endearing language I had used during our marriage. We finally said goodbye, and this was the last time that we talked for several years. The next morning, I was able to get a seat on a different airline, and I returned to Houston in the afternoon.

After that, I was able to forget about Don most of the time. I attended CAA functions where people often mentioned him, usually to ask about our marital status. Mostly they were friends and admiring acquaintances, but I was shocked by those who condemned what they saw as his arrogance in deserting the museum. Well-educated, sometimes wealthy individuals, they knew nothing of the challenge that he faced in writing a new kind of fiction.

As often as possible, I drove out to Collier Airfield to practice takeoffs and landings and sometimes just flew around Houston, occasionally circling over my sister's new home in the Cypress area. I avoided metropolitan centers and flew on the west side of Houston. Whenever possible, I accompanied a more experienced pilot on local trips, in either a small Cessna or occasionally in a twin-engine plane. One weekend, I flew with a friend, Robert Barstow, down the eastern coast of Mexico to Veracruz. Bob's father had been a barnstorming pilot in the 1930s, had known Charles Lindbergh, and, like many of these young men, was killed in a plane crash. Bob was one of the heirs of Dow Chemical and had a trust fund that he invested largely in building a small aviation company. He was a dealer of Moody Aircraft, a sleek little plane in which we sometimes flew.

Flying all the way to Veracruz took us over dozens of small fishing villages along the coast, with miles of clean white sand where we could have landed easily and safely, to Tampico, where we spent one night, refueled, and then departed for Veracruz. Although there were mountains inland, it was not until we approached Veracruz that a range came down into the water. The beaches abruptly disappeared, we climbed much higher, carefully avoiding downdrafts, and finally, with Veracruz in sight, we descended into the city. During the last hour of the flight, I had my first encounter with a threatening thunderstorm, which we managed to fly around. We were flying entirely by visual flight rules; our charts for Mexico were not of much help, and there was very little assistance from flight controllers on the ground.

Flying was adventurous, but like sports car driving and sports car races it was a seductive distraction that I knew I had to give up if I were to pursue my doctoral program. Also our agency had grown, with an increasing number of industrial accounts among our clients; I preferred these to most of the consumer and service companies that we represented.

Even though the agency still had debt, we had assets as well. Odell and I had purchased the building at 5 Chelsea Place in 1964; this was the building to which we had moved in 1961. But managing our finances continued to be difficult. Bank loans for business were almost impossible for women to obtain, regardless of what you had already done. In our first experience we asked Fannin State Bank, where we had an agency account, for a small operating loan, and the officer explained it would be impossible because we were both women. We each had a bachelor's degree and I had a master's as well, but the young man pointed out that I was still of child-bearing age and therefore not an acceptable risk. We were shocked, especially since there was little doubt that each of us had an annual income that was easily double his own.

Finally, we turned to our mother for a loan. We did not try to obtain another bank loan until the president of Reagan State Bank, who had two daughters in professional positions and understood many of the barriers facing us, supported our request for a loan from the Small Business Administration.

We continued to rely on Pete Barthelme to write for our agency, even after he accepted an offer from Aylin Advertising, one of the city's more prominent advertising firms. Ours was still a small firm, so when one of the principals at Aylin called in search of a writer, I encouraged Pete to apply. He was talented and confident of his skills; when asked by the president of Aylin, Bob Aylin, if he could write a news story, Pete replied, "Certainly, I read one once."

Throughout these years, Pete wrote numerous articles for magazines, especially for fishing publications. Before much longer he began a series of mystery novels set along the Gulf Coast. Pete continues to be a serious fisherman, and in the 1990s he moved his home and office to Seadrift on the Gulf of Mexico, not far from Victoria, Texas.

In the 1960s, Pete and his wife Lillian had two daughters and a son, Pete. I occasionally visited Lillian and Pete at their home, and Don's mother sometimes brought the children by our offices when she took them to see Lillian's father, Dr. Stephen Foote, whose practice was housed in another restored mansion across the street on Chelsea Place.

Although it would be a few more years before Frederick joined our agency, we saw him fairly often. Rick had studied architecture at Tulane University but gave it up for art; in Houston he was experimenting with media, creating "happenings," and working on minimalist art. In the 1960s, Rick was in the first important local exhibition of minimalist art at the Louisiana Gallery in Houston. He would later spend time in Manhattan, attracting enough interest in his work that he was among a group of young artists of this era to exhibit at the Museum of Modern Art.

I did not know in the early 1960s that Rick was writing fiction as well, but by 1970 he had done enough to publish a collection of short fiction entitled *Rangoon*. With his humor and acute understanding of his generation, Rick described the central thesis of *Rangoon* as the "thunderous acceptability" of the "human lack" of condition.

Steve meanwhile completed high school and graduated in the first class at the new Jesuit Preparatory Academy in 1965. He went off to Boston University for his first year, but like Pete, Steve preferred Texas and returned to study at the University of Texas in Austin the following year. He too was soon writing and publishing both short fiction and essays. By the end of the 1960s, he had published stories in the *Transatlantic Review* and the *Massachusetts Review,* along with numerous pieces in the *Texas Observer.*

I frequently saw Joan Barthelme as well in the 1960s; she had returned to Houston from the East Coast to work in advertising and public relations. Like her brothers, she was endowed with remarkable talent and quickly earned a reputation in the agency world. Before long, she became engaged to George Bugbee, a talented pianist and writer whom I had known in journalism and public relations circles since the 1950s.

Joan and George had two sons, and in her commitment as a mother,

Joan gave up her full-time career for a while. She later joined Pennzoil in Houston and became a senior vice president in publications, the first and only woman on the "executive floor" of Pennzoil. She stayed with Pennzoil until retiring several years after Don's death. No other woman in Houston held a comparable position even as late as the 1980s. The continued discrimination against women at the executive level, at least in Houston, had not really improved much by the 1990s, but like her four brothers, Joan possessed such talent and wit that she became an exception in this almost wholly male world.

With stories appearing often in the *New Yorker,* Don now had an international audience. When his first novel appeared, it was reviewed immediately by major publications in the United States. Translated into several other languages, *Snow White* became famous abroad as well. While in Europe, Don had written letters describing his failure in getting this first novel going, but he had actually started *Snow White* and was almost finished when we talked in 1966. This work actually replaced the novel that he told Herman Gollob he would develop from "A Shower of Gold." Don was uneasy about having enough material in the short story for a work of that length and instead developed a theme to tell the story of his own emotional life, a tale in which he could bring in observations on contemporary culture. The completed work finally appeared in the *New Yorker* on February 18, 1967, for which the magazine paid him twenty-five thousand dollars. Meanwhile, Atheneum had mailed bound galleys of the novel to reviewers and the bound book was distributed by the publisher in March.

Don's contemporary version of the fairy tale explores his own love life before he met Birgit. In *Snow White,* Don created a heroine who serves as a vehicle for Don to examine himself as well as the world he satirized. Incidents were suggested by other experiences and observations as well. For example, the description of the college that Snow White attended and the courses she studied were probably suggested by Don's classes at the University of Houston.[1]

Seemingly a tale of a young woman seeking her Prince Charming, the novel alludes to both Don's relationship with his first wife Marilyn and our life together. Although the book's title suggests that the novel is about a woman's experience, it largely deals with Don's own inner struggles with marriage and ultimately his decision to give up the notion of "romantic" love.

Don used his own complex personality as a basis for the characters of Bill, Paul, and Hugo; in earlier stories, he created multiple characters to depict aspects of himself, but in *Snow White* his introspection is impressive.

By adapting the fairy tale structure to an ironic mode, he could both examine his own feelings and imagine the reactions of the girl cast in the persona of Snow White. During our courtship, Don told me of a group of male graduate students who were part of his first wife's circle of friends at Rice University. Years later, one of these friends wrote a note to me in which he said that it was possible to identify which "dwarf" portrayed each of them.

Among the allusions to our relationship, the speech at the end of *Snow White* seems clearly in response to my reluctance to give up my perception of him as "Prince Charming." Paul, who plays this "Prince Charming" role, is dead at the end, and the narrator observes that it is not a good idea for Snow White "to cast chrysanthemums" on his grave. There is "nothing in it for her, that grave." It was true that there was nothing left for me in what I had thought was an ideal relationship with Don.

When I first saw the published novel itself, I felt betrayed that he dedicated it to Birgit. It now seems strange that I should have been surprised, but I was furious enough at the time to rip out the dedication page and to scribble a note that I mailed to Don immediately. He replied in a dispirited, sad tone that he was sorry I had not liked his dedication and that the book was not selling anyway.

Snow White brought him new notice; it was generously received by both scholars and students and almost immediately began to appear on university reading lists throughout the country. In spite of Don's gloomy prediction for the novel's future, the paperback edition sold widely and has continued in print for more than three decades.

AFTER OUR TELEPHONE CONVERSATION in New York in 1966, I neither saw nor talked to Don for several years. His brothers and friends mentioned him often, but it was not until the spring of 1972 that we saw each other once again.

I was now spending most of my time at the agency and was working at my desk when he suddenly walked in. For a moment I did not see him; when I finally looked up, he was standing there grinning at me. We just looked at each other. The first thing I said was, "I've thought of you mostly with love and affection." He replied, "Me too." I told him that he hurt my feelings terribly when he dedicated *Snow White* to Birgit. He said my letter hurt him as well. By then I was standing; I kissed him on the cheek and then we hugged and laughed. The passion of ten years earlier was gone, but the moment was one of joy anyway.

During the intervening years, since the late 1960s, I had thrived on my doctoral work and university life three or four days each week. It was in sharp contrast to the world of advertising, but the contrast intensified my interest in everything I did. Except for several artists, the only other friend I usually saw in Houston was Marjorie McCorquodale, a professor at the University of Houston.

With the publication of *Come Back, Dr. Caligari* and *Snow White,* as well as the routine appearance of his short stories in the *New Yorker,* Don had achieved such fame that his name now appeared on reading lists in contemporary or American literature classes at the University of Texas, and younger faculty as well as graduate students often asked about him. I answered their questions and discussed his work, but my own program was demanding and I seldom thought of what we had lost.

In Austin, this era was enlivened by the counterculture movement and student demonstrations against the Vietnam War. Finally, the bombing of Cambodia and the shootings at Kent State University kindled a reaction that swept the campus overnight, arousing thousands of students to gather in front of the university's tower and to remain there night and day. This was also the time of the Black Panthers and of new liberal organizations concerned with ending the war.

When a huge rally and a parade were organized for a march through the city to protest the bombing of Cambodia, the Austin City Council refused to grant a parade permit. Students became more restless, and National Guard troops were sent in to stand just off campus, with bayonets ready to stop any movement toward downtown. But when the marchers decided to give up the parade and to walk on the sidewalks to the Texas capitol, the city gave in and granted a permit.

Thousands of students, faculty, and friends marched to the capitol and then returned to the campus. Along the way, banks, government offices, and businesses closed their doors, afraid of the kind of violence other areas of the country had experienced. It was, however, a subdued and serious event, with the marchers walking quietly and singing what had become the slogan of the antiwar efforts, "Give Peace a Chance."

Meanwhile, in Houston, antiwar resistance and the growing counterculture movement were present, but quieter. In the late 1950s, a small but entrenched community of artists in Houston began to rebel against established cultural behavior and values. More and more male artists grew beards and wore their hair longer. Although women, in the art world as well as the business world, were a little more casual in their dress for informal occasions, often wearing slacks or even blue jeans, most continued to wear traditional attire for all occasions. Also, in the art world, most people expected greater freedom in their personal and sexual lives. In the 1960s, the word "hippie" was used to describe those influenced by the changing values of the counterculture movement. By 1970, the changes were pretty well established in the museum district, as well as on university campuses, but throughout much of the business world, nothing had changed.

Odell and I had sold our building on Chelsea Place by this time and moved our offices to the Great Southern Building on Buffalo Drive. It was here that Frederick Barthelme, who had recently moved back to Houston from New York, came by one day in the early 1970s to inquire about joining our firm. We had other talented writers at the agency, but no one with the imagination and humor of a Barthelme. Pete no longer created campaigns for us and would soon form his own agency; for the present, he was still an officer and a member of the board of Goodwin, Dannenbaum, Littman, and Wingfield.

Rick's arrival at our building revealed how most people in Houston were not cognizant of the cultural changes taking place in our own city. Although we were located only a mile or so from the center of the art world in the Montrose-museum area, owners and tenants were totally unprepared for Rick's arrival.

When he first came to visit us at the Great Southern building, Rick had long hair and was dressed in casual clothes that included sandals. At the entrance, he was stopped and questioned with disapproval by the insurance company guard. But there was little that anyone could do about how he or any individual in our firm dressed. Rick thought the incident funny, but I was shocked when I heard of the building owners' objections; we were a long-term tenant with no agreement on dress code for the building. I knew, of course, that the company was an old-fashioned, staid organization with rules for everything for their own employees.

Before long, however, Rick's charm and humor won the affection and acceptance of everyone he encountered. Rick was, in fact, quite traditional in other facets of his life. After he joined Barthelme-Moore Associates, he bought a handsome Brooks Brothers–style three-piece navy blue pin-striped suit that would be appropriate for calling on clients.

Rick was a rebellious young teenager when I first knew him, about a decade and a half younger than Don, but I could see in Rick the influences of a changing culture. He was a handsome young man, tall and attractive with the well-groomed, buttoned-down collar look of his elder brothers. In fact, in the early 1960s, he was an ideal model for an advertising campaign that we produced for a new academy in data processing.

In his own work in painting, Rick was already interested in the new trends in contemporary art; before leaving for New York, he was part of the avant-garde group then working in Houston. Among them was Jim Love, a Houston sculptor recognized for his imaginative and funny pieces created out of found junk. Jack Boynton, whose beautiful abstract paintings were very much in the tradition of the New York art world, only later began to look at other media and other materials.

The other friends we had known in the early 1960s—Robert Morris, now in Connecticut, and Guy Johnson, who had worked and taught in Baytown but was now on the East Coast—not only worked with collages but were willing to use recognizable figures in their work. Dick Wray, who remained in Houston, experimented with textures and the use of other media along with paint.

Rick, however, was younger and one of the new group of minimalists, in painting as well as in writing. I had no idea that besides his interest in art and music, he was also developing his own style of writing fiction. He read widely, including the new and experimental work by the writers of Don's generation—John Barth, John Hawkes, Thomas Pynchon, and others. And now he was breaking away and writing what would lead to another stage of postmodernist fiction.

Rick was uncommonly well suited to advertising. Although he made no pretense of having expertise in any one field, he could talk to corporate executives with enough sensitivity and humor to establish rapport as we talked about their goals. He worked easily with our staff artists as well. Before long, he was at work on most of our accounts and designing a campaign for our agency as well.

After completing my course work at the University of Texas, I began doing research for my dissertation on William Faulkner's *Pylon*. I gave up my apartment in Austin but continued to do research at the Ransom Humanities Research Center. I had undertaken to study all stages of the manuscript, which for Faulkner meant holograph, typescript, and galley proofs, besides early short stories that Faulkner might have incorporated into the manuscript. The Humanities Research Center had a large collection of Faulkner materials, among them the page proofs of *Pylon*.

And now, in Houston, Don was back in my life.

His appearance had changed, but not dramatically. He was slender and his walk was still buoyant, almost jaunty, but the boyish look was gone; he now had a reddish beard and his hairline had noticeably receded. At first, I did not see the most dramatic alteration—the indentation in his upper lip was removed so that it was smooth and straight. The cupid mouth he had inherited from his mother was gone. A cancer caused by smoking had developed just above his upper lip, and he lost the cleft when it was removed.

Don's daughter Anne was in Houston with him, and they were staying with his parents; he and his sister Joan, who now had two sons, were planning to take their children to the Astroworld amusement park the following day and asked me to come and bring my nephew Lee Vandruff. But I could not go, so we made a date for lunch the day after.

We met at the Courtlandt Restaurant on Francis Street, a French restaurant in our old neighborhood. It was off Smith Street, not far from Don's 1956 apartment on Burlington Street and just a few blocks from where he and I first lived on Hawthorne Street.

After our first emotional greeting, Don retreated a little from this instinctive response to our reunion; he did not seem comfortable yet with the fact of returning to Houston. He wanted to be with me and to talk but seemed apprehensive of getting too personal or at least wary of becoming nostalgic or sentimental.

But by the time we began lunch, we both relaxed and talked about what had happened since our divorce. His marriage was difficult from the first and after a year or so, mostly sad and unhappy. Don wanted to talk about it, but I discouraged him and that day he talked mostly of his work and Anne. It was a festive reunion, and we stayed at the restaurant for much of the afternoon.

He was as dissatisfied as ever, especially with his achievement in writing. He was not unhappy with the work itself but with what he felt was limited recognition for it. Don received such praise and acclaim in newspaper and magazine reviews that I was surprised at his disappointment. He said that most people did not read him. He knew that his audience was made up of readers of the *New Yorker,* especially on the East Coast and in Europe, as well as faculty and students on college campuses across the country—an elite but relatively small audience. He was still unknown by most people in Houston outside of the arts and the academic world. I reminded him that this often was the fate of the best writers. William Faulkner was among those who at first received greater recognition in Europe than in his own country. Even F. Scott Fitzgerald was once out of print.

By now, most young writers at universities were interested in imitating Don's style just as they had attempted to imitate Hemingway's. But Don wanted more than this. He did not complain about being overlooked for major awards, but a major literary award would have represented an acceptance that he did not yet have. Although Don received the National Book Award for a children's book, he did not recognize it as meaningful for his work.[1]

Nor was Don disappointed solely with sales. He really wanted readers that he could respect. When *City Life* was chosen as an Alternate Selection of the Book-of-the-Month Club, Don was "reserved" about it. After asking his editor, Henry Robbins, at Farrar, Straus if there was "some way we can politely turn down" the offer, Robbins talked him out of rejecting it. Roger Angell, his friend and editor at the *New Yorker,* congratulated Don on the Book-of-the-Month Club deal, but from Don he "met silence." Roger then told Don that he thought that Don did not "want to be discovered."[2]

Even though Don had told me that most people did not read his work, I have no doubt that he believed that being known as a Book-of-the-Month-Club author would not give him the kind of readership he wanted. It must have seemed an almost sinful lapse from his own standard of perfection.

Besides *Come Back, Dr. Caligari* and *Snow White,* Don had by now published additional collections of stories and parodies. *Unspeakable Parodies and Unnatural Acts* in 1968 was followed by *City Life* and then *Sadness. City Life* was published in 1970 and was named one of the Year's

Best Books by *Time* magazine. *Time* described the collection as written with "Kafka's purity of language and some of Beckett's grim humor."[3]

Don continued to be interested in newspapers and magazines and told me of a new tabloid called *Fiction* that he and a friend, Mark Jay Mersky, a professor of English at City College, initiated. Mersky was the editor and Don was in charge of layout and design. They had already obtained contributions from several prominent writers, among them John Barth. Don also contributed fiction, but it was the job of makeup editor that gave him the greatest pleasure. In March, 1972, the first issue had appeared.

At the restaurant in Houston that first day of Don's return, I learned that Don and Birgit were now separated and getting a divorce, and Birgit had returned to Copenhagen to live. Anne was with Don on this trip, but she was to go to Europe to live with her mother. He was very sad about being apart from his daughter and told me that his primary concern was how to live in the future separated from her much of the time.

He had just published *The Slightly Irregular Fire Engine,* the book for children that later won the National Book Award. He first read the manuscript to his daughter. Don was inventive in finding ways to entertain Anne and often made toys for her that she could pull around the flat. He told me that she wanted a dog, but even though he had owned one as a child, he would not give in to having one in the apartment. Anne also asked for a pony, but apparently Don was able to persuade her that this was impractical in Manhattan.

Now six years old, Anne wanted to live with her father, but Don explained that she would have to live with her mother until she was thirteen. At that time, she could make her own decision; before then, she would spend summers with him. It was wrenching for Don, but he thought she should not be separated from Birgit. Don had promised Birgit that he would "deliver" Anne in June but did not know yet how he would manage it. In fact, he was thinking of living in France, where the train ride to Copenhagen was only overnight. In 1965, he had not wanted a child, but as it turned out, this child had given him a purpose. He emphatically stated that he "could not have made it without" Anne.

He finally spoke at length about Birgit and what had happened in the spring of 1965. In New York, their marriage quickly became sad and unhappy. Birgit enrolled for classes at the New School in New York, and perhaps to illustrate the nature of their relationship, he said she asked him for permission to have an affair with one of her professors. In telling of this, Don seemed to insist that he no longer expected marriage to provide an "ideal relationship," a theme he returned to in our conversations over the years that followed. This theme was also expressed in the death of Paul in *Snow White;* in the novel, however, the "heroes depart in search of a new principle," whereas Don seemed unclear about a "new principle" other than his love for his daughter.

Don described how Birgit's illness affected her behavior. After she returned to Denmark, it was not unusual for her to telephone to ask for help with some problem, even to tell him that she was unable to find her checkbook and ask what she should do. Although Birgit was pregnant when Don asked me for a divorce in 1965, I never forgave him for the abrupt manner in which he gave up our marriage; now, in 1972, I could only listen to what he told me. I was never able to feel sympathy or concern for her condition. I later learned from friends in New York and in Connecticut that her manner was like that of a child and that Don treated her like one.

That first day, he also talked of Birgit's family in Copenhagen, especially her father and sister. Don was particularly fond of her father, a university professor of chemistry at the University of Copenhagen. He described him as kind and intelligent and then declared, "I wish he had been my father." This statement was such a sweeping rejection of the elder Barthelme that I found it difficult to believe Don truly felt this way. Birgit's father saw her mother suffer through the difficulties of the disease that now afflicted Birgit and must have recognized that Birgit was already developing the symptoms that would worsen rapidly over the next few years. He seemed to readily accept Don's relationship with his daughter and in this sense was not disapproving in the way Don's father probably would have been in similar circumstances.

I saw Don as frequently as possible before he returned to New York. And then in December, I saw him during the annual meeting of the Modern Language Association in Manhattan, where he was scheduled to speak at one of the sessions. He had stayed in New York for the holidays but had broken his arm and was in a foul humor; the arm was aching, but mostly he did not want to give the talk at MLA. At lunch, as we talked about people we both knew, he was better. Odell was in New York with me, and he was glad to see her. The conversation covered all our shared friends in Houston, the CAA, and the latest on our families. Don wanted to know about everyone and everything that was taking place in Houston. Although we had both cocktails and wine with lunch, it was the week between Christmas and the New Year and a special occasion, so I thought little of Don's drinking.

I had been on leave from Dominican College and planned to return there when I completed my doctorate. Instead, in the fall of 1972, I accepted an appointment with the Department of English at the University of Houston. As at most universities, the students in creative writing were excited about Don and his work. It was not unusual for a student to drop by my office to show me a story that he or she had written that was an effort to develop a style resembling Don's. The director of the creative writing program explained that students throughout the country were now attempting to imitate Don's work.

Meanwhile, I was still working on my dissertation on Faulkner's *Pylon*, the story of barnstorming pilots in the 1930s. *Pylon* had been neglected by scholars, so a critical and textual study of it became a demanding task. All in all, for a few years, I was satisfied with both my academic work and with what we were doing at the agency.

In 1973, I visited the University of Virginia, where a major Faulkner collection resided. I knew that the typescript of *Pylon* was in their archives, along with Faulkner's letters for this period of the 1930s and typescripts of short stories that sometimes had texts of earlier stories on the back of pages. In typing a manuscript and in his effort to economize, Faulkner never hesitated to use discarded pages of earlier work.

I had not yet located the original holograph of the novel, although other scholars believed one existed. I had already visited the University of Mississippi but found very little that I could use. As it turned out, the handwritten manuscript was located in the Faulkner home in Oxford—in a box of manuscript materials under the staircase. Ownership of the contents of the box was being litigated, so the materials were not yet available for study. Jill Faulkner, however, had a photocopy of her father's holograph of the novel, and she kindly gave me access to it.

During this period, Don often returned to Houston. We usually managed to see each other at least once while he was in town. His finances continued to plague him. He had assumed all financial responsibility for both Birgit and his daughter; without a professional career, she could not provide any income whatsoever. He had by this time turned all of his financial matters over to an accountant and could spend only what the accountant approved. Nevertheless, his income was always inadequate; in fact, according to the elder Barthelme, Don asked for money again for his move to Houston in the early 1980s.[4]

In the 1970s, Don was usually in Houston without a car, so one day when I picked him up at an apartment on Richmond Avenue for which he had a short-term lease, I arrived late and he was drinking wine. Although he commented on it, I did not really see it as a problem at that time. But later, during another trip to Houston, he brought up the matter of drinking again.

I had just returned from Austin and did not know that Don was in Houston to address the Southwest Writers Conference until I saw him at a party at the home of Marjorie McCorquodale. Don was at the party with Pat Colville, with whom he had developed a close relationship after our separation in the 1960s. Pat, an artist and a member of the faculty of the University of St. Thomas, and her writer husband were now separated, so she and Don were dating.

A few days after the party, Don told me that he and Pat had quarreled over his drinking at Marjorie's party. I was surprised because I had not noticed. I was there that evening with Samuel Southwell, a professor of English and chairman of the department at the University of Houston, and the four of us had talked in a group for an hour or so. I could not recall Don drinking excessively; in fact, he was clearly sensitive to everything around him and I was reminded of being with him at parties in the years that we were married.

That was the first time that Don had met Sam, but he knew that we were considering marriage. I saw him looking closely at Sam and a few days later, when he asked what Sam had said about him, I replied that he thought Don seemed "noble and graceful." Clearly satisfied with the description, he said of Sam that he "looked quite strong." Later, after Sam asked about Don's opinion, I repeated this and he too was satisfied.

When Don joined the faculty of the University of Houston in 1981, they became friends and remained so until Don's death. In describing Sam to Don, I told him of his background in philosophy and that he was familiar with the work of all the philosophers in whom I knew Don was interested. I added that he had even read all the work of Kenneth Burke, an intimidating task for most people, even scholars. Don laughed because he had probably read only chapters from some of his books, enough to extract the ideas in which he was interested, a challenge in itself.

During this period, Don occasionally talked about his university teaching in New York. His first position was with the State University of New York at Buffalo, an appointment for which John Barth recommended him. But Don continued to live in Manhattan, commuting every week to Buffalo. He soon found that the time required to commute, together with the extremely cold weather, were intolerable.

In the 1970s, he became a distinguished visiting professor of English at the City College of the City University of New York. He talked about the problems generated by the open admissions policy at the City College, problems that he felt made it almost impossible to teach creative writing. I don't know if he later changed his mind, but I could imagine that for Don, whose fiction drew from the immense resources of his own reading, such poorly prepared students would have been difficult to instruct.

Don still sought perfection in his writing, but it seemed to me that he was no longer the purist that he had once been in demanding perfection from his fellow artists. After I expressed disappointment with one of Kurt Vonnegut's novels, he defended Vonnegut more vigorously than I would have expected. What Vonnegut was doing was worthwhile, he refused to give in to criticism, and he was trying to support himself with writing. Vonnegut was his friend, and Don admired most of what he wrote; he also had a special feeling for writers who were able to successfully cope with the challenges of living and publishing in New York.

As he talked of the difficulties of trying to succeed in the creative world of New York, Don mentioned a friend and neighbor who was a famous actor on a daytime soap opera. He described him as the actor who portrays Victor on "The Young and the Restless." I had never watched a daytime soap opera and had no idea that he was referring to Eric Braden, a famous actor with an established reputation in films as well as in television. Braden told him that there was very little challenge in the role, that "he sometimes confused the character of Victor with himself." When I asked why the actor did not give up the show and look for a role that would challenge him, Don replied rather impatiently, "It's because he wants to act, that's what matters to him."

He mentioned other friends, among them Grace Paley, of whom he was especially fond and who lived across the street from him. In Manhattan, instead of being isolated as he was in Houston, he was in the midst of some of the world's greatest creative talent.

In 1975, Don published what I believe to be his best novel, *The Dead Father*. One section of the work, "Manual for Sons," appeared first in the May 12, 1975, issue of the *New Yorker*. In the novel, Don examined every aspect of the father-son relationship. Even though I continued to admire *Snow White* for its originality and for his honesty in the treatment of his own experience, *The Dead Father* is an even more important literary achievement. I recognized in it, of course, the difficulties of his relationship with his father. And it provides some understanding of what Don himself tried to achieve as a father.

During these years, the agency business continued to grow; we still represented real estate and financial accounts, but our major clients now were industrial companies. This level of activity was sometimes a formidable challenge for our small staff of fewer than ten people. And when an energy crisis caused a major recession, we were affected along with some of our larger clients.

Rick worked with us during this period, but other agencies were aware of his extraordinary talent, and around 1975 he accepted an offer from a larger firm. Eventually, however, Rick applied to Johns Hopkins University to study with John Barth and earn a master of fine arts degree. After that he joined the faculty of the University of Southern Mississippi in Hattiesburg, where he directs the Center for Creative Writing.

Rick has written a number of novels and is recognized as one of the leading minimalists. In the 1980s, the *New York Times* published a long essay, a kind of manifesto, that Rick wrote on minimalism. It is a sagacious and full discussion of the emergence of a new kind of postmodernist writing.

Meanwhile, Steven Barthelme had begun working with us around 1970, while I was still living in both Austin and Houston. The youngest in the family, Steve completed his degree at the University of Texas and wrote essays and fiction for the *Texas Observer* and other magazines. He decided to remain in Austin instead of returning to Houston, but he continued writing for most of our accounts, and this long-distance arrangement created few difficulties.

As I completed work on my dissertation, I planned to return to Dominican College to teach at least one or two classes. In the 1960s, we had developed an interdisciplinary program that was limited to a small number of students; the college now was planning to make it available to all students. However, in the 1970s, women's colleges throughout the country were struggling for survival, and before long Dominican College became a casualty of this trend.

About this time, Don told me of a girl he was dating in New York, Marion Knox, a writer who focused on education. Although reluctant to marry again, he was considering it. He said that Marion wanted marriage and he thought it was the "right" thing to do. He seldom mentioned her after that, but one day in 1978 Steve Barthelme called to tell me that Don was planning to marry and Steve thought I should know. A few days later, I called New York to wish Don well. He was pleased and then laughed because the marriage was to take place that very evening. In fact, he was delighted that his mother and father were in town for the ceremony. He was at that moment "scrubbing the john" as part of cleaning the apartment for the occasion.

He was clearly pleased with his decision, and not long afterward he published "The Leap," a story exploring his commitment to marriage once again. There is no suggestion of the "mystery" of a girl to give meaning to the story, but rather the meaning comes from love, possibility, and a "leap of faith." In the story, the two speakers, both voices of the author, begin a conversation this way:

—Today we make the leap to faith. Today.
—Today?
—Today.
—We're really going to do it? At last?
—Spent too much time fooling around. Today we do it.
—I dont know. Maybe we're not ready?
—I am cheered by the wine of possibility and the growing popularity of light. Today's the day.
—You're serious.

and end it with:

—A wedding day.
—A plain day.
—Okay.
—Okay?
—Okay.

In the personas of two speakers, Don explores love in the context of the human condition and finally comes to a decision to try marriage once again. At one point, he appears to evoke an earlier relationship, probably ours, when he says, "tortures unimaginable, but the worse torture of knowing it could have been otherwise, had we shaped up."

In examining his own tormented mind and emotions, the speaker alludes to Søren Kierkegaard: "Purity of heart is to will one thing. . . . Here I differ with Kierkegaard. Purity of heart is, rather to will several things, and not know which is the better, truer thing, and to worry about this, forever."

After more observations about love, the speaker ends with the plan to "try again," in other words, to try marriage again.[5]

In September, 1981, Don returned to Houston for his first semester of a distinguished professorship in creative writing at the University of Houston. I had talked to him but had not seen him for about two years; before he left New York, we made plans to meet for lunch once he arrived.

Don was staying at Pete Barthelme's home while he was in Houston. He was to be in Houston until Christmas and then spend the spring in New York.

Pete lived in a small modernist house at Bissonnet Boulevard and Shepherd Drive, about a mile from the Museum of Fine Arts. As I turned into the drive, Don was watching through a large window overlooking the entrance; he saw me and quickly walked out and stepped into the car. We laughed and hugged, delighted to see each other. Don handed me a copy of his new *Sixty Stories,* a beautiful collection of what he thought were his best stories. As we talked, I saw the spirit and exuberance of a younger Don.

Pete Barthelme was now divorced, and his elder daughter was living with him. Don's wife Marion, whom he had married in 1978, had remained in New York, so Don was alone.

We drove to Ruggles Café, a popular restaurant on Westheimer Road in our old neighborhood. Built a few years after we moved away, the café was just four blocks from our home on Harold Street. We had taken walks along these streets almost every evening, and this was where Don walked when he took a break from writing the *Dr. Caligari* stories in the mornings. We were not far from Courtlandt Place, a long block of mansions that survived only because the street was eventually declared a historic community and iron gates were placed across the entrances.

Ruggles was a fashionable dining place in the 1970s but was now beginning to decline; although the property was more expensive than it had been in the early 1960s and into the 1970s, the area had few renovated mansions and more apartments, and on Westheimer itself there were block after block of shabby storefronts. It was a typical inner-city scenario of decline and change. Ruggles, like other businesses in this neighborhood, depended largely on tourist traffic; on weekends, crowds of pedestrians gave it a bohemian look.

Montrose by this time boasted a very large population of gay men and women; the district had long been an attractive place for gay residents. In the late 1950s and into the 1960s, a large number of designers and decorators, along with architects and other professionals, had lived discreet homosexual lives there. At that time, gay men often married women in order to maintain the appearance of a conventional lifestyle. But by the early 1970s, the change was apparent. Odell and I lived in townhouses near Montrose Boulevard and the University of St. Thomas and were acutely aware of the increasing and openly gay population.

The changing character and appearance of the area was such that many residents preferred to refer to it as "the museum district" or the "museum and St. Thomas University," rather than the "Westheimer and Montrose neighborhood." Montrose Boulevard itself, extending from around Westheimer to the Museum of Fine Arts, continues to be an attractive drive with more and more fashionable restaurants constructed every year. But owners and patrons usually prefer to distance themselves from the connotation of the "Westheimer" name.

Don now had a little gray in his hair and a beard that Charlotte Phelan, a *Houston Post* reporter, described as "somewhat Amish." Dressing in a way that had become customary for him, a plaid sports shirt with khakis, he had added cowboy boots to the picture on this day. He had gained a little weight, but just in his waistline, so that his six-foot height still gave him a slender look; in fact, he occasionally assumed the erect and proud carriage that evoked a younger Don. His hands, with their long slender fingers, were still young, and like his mother he had handsome clear skin.

At lunch, his manner was enthusiastic and often cheerful as we talked about our lives and our work. But as the conversation turned to the people we both knew, some of whom had now died, I felt that he needed to be in Houston again for a while. He was fifty years old and was sad that a friend since the 1950s, Mary Anne Hayes, had died. At the University of Houston, where she had joined the staff of the news office when I was still there, Mary Anne had worked with Don on *Forum* and was managing editor when she left the university. She studied philosophy at the New School in New York before moving to Paris, where she later joined the editorial staff of the *International Herald Tribune.* The last time I saw her was when she returned to Houston to visit her brother, whom she knew would, because of a genetic trait, undoubtedly develop a brain tumor and die from it before she could return.

After learning a few years later that, like other members of her family, she too had a terminal brain tumor, Mary Anne returned for a final visit to the States; in New York, she spent time with Don and his family. Don met Mary Anne at the airport when she arrived from Paris, and since she was under heavy medication, he had stayed close in order to take care of her. When she was ready to leave, Don accompanied her to the airport for a flight to Houston to visit Farris Block, who was still on the administrative staff of the University of Houston. Her visit and subsequent death had deeply affected Don.

That same day, Don talked as well of Tom Hess, who had become his closest friend in New York. Tom had died at fifty-six of a heart attack; he "just suddenly fell over onto his desk," Don said.

He asked about everyone he could think of and told me of other acquaintances. He had stayed in touch with Pat and Georgia Goeters and sometimes saw Pat in New York. They were no longer together, though. Pat was practicing architecture in California, "afraid to marry again" and "wants no more children," Don said, and Georgia was living in Hartford with their six children and working at Yale University.

Don quoted Pat as saying that his sons were "enrolled in junior college with earning money as their goal." They were "anti-intellectual with no self-awareness," and Pat was puzzled and confused about it. Don thought it was ironic that Pat should not understand what had happened; he recalled the years of financial struggle and difficulties in which the Goeters children had grown up, a background that Don thought could easily explain their behavior. Don knew, of course, as I did, that Pat had received a considerable inheritance, but even that together with his professional income could not have covered his lifestyle.

Robert Morris and Gitta were still in Connecticut; Bob was teaching and Gitta was working for a newspaper. Guy Johnson now lived with his second wife, who was Dutch, in Amsterdam. According to Don, he was still doing the same style of satirical painting as he had in the early 1960s. Elaine de Kooning and Bill de Kooning, separated for many years, were together again; he was ill and she was taking care of him.

Anne was then living with her mother in Copenhagen but was planning to come to the United States for college. She was not quite sixteen and spent every summer and Christmas with Don. He was glad that she was in school there and not in New York City, where, according to Don, the schools were "hell holes."

When I asked about his fourth marriage, to Marion, he said that Marion was expecting a child in January. He was wary of having a child at his age but said that Marion "wore me down on it."

A few of his friends were still working at the University of Houston; among them was Farris Block, who was in China that fall. Outside of the university, Don was particularly interested in the other artists he had known. He was looking forward to working with sculptor Jim Love on a joint project. But when I asked about Jack Boynton, to whom he had once said—with both honesty and affection—"you sure are an illiterate bastard," Don just looked discouraged and told me what happened. He had encountered Jack at Butera's Grocery on Bissonnet Boulevard, and Jack had enthusiastically told him of his interest in the work of California guru Carlos Castaneda. Apparently Jack was not aware of Don's parody of Castaneda in "The Teachings of Don B: A Yankee Way of Knowledge," a story that first appeared in the *New Yorker*.[1]

Don explained that he was working on a novel to be entitled *Ghosts*, which he hoped to complete by the following May. He said little more after that, but it later occurred to me that he planned a novel that did not materialize. When he first told me of his plans to be in Houston in the fall, Don said that he looked forward to our having "lots of long afternoon lunches." I thought little of it, other than that Don was happy to be returning to Houston for a few months. But when Don published "Construction" in the April 29, 1985, issue of the *New Yorker*, I recalled the conversation. The story was one of only two instances in which Don used the name Helen for a character after I asked him to avoid it in the early 1960s.

In "Construction," Don introduces the character of Helen in a context that clearly is the beginning of a longer work. In the story, the speaker anticipates traveling to California, where he looks forward to exploring "the mystery of Helen." Don probably believed our talks would yield material for this work, but as far as I know this did not happen.

The first time Don used my name in a story was in "The School," published in 1976. This story was undoubtedly suggested by our reconciliation when he suddenly appeared in my office in 1972. The story tells of an elementary school class in which everything dies, animals and even people, and the children tell the teacher "we don't like it." The children ask the teacher to "please make love with Helen," the teaching assistant, because they "require an assertion of value, we are frightened." The teacher had already told the children that "life is that which gives meaning to life." After the children asked for a demonstration of love, "Helen came and embraced" the teacher, he "kissed her a few times on the brow," and then "there was a knock on the door" and "the new gerbil walked in." After that, the "children cheered wildly." Our continued affection for each other after years apart meant a lot to Don that day in 1972. And then in "The School," he used a gesture of love to create meaning and thus value.

As it turned out, we saw each other often, but I believe it was simply too late to have the kind of conversations that would have provided the material he needed. The novel he did publish in 1986 was *Paradise,* a work in which I was disappointed and that I found much less challenging than his other novels. Nevertheless, it reflects both the hope and the despair that Don seemed to feel in the 1980s.

Paradise is the story of Simon, a middle-aged architect whose most recent wife has departed; the novel portrays the character's relationships with three young women who all live together with him for a while. Don used such familiar style devices as Q and A exchanges interspersed throughout the narrative. Simon seems dispirited much of the time, but Don frequently ends a scene with a surprising turn. At one point, Simon looks out the window and sees two men beating a cop who is a "black woman, slight of build." After he intervenes and the pretty young policewoman continues her beat, Simon returns to his apartment and thinks "Death may haunt Calcutta's streets, but teeming city throbs with life." Near the end of the novel, Simon says that he has "hope. . . . Not a hell of a lot of hope, but some hope."

On that day in September, 1981, we returned to Pete's home after lunch for an interview Charlotte Phelan was doing for the *Houston Post.* Later, he would drive one of Pete's cars to pick up his eighteen-year-old niece after school. She had just returned to live with Pete in order to finish her senior year at Lamar High School. In living there with both of them, Don described it as crowded and "sort of like the barracks." But I could see that he was gratified by the task of taking care of her. Pete was off on a fishing trip, and Don's responsibility was to drive his niece to school, pick her up, prepare dinner, and all of the duties that he called "uncle-ing."

I stayed with him as he waited for Charlotte to show up for the interview, and by then he drank only wine. He told me that since he was to drive one of Pete's cars to pick up his niece after school, it was important to be sober. He had spent the morning at Pete's house washing windows and proudly pointed to the clean windows. I remarked that he had always been a meticulous housekeeper.

Charlotte arrived, and I left them to the interview. In her article, Charlotte described Don as having "a certain serenity." I do not believe this was an accurate observation. He was pleased with the new professorship at the university, but I would never have described his manner as "serene." I had become more conscious of his drinking and believed that his controlled manner may have been deceptive, creating a screen behind which no one could see him clearly.

On another day when we were at lunch, Don seemed nervous instead of serene; when I asked him about it, he replied that he was "nervous in the world." He admitted that he would like to be back in New York, that he would like to say goodbye to his students and return immediately to his Manhattan home. But he had to earn money. He had to teach at the University of Houston to earn money.

Don's pessimistic vision occasionally slipped out in a remark about his own alcoholism or the condition of being a writer. As we talked about the research I had done on William Faulkner, I told him of Faulkner's daughter Jill and her interest in what I wrote. I mentioned a well-known incident in which Faulkner compared himself to Shakespeare. Jill Faulkner had asked her father not to drink and pleaded with him to "think of me." [2] I was sympathetic with Jill, but Don reminded me—with intense feeling for Faulkner—that Faulkner had replied, "Nobody remembers Shakespeare's children."

Although we had not been discussing Don's drinking, there was no doubt in what he said and in the harsh, angry tone that he used that he had no sympathy for Jill. He clearly identified with Faulkner as well as Shakespeare and the privileges that such talent deserved. Almost fiercely he added, "You cannot take an alcoholic's booze from him."

Before long his second daughter, Katharine, was born, and I was sure that he was happy about it; he did not need to take care of Katharine as he had Anne, but he occasionally recalled something she had done. One day, when Marion was not at home, he was taking care of her in their second-level flat in Houston, and writing as well, when "she was suddenly gone" before he was aware of it. When he went downstairs, he found her going down South Boulevard, already about a block from home.

Anne was now living with Don in the United States, in both Manhattan and Houston. While Anne was still in Copenhagen, her mother had committed suicide by jumping out of the high-rise apartment building in which they lived. Don said very little about Birgit's death other than to express compassion for her illness and her decision to end her life.

Each time we met, Don brought up his personal life. He said one day that "marriage is not an ideal form, as we both know." When Marion wanted to have another child, he replied that "maybe what you need is another husband." This comment was cruel, but in our conversations Don had been increasingly cruel about marriage. I have no doubt that he was mostly very kind and gentle in his relationship with Marion. It seemed a kind of dilemma for him, the sense of responsibility and morality that his Catholic background had given him, and the reality of his mostly sad and despairing inner life.

In New York, he had an affair with the young wife of a renowned European novelist and observed that "there were all kinds of feelings of guilt for both of us."

Don was probably as happy at the University of Houston as he could be anywhere. He seldom discussed his teaching methods or how he felt about teaching, but he occasionally said something about advice that he gave to his students. He warned them *not* to write about weather. And he told them over and over that he did not want to read about anyone feeling bad: "If you feel bad, don't tell me." He occasionally boasted about his students; he was satisfied that they were doing good work and bragged of their successes in publishing. One day, he boasted of a thirty-five-thousand-dollar advance that a woman student had received for a novel. Just as he must have encouraged and helped his students, he certainly would have not "suffered fools" in the classroom. In fact, if necessary, he would interrupt a student reading a story with an abrupt "that's enough . . . you may sit down."

There was little doubt at this point that alcoholism was now a problem for Don. One day when we were having lunch at a restaurant on West Gray, Don commented that his only criterion in choosing the restaurant was that "they have booze." He drank wine during lunch, as well as martinis before and after lunch. I could occasionally see the Don I had known, but in appearance he was turning into an older man. He seemed to consciously develop this look. His red beard from the 1970s was now gray and much longer, giving him the look of an aging patriarch. He told me that a little girl in a Manhattan grocery store had pointed at him, telling her mother to "look at that old man."

At the beginning of 1983, Odell and I moved our offices from Houston to our home on Lake Conroe, a house that we had purchased and from which we knew that we could commute to Houston for client meetings. Although a devastating economic decline that spread throughout Texas by the late 1980s was already emerging in Houston, few people recognized it as anything more than the effect of an oil crisis that had begun in the 1970s.

But our experience in financial, industrial, and real estate accounts made us sensitive to the problems that would soon overwhelm the entire state, problems that affected every business in Texas before the decade ended. Deregulation of the savings and loan industry together with inflated prices in real estate eventually resulted in the collapse of a large number of financial institutions. In the early 1980s, we could not have imagined the near disaster that finally developed in the Houston and Texas economy, but we saw that we should reduce our overhead as quickly as possible. As it turned out, we made enough changes to continue our business quite successfully out of our Lake Conroe office for several more years. And for the first time since 1960, Odell and I both enjoyed the freedom of a new lifestyle.

The lake was formed by the creation of a dam on the San Jacinto River, making it a beautiful recreational area with dense forest surrounding much of it. We lived in a neighborhood developed on the north end of the lake, property that was once a large ranch owned by Frank Horlock, a prominent Houstonian who owned the Pearl Beer distributorship. We bought a boat especially for our teenage nephew, Lee Vandruff, and on weekends and during the summers he and his friends were frequently at the lake. We lived on Lake Conroe until 1986, when the recession had deepened to the point that there was very little business for advertising agencies anywhere in the state.

After moving to the lake, I sometimes drove into Houston, fifty miles south of the lake, to meet Don for lunch. This is what I did the last time we were together. After I picked him up at his flat on South Boulevard, we drove a few blocks to Anthony's, a fashionable restaurant on Montrose Boulevard near the Museum of Fine Arts.

We talked that day of the economic problems in Houston; his brother Pete still had his advertising agency and had told him what was happening. Don was as courteous and proper as always, but during lunch, I was acutely aware of how much he was drinking. Before we were finished eating, he ordered a martini to drink while I had coffee. It seemed, however, not to affect his public demeanor at all. I do not believe that most people, even other members of the faculty at the University of Houston, were aware of anything other than what seemed a kind of aloofness in his manner.

After we left the restaurant, I drove through two of our old neighborhoods off Montrose Boulevard; the apartment building in which we had lived on Richmond Avenue was still standing, an ugly, unimposing exterior. Don and I commented on the strangeness of seeing it there. We were extremely happy when we had lived there, so it was a little unreal to discuss it in such a dispassionate way. Our conversation was never sentimental; if there was any chance of nostalgia, Don quickly evoked reality with an ironic observation about life.

I was driving my sister's sports car, and he commented on it and the fact that he drove an old car. Ever since the philosopher Maurice Natanson alluded to Don's "affinity for sports cars" in the late 1950s, a comment that Don had thought was a condemnation of his lifestyle, he talked about making a choice between writing full-time or such luxuries as "owning a Jaguar." I doubted that the car he now drove mattered to him at all and assumed that he was just making a dispassionate comment on his own life.

When we returned to his home that afternoon, he looked especially unhappy. He had begun to look like an old man; his demeanor as he walked away was somber and dispirited. I sat in the car and watched him go up the walk to the front door of his building, his shoulders a little slumped. I was reluctant to leave, but after a few moments I sadly drove away. Although I talked to him whenever I could after that, this was the last time I was to see Don until he was in a coma and near death at M. D. Anderson Cancer Center in the summer of 1989.

When I last saw Don, I had already begun to think of teaching again and had applied for a position at Texas A&M University in College Station. I received an appointment to the Department of English in 1987 and began living there that summer. I continued to talk to Don but was shocked when Sam Southwell called to tell me that in the spring of 1988 Don had undergone throat surgery for cancer just above the larynx. I knew that Don had continued to smoke even after losing part of his upper lip to cancer, but he had not mentioned any problems each time we talked. His brother Pete had recently gone through the same surgery and was recovering when Don went to the hospital. Pete described the cancer as "squamous cell carcinoma of the pharynx . . . metastasized to lymph glands and other structures . . . on the right side of the neck."[3]

Before I learned of Don's throat cancer, I had planned to be in Houston and to have lunch with Don in 1988, but my mother died in early July. I had just completed a class for the first summer session at Texas A&M and was planning to drive to Houston the next day to see her when my sister Margo called to tell me. I immediately drove to Houston and spent the next few weeks with my sister. Since 1980, our mother had lived here in an apartment wing that my sister had built for her. We made arrangements for the funeral services, called members of the family, and talked a lot about the past. It was a sad time for me, and I did not contact Don until after the funeral.

He was not at home when I telephoned and it was not clear when he would return, but before long Don called to tell me that he had been at the Spring Shadows Rehabilitation Center recovering from what he termed "alcoholism." He was giving up smoking as well. I did not understand how difficult recovery from both addictions must have been nor how much pain he had already gone through with his throat cancer.

Don had been very fond of my mother and understood how much she meant to me and how much I missed her. After a while, he told me more about himself. He was trying to refrain from both drinking and smoking but was finding it difficult. As we talked, he said nothing of his physical condition, not even how much weight he had lost after the surgery.

Don's yearning to edit his own publication had persisted even after he rejoined the University of Houston to teach. He had introduced the idea of starting a new daily newspaper in Houston to George Christian, who was now book editor for the *Houston Chronicle*. George tried to point out the difficulties of developing an organization, of financing it, and of building circulation, all problems that George believed were insurmountable, but Don talked about it again when they last met in 1988.

George was shocked to see how much Don had changed from the surgery and described him as "very unhappy." George was at Don's home for lunch when Don told him several times that he wanted to die, "to go to sleep and never wake up." Marion was in the apartment and entered the room occasionally, but in her presence Don altered his demeanor so that he would not reveal his feelings. George said that "as soon as she left, Don resumed talking about how miserable he was."[4]

A few years earlier, when Mary Christian first saw Don after he began teaching at the University of Houston, he had greeted her cheerfully with, "Hello, I'm going bald, I'm going fat," as he put one hand out to shake hands and the other to hide his bald head. And now he repeated to her what he had said to George, that he just wanted "to go to sleep and never wake up."

After his throat cancer surgery in the spring of 1988, it became a little more arduous for Don to lecture at the university; he frequently coughed and cleared his throat during class. Students and faculty described him as "gaunt and thin." But I did not know this. In July, his voice was quite strong, and he gave no hint of how much the surgery had affected him. In a telephone conversation I had with him after my mother died, I promised to get back to Houston during the fall term so that we could have lunch and talk. I could not return before the Christmas holidays, however, and made plans instead to see him in the summer of 1989.

Don returned to Manhattan at the end of the fall term, and in the spring he and his family were going to Rome, where Don would teach at the Roman Academy and receive an award for his work in fiction.

While they were in Italy, there seems to have been no indication of the depression or desire to die that he had expressed to George Christian in Houston. His letters to his parents described where they lived and trips they took, with nothing to suggest anything other than pleasure in seeing the beauty of the country.

The villa in which they lived, as well as the academy where he taught, were "set on the top of a hill." The size of the villa was impressive, with a living room "45 feet by 18 feet." There was a small terrace off the bedroom, so that "just looking out of the window in the morning is a great joy." It had "shabby, old furniture and old paint." Another scene he found spectacular was from the terrace of the Hotel Carso Belvedere, where they had breakfast.

They took a trip to "a tiny town called Ravello on the Amalfi coast which turned out to be the most beautiful place I've ever been," Don wrote. Accompanied by Marion's mother and father, who were there for a visit, Don described seeing Vesuvius on their return trip.

He talked to his brother Rick while in Rome, but gave no indication that he was now extremely ill. Edward Hirsch, one of Don's colleagues at the University of Houston, was also in Rome; he had dinner there with Don and later talked about how happy Don had been.[5]

That spring Don was working on the book that would become *The King;* he planned to "get it to the publisher at the end of the month." After reading *The King,* I found it difficult not to believe that Don knew he was writing his last novel and the final story of his own life.

After their return to New York in May, Don was losing weight, but Marion could not get him to eat. She tried preparing special dishes to encourage him, but he told her bluntly to "leave him alone."[6] He was also drinking again, more than a bottle of wine each day.[7] In June, he was persuaded by Marion and his family to return to Houston to see the doctor who had performed the throat surgery. But after initial tests, the doctor said everything was okay, that there was no recurrence of throat cancer. Then Don was examined by his internist, who found a large tumor in his chest but advised Don that it was so large, nothing could be done.

Before Don had been admitted to the hospital for the tests, Pete received a telephone call from Don asking him to come over to his apartment on South Boulevard. Marion was not in town and Don was planning to pick his daughter up from school; he wanted Pete to go with him on a "test drive to see if he could function as a driver." Pete arrived to find Don "not really coherent"; the test was a "terrifying" drive, and Pete quickly stopped Don and took over. He then called Joan at her office at Pennzoil to go with him to take Don to the doctor. Don was immediately admitted to the M. D. Anderson Cancer Center, where he remained until his death.

After more tests, they learned that the cancer had spread throughout his body. His organs were affected and his bones had been attacked, so now large quantities of calcium were going into his blood. This condition caused him to hallucinate and become paranoid. Rick described him as "terrified" at one point.

Following a period of tests and treatment for calcium, Don was conscious for a day or two, around July 13. He talked to Marion and began to make plans with her for chemotherapy treatments; he also asked her to call the Department of English at the University of Houston to tell them the status of his illness and that he did not know yet when he would return. Marion asked if he wanted her to say he would be there for fall classes and he said no, not to be "overly optimistic." At one point, he asked her if she was scared and Marion, who was actually terrified, replied that she was not.

At first, Don was in and out of consciousness, but soon he was unconscious most of the time; he occasionally recognized someone but seemed not to gain consciousness at all the final few days. He was receiving heavy doses of morphine and had difficulty breathing. He was surrounded by medical equipment that helped him to breathe, but one by one, his organs were breaking down, ceasing to function. Everyone knew that he was dying.

I was in Houston when I learned of Don's condition on Thursday, July 20, 1989. I was visiting my sister Margo after completing the first summer session of classes at Texas A&M University. That evening, Margo drove with me to the hospital, where Don was in intensive care. When I saw him, he was attached to life-sustaining equipment and in a coma from which he did not awaken. Even with the equipment covering most of his face, he looked peaceful. His face was lined and his hair and beard were white, but otherwise he looked normal.

At the hospital, I met Don's daughter Anne for the first time. She was a tall, attractive girl, now twenty-four years old. She wanted me to know that she had "heard of me all her life" and that "it was all good." She went on to tell me that she had asked her father a number of times if she could go with us to lunch and that he had answered with a dramatic "NO!" I recognized the emphatic but playful tone that Don used and I thought what an exceptional father he had been.

After Don's death, Pete told me that he was never sure that Don's doctors had found the "original cancer" the preceding year. Pete himself had a second operation for cancer after his surgeon found the primary source, but he did not know if the further spread of Don's cancer "could have been caught." Don was "considerably weakened" by the surgery in 1988, more than Pete had been, even though Pete had suffered heart attacks and undergone both heart and cancer surgery. Pete also pointed out that Don's recovery from throat surgery in 1988 could have been complicated by alcohol withdrawal.

Pete told me that the doctor enumerated all the problems, the breaking down or loss of function of all his organs. Pete had developed an honest and realistic way of analyzing events and was graphic in describing the enlargement of Don's kidney and other problems. He wanted me to know there was no hope and said several times that he would like to say something that would comfort me but could not. He told me, as he had told his mother, "There is not going to be a miracle."

Don died on Sunday, July 23, at 5:15 A.M. When I talked to his mother on Sunday afternoon, she told me that she had asked one of the doctors if he had ever seen a miracle, assuming he had not, and the doctor replied that "yes, he had." She retained some hope from this, but when she saw Don Saturday afternoon, she gave up all hope. She also did not want him to "suffer the pain of chemotherapy," which had seemed a possibility just a week earlier.

Don was cremated Tuesday, July 25. Marion was planning a private memorial service at a later date for family and close friends. Joan wanted the former bishop of Houston and Galveston to come from his current diocese in Austin to speak, especially for their mother; Pete told me that all four sons had left the church, but they understood and respected Mrs. Barthelme's total commitment to the Catholic church.

When I talked to Rick during the week, he said that it was so horrible that all he could do was to try to make jokes that Don would have liked. When I telephoned, he had been "poking around the ashes in the fireplace, trying to see if Don was there." Concerning plans for the service, he said it might be at the Rothko Chapel, the University of Houston chapel, or the Rice University chapel. Then he added that there would be "services at all three place, and that tickets would be given out—and there would probably be a scalping of tickets, in fact, [he] would probably scalp his."

His humor did help; I recalled how much I had missed Don. Each Barthelme had a different kind of humor, but all were unique, and I have never known anyone else like them. I have no doubt that Don would have enjoyed Rick's way of dealing with his death at that moment.

A service was held a short time later at the Rothko Chapel, next to the University of St. Thomas campus. Roger Angell, a close friend of Don's and editor at the *New Yorker*, gave an admiring eulogy that I think Don would have liked. He described Don's insistence that no one change his stories. I knew from Don that, in fact, he had valued Roger's recommendations.

There were other memorial services later, one at the University of Houston and another in Manhattan. And since Don's death, memorial fellowships have been established in his honor at the University of Houston. The best known is one established by James A. Michener — the Michener Fellowship in honor of Donald Barthelme.

When Don's novel *The King* was published posthumously in 1990, George Christian, then book editor of the *Houston Chronicle*, received a review copy of the publisher's proof, which he mailed to me to read. I was struck by how perfectly fitting it was as the farewell to Don's life and work.

In *The King*, both George and I saw characteristics of Don himself, especially of the young Don we recalled from years earlier. Don's ideas are expressed in the character of King Arthur and of Lancelot as well. We were moved as we recognized that Lancelot dreaming of Guinevere sharply evoked Don himself.

The genius of Donald Barthelme can be seen clearly in *The King;* in it, he provides us with a moral lesson that is given weight through the myth of King Arthur. Although no one in the twentieth century had an answer for the nuclear question, Arthur has a solution that is typically Barthelme: He makes a decision that seems possible in the world imagined by Don. The king, whose knights are still in quest of the Grail, refuses to use the Bomb to defend the Allies against their enemies. He says instead, "I cannot allow it. It's not the way we wage war. . . . The essence of our calling is right behavior, and this false Grail is not a knightly weapon. I have spoken."

Lancelot says that Arthur's decision "restores my faith in shouldness and sets a noble example for all the world." The theme of man's responsibility expressed in "shouldness" and "noble example" is given powerful eloquence in this scene, and like many of the ideas and themes that recurred throughout Don's writing life, it can be traced back to his early stories and to his own life and beliefs.

Notes

CHAPTER 1. FIRST ENCOUNTER

1. Quotations from and other references to Joe and Maggie Maranto are based on my personal knowledge and on an interview at their home in Stamford, Connecticut, in May, 1993.

2. Historical information on the Barthelme family is based on conversations with Don and with members of the Barthelme family beginning in 1956, from interviews with Don's parents from 1991 to 1996, and on conversations with his brothers and sister. Quotations from letters that Don wrote to his parents are cited in the text. Other quotations by members of Don's family are cited in the text.

    All other quotations and information about the family are based on personal experiences.

3. Donald Barthelme, "A Shower of Gold," in *Come Back, Dr. Caligari* (Boston: Little, Brown, 1964), p. 183.

4. In reply to my request, Sister Huberta Gallatin, who was then living in Shreveport, Louisiana, wrote a letter dated August 12, 1992, recalling her experiences with Don when he was a student at St. Anne School in Houston.

5. Herman "Pat" Goeters, interview by author, May, 1993.

6. Donald Barthelme, "Overnight to Many Distant Cities," in *Forty Stories* (New York: Putnam, 1987), p. 219.

7. Goeters interview.

CHAPTER 2. NEVER SUFFER FOOLS

1. Quotations and other references to Herman Gollob are taken from personal experience, from two interviews with Herman in his office at Doubleday in New York in May, 1993, and letters as cited in the text.

2. Maggie Maranto interview.

3. This and all references to Herman "Pat" Goeters are based on my own knowledge, on discussions with Don's father, and on an interview with Pat in May, 1993.

CHAPTER 3. A DRAFTEE SEARCHING FOR A "COOL SOUND"

1. This letter and others addressed to Joe Maranto are from Joe's personal files.

2. This information is from a letter from Donald Barthelme to his family. This and all other letters to his family are in their private files.

3. "Thailand," in *Sixty Stories* (New York: Putnam, 1981), pp. 433–36.

Chapter 4. Then Wear the Gold Hat

1. Hubert Benoit, *The Many Faces of Love,* trans. Philip Mairet (New York: Pantheon Books, 1955).

Chapter 5. Discovery of *Godot*

1. "Bishop," in *Sixty Stories,* p. 449.

2. "Florence Green is 81," in *Come Back, Dr. Caligari,* p. 14.

Chapter 6. Life with a Literary Genius

1. When Ann Boynton finally succeeded in taking her own life in 1963, I called Don in New York to tell him. Don asked what he should do; I suggested he simply call Jack but was surprised that he did not instinctively know what to do.

Chapter 7. *Forum:* Working in a Vacuum

1. The correspondence between Walker Percy and Don was originally in my Donald Barthelme files. It is now with the Percy Collection in the Wilson Library at the University of North Carolina at Chapel Hill.

   All other correspondence quoted in this chapter is in my Donald Barthelme files. In some instances, there are also copies in the Donald Barthelme Collection at the University of Houston.

2. The Percy Collection includes several versions of *The Moviegoer;* the revisions are so extensive that it is easy to see why Percy did not wish to edit it further.

3. The original version of the conclusion of chapter 2 of *The Moviegoer* was in my files and is now at the Wilson Library.

4. This letter is at the University of North Carolina. *Zuruck an die Sache,* meaning "Back to Things," was the motto of the phenomenologists, following Edmund Husserl, who obviously influenced Percy. That is, back to things of this life-world as reality more authentic than the abstractions of the science-world. In the context of Percy's letter and this phrase, the reference to Plato could only mean abstract theorizing. See Jay Tolson's *Pilgrim in the Ruins: A Life of Walker Percy* (New York: Simon and Schuster, 1992) for numerous references to Percy and Catholicism.

Chapter 8. The Creation of a Strange Object

1. Quoted in *Paris Review* 23, no. 80 (1981): 187.

Chapter 9. The Writing of *Come Back, Dr. Caligari*

1. "The Genius," *Forty Stories*, pp. 17–23.

2. After Don joined the faculty of the University of Houston, he and Sam Southwell became close friends and frequently had lunch and enjoyed talking about a wide range of topics. Sam is a scholar of Victorian literature who has published a work on Robert Browning, but his other publications include a novel that he wrote in the 1960s, as well as a philosophical study of Kenneth Burke. He encouraged me to write this account of Don and has been helpful in recalling Don's observations and thoughts throughout the 1980s.

3. Ehrenzweig, *The Hidden Order of Art* (Berkeley: University of California Press, 1967).

4. *Paris Review* 23, no. 80 (1981): 182, 203.

5. Walker Percy, "The Man on the Train," *Partisan Review* 23, no. 4 (fall, 1956): 489.

6. Angell used this anecdote in the eulogy he gave during a memorial service for Don at the Rothko Chapel in Houston in 1989.

7. "Not-Knowing," *Georgia Review* (fall, 1985), p. 514.

Chapter 13. New York at Last

1. The foundation conducts the Creative Arts Program of the Edgar Stern Family Fund of New Orleans.

2. Don's letters from New York during this period include some to me, but most of them were to his parents. When he and I talked on the telephone, he told me much of what he told his parents in correspondence. Also, here and throughout this study, I am using diary notes from my files.

Chapter 14. Loss and Possibility

1. "Down the Line with the Annual," *New Yorker,* March 21, 1964, pp. 34–35. The story was collected in *Guilty Pleasures* (New York: Farrar, Straus, and Giroux, 1974).

2. Almost a decade later, in 1971, when Bly and Michael Hamburger were at my home for a dinner party during a poetry festival at the University of Texas in Austin, Hamburger asked Bly why Don and I were divorced. Bly replied that "Helen's a lady, but Don is not a gentleman."

3. "For I'm the Boy Whose Only Joy Is Loving You" was a story Don wrote in Houston that gives insight to his own inner feelings at that time. Its characters anticipate those in *Snow White*.

4. Larry Rivers was one of the leading younger artists in the United States, including the New York art world. Don was unhappy with his cover for "Location."

5. Gollob interview.

6.   The information about Lynn Nesbitt's suggestion that Don travel the world comes from the interview with Joe and Maggie Maranto in May, 1993.

CHAPTER 15. A NEW LIFE BEGINS FOR DON

1.   This letter and all of the letters Don wrote to me from Europe are in my private files.

2.   Although I knew nothing of Birgit's pregnancy at that time, I later learned that he had written to his parents about it in the late spring, at the same time that he mentioned the story "The Game."

3.   The second story was undoubtedly "Edward and Pia." "Snap Snap" was published in the *New Yorker* on August 28 and "Edward and Pia" on September 25. The latter includes a girl who is pregnant and vomiting; it was still characteristic of Don to include personal experiences in his stories. Don's next *New Yorker* story was not published until "This Newspaper Here" appeared the following February 12. Don was then working on *Snow White*, a novel that was first published in the *New Yorker* on February 18, 1967, and then published in book form by Atheneum in March, 1967. "The Affront," which Don mentioned in another letter and which ran in *Harper's Bazaar* in November of 1965, became a part of *Snow White*.

4.   Donald Barthelme, Sr., interview by author, Houston, in 1996, just two weeks before his death.

CHAPTER 16. CASTING CHRYSANTHEMUMS ON HIS GRAVE

1.   Among the faculty of the university that had been assembled by the late 1940s there were former public school educators, including those who made up the faculty of the junior college that became the University of Houston. There were also faculty from more established universities, including several from Harvard and other Ivy League schools. The more ambitious among them had imagined building a great university of the South, but in the early 1950s, a more practical institution was needed. With its large and growing student body, the University of Houston wanted to serve all students. Besides the traditional colleges, there was a College of Technology which was largely a trade school. The university had yet to develop the College of Law and other professional programs for which it has since become distinguished. Such material as this provides some of the background for *Snow White*.

CHAPTER 17. DON ENTERS MY LIFE AGAIN

1.   *The Slightly Irregular Fire Engine*, published by Doubleday in 1971, was Don's only book for children. He told me that he wrote it for his

daughter Anne and that he read it aloud to her to get her response but that she was not particularly impressed by it. This is probably an exaggeration by Don, but I have no doubt that Anne was the only reason for his writing the book.

2. Richard Schickel, *New York Times,* August, 1970.

3. *Time,* January 4, 1971, p. 76.

4. Donald Barthelme, Sr., interview.

5. "The Leap," in *Great Days* (New York: Farrar, Straus, and Giroux, 1979), pp. 145–54.

Chapter 18. The Final Years and *The King*

1. This story is included in *The Teachings of Don B.: Satires, Parodies, Fables, Illustrated Stories, and Plays of Donald Barthelme,* ed. Kim Herzinger, with an introduction by Thomas Pynchon (New York: Random House, 1992), pp. 3–10.

2. This anecdote is recounted in Joseph Blotner, *Faulkner, a Biography* (New York: Random House, 1974), 2:1204.

3. This information came from interviews with Peter Barthelme after Don's death, the last interview being in 1997.

4. George Christian, interview by author in 1991. This and other quotations are from interviews that I had with George in 1989, 1990, and 1991. At that time, George was book editor of the *Houston Chronicle.*

5. After Don's death, Edward Hirsch told Sam Southwell about his visit with Don in Rome, and I learned of the visit from Sam.

6. I learned in July, 1989, from Marion Barthelme that Don had been refusing to eat.

7. Frederick Barthelme told me in Houston on July 20, 1989, of Don's drinking during that period. My account of Don's death is taken from conversations with Rick, Steven, Pete, Don's mother, and Marion.

Index

Aalto, Alvar, 9

Abstract Expressionism, 139

Absurd, Theatre of the, 105, 109, 119–20

A Clockwork Orange (Burgess), 106

Acta Diurna, 71

"The Act of Naming" (Percy), 72, 73

advertising: as career for women, 44; Don on, 32

advertising agency: creative director, 134; loan difficulties, 162–63; 1960s, 37, 43, 67, 90, 124–25; 1970s, 167, 169, 175–76; 1980s, 184–85; problems in leaving, 130; working from New York, 141; writing for Helen's, 98–99

"The Affront," 156

Against the American Grain (Macdonald), 137

Albee, Edward, 58, 106, 111, 115, 119–20

alcoholism, Don's: development of, 134, 141, 172, 173–74, 182–84, 185; recovery, 186; return of, 188

"Algeria" (Sartre), 80–81

Alleg, Henri, 80

Alley Theatre, 120

Allred, John, 86

Alpaca (Hunt), 98

American College Public Relations Association, 126

The American Communist Party: A Critical History (Coser and Howe), 76, 77

The American Dream (Albee), 119–20

Angell, Roger, 108, 191

antihero, 99, 105

antirealism, 95, 106, 137

Antoinette, Sister Mary, 126

architecture: Don on Seoul, 25; and father, 7–8, 17, 52; Japanese, 27; Kipling Street home, 64; and P. Goeters, 131; of second marriage home, 48

army tour, 22–34

Arrabal, Fernando, 109, 119

art: incorporation into text of articles, 78; literature as pure, 117

Art and Literature, 155

"Art and the Philosopher" (Collins), 72

artistic community: Barthelme participation in, 51; Houston in 1960s, 56, 57, 65; Houston in 1980s, 181; New York, 138–39; 1970s developments, 168; writing on Houston, 18–20

audience, from *New Yorker,* 170

The Automobile Graveyard (Arrabal), 109, 119

avant-garde drama, 119–20

Aylin Advertising, 162

Bancroft, Charles, 66

Bardley (pseud. for Don), 5, 18

Barnstone, Gertrude, 124

Barnstone, Howard, 124

Barstow, Robert, 161–62

Barth, John, 25

Barthelme, Anne (daughter), 171, 180, 183, 189

Barthelme, Birgit (third wife), 159, 160–61, 169–70, 171–72, 183

Barthelme, Donald: alcoholism of, 134, 141, 172, 173–74, 182–84, 185, 186, 188; appearance and manner of, 3, 179; artistic environment of, 55–57; and CAM, 110–12; and Catholicism, 10–12, 41, 59, 75; character of, xiii, xvi; charisma of, 4–5; childhood and youth, xiv, 7–10, 13; confidence of, 19; creative process,

Barthelme, Donald (*continued*)
xiii,xiv, 90–101, 103, 104; death of, 190;
depression of, 186, 187; as director of
CAA, 119–24; distancing from people,
109; editing ambitions in Manhattan,
126–32; European trips, 152–55, 187;
and father, 18, 52–54, 56; and father-
hood, 66; and finances, 60–61, 126–27,
129–30, 133–34, 141, 158, 173; first
meeting with Helen, 2–4; and G.
Christian, 16; and H. Gollob, 15–16;
high moral sense, xv; at *Houston Post*,
19–20, 36; idealism about relationships,
40–41; illness, 186; "imagining the
worst," 40; lamenting loss of friends,
179–80; on literature, 108–109; loss of
children, 51–52, 59–60, 61–62, 66;
Mexico adventure, 12–13; move away
from home, 20–21; move to New York,
133–40; New York City Writers Conference, 112–18; and P. Goeters, 12–13,
17–18; and parents, 52–55; personal developments, 1970s, 173–74; as "Prince
Charming," 165; psychoanalysis,
65–66; reluctance to return to *Post,* 32,
33; return trips to Houston (1970s),
166, 169–70; romanticism, 40–41, 42,
164; and S. Southwell, 174; search for
writing home, 66–68; and smoking, 91,
169, 186; talent for recognizing new
ideas and new writers, 81; teaching career, 58, 174–75, 178, 184; on wealth,
48, 63–64; wit of, 15–16, 95; and
women, 16–17. *See also Forum; Location;* marriages; writing; writing style
Barthelme, Donald, Sr. (father): vs. Birgit's father, 172; criticism of apartment,
61; disapproval of New York move,
131–32; in Don's youth, 7–9; financial
assistance, 134; and Helen's miscarriage, 51–52; as mentor, 17–18; and
modernist theories of architecture, 8;
and music, 52; and photography, 63;
pressures placed on Don, 52–54, 56,
108; search for Don, 13

Barthelme, Frederick (brother): acceptance of outside agency offer, 176; after
Don's death, 190; birth of, 9; borrowing
of sports car, 156–57; family dynamic,
53; literary achievements, xiv; prior to
joining Helen's agency, 163; role in
artistic community, 167–68
Barthelme, Helen Bechtold (mother),
7–8, 52, 53, 54–55, 157, 158
Barthelme, Helen (née Moore) (second
wife): career attitudes, 141–42; and
cooking, 23, 49, 50; courtship by Don,
35–43; development of relationship
with Don, 6; domestic life, 48–51; on
Don's death, 190–91; as editorial consultant, 92, 102–103; financial difficulties, 60–61, 126–27, 129–30, 133–34;
first meeting with Don, 2–4; flying lessons, 150, 161; graduate work, 160, 166,
169; in Houston without Don, 145–46;
loss of children, 51–52, 59–60, 61–62,
66; move to Lake Conroe, 184; move to
New York, 135–36; moving in Houston,
148–49; reaction to divorce, 158, 159;
return to Houston, 144; separation from
Don, 133; social life with family, 55–56;
study of Langer, 46; support of Don's
writing, 90–91; teaching career, 58,
116, 125, 142, 172–73, 176, 186; troubles
in marriage to Don, 137–38, 139–40,
144, 145–46, 151, 154–59. *See also* advertising agency
Barthelme, Joan (sister), xv, 8, 11, 53, 87,
163–64
Barthelme, John (grandfather), 8, 13
Barthelme, Katharine (daughter), 183
Barthelme, Lillian (née Foote) (sister-in-
law), 125, 131, 163
Barthelme, Mamie (grandmother), 55,
62–63, 130
Barthelme, Marilyn (née Marrs) (first
wife), 22, 32, 33, 36
Barthelme, Marion (née Knox) (fourth
wife), 176, 177, 180–81, 187, 188, 189
Barthelme, Peter (brother): birth of, 9; and

Contact, 93

Contemporary Arts Association. *See* Contemporary Arts Museum

Contemporary Arts Museum (CAM), 56, 66, 102, 110–12; Contemporary Arts Association (CAA), 110, 111–12, 119–24, 129, 130

cooking, 23, 49, 50

Corrigan, Robert W., 106

Coser, Lewis A., 76–77

Cougar, 5, 18

counterculture movement, 166–67

Crawling Arnold (Feiffer), 119–20

creativity: creative process, xiii, xiv, 90–101, 104; theories of, 104–105; unconscious as source of, 106–107. *See also* writing style

critics, literary: on *Come Back, Dr. Caligari,* 152; dominance of New Criticism, 99; Don as, 24; of Goeters' writing style, 27

Crittenden, Lillian, 39

Cullen, Hugh Roy, 70

cultural environment of Don's youth, 9. *See also* artistic community

Dabney, Sarah, 115–16

daily routines, 49–50

Darling, Edward, 79–80, 81

"The Darling Duckling at School," 93. *See also* "Me and Miss Mandible"

The Dead Father (Barthelme), 175

The Death of Ivan Ilych (Tolstoy), xv, 46–47

"Defining the Two Worlds of Man" (Natanson), 71

de Kooning, Elaine, 112, 128–29, 138–39, 180

de Kooning, Willem (Bill), 138, 180

de Menil, Dominique, 80, 110

de Menil, Jean, 56, 80, 110

Denmark, 153

design and layout. *See* layout and design

dissatisfaction theme, xiv, 108, 117

divorce: and Catholic Church, 41; Don's

from Helen, 154–59; Don's from Marilyn, 40; Helen's from Gilpin, 38–39, 40

domestic life in second marriage, 48–51

Dominican College, 58, 123, 125, 126, 129, 176

Dostoevsky, Feodor, 101, 111

"Down the Line with the Annual" (Barthelme), 95

drama: CAA promotion of, 111–12, 119–20; contemporary dramatists, 106; Don's interest in, 18, 32; dramatic readings and Don's writing process, 92, 103; Theatre of the Absurd, 105, 109, 119–20

Eames, Charles, 9

Eames, Ray, 9

editing careers, ambitions in Manhattan, 126–32. *See also Forum; Location*

"Edward and Pia" (Barthelme), 196n 3

Ehrenzweig, Anton, 104–105

Eliot, T. S., 94, 99

entertaining, 39, 49–50, 61. *See also* social life

essays, "The Case of the Vanishing Product," 98

Evans, Richard I., 76, 82

Ewing, Betty, 44

existentialism, Don's interest in, 46–47

experimental fiction, 105–106

Faulkner, Jill, 183

Faulkner, William, 26, 169, 173

Feiffer, Jules, 119–20

Fiction, 171

Fiedler, Leslie, 82

films: influence on Don, 25, 27, 37, 93, 101; reviews of, 20

financial issues, 173; Don's optimism about, 141, 158; with Helen, 60–61, 126–27, 129–30, 133–34

First Person, 93

Fitzgerald, F. Scott, 41, 94, 100

"Florence Green Is 81" (Barthelme): and creative process, 105, 127; and dissatisfaction theme, 108; models for characters, 94, 117; publication, 133, 146; and surrealistic art, 56

flying of airplanes, Helen's, 150, 161

Flynn, Errol, 101

Foote, Dr. Stephen, 163

Foote, Lillian (Mrs. P. Barthelme) (sister-in-law), 125, 131, 163

Ford Foundation, 85

"For I'm the Boy Whose Only Joy Is Loving You" (Barthelme), 147

form and content, 99–100

Fort Lewis, Washington, 23

Forum: contributors, 39–40, 48; disillusionment with, 65; Don's engrossment in, 46; Don's work on, 70–89; Don's writing in, 97; founding of, 36; philosophical influence, 45

From Baudelaire to Surrealism (Raymond), 52

From Here to Eternity (film), 25

From Shakespeare to Existentialism: Studies in Poetry, Religion, and Philosophy (Kaufmann), 81

Fuermann, George, 152

Fuller, Richard Buckminster, 111

Gallatin, Sister Huberta, 11

Galveston, 8, 55

"The Game" (Barthelme), 155

Gargantua and Pantagruel (Rabelais), 52

Gass, William H., 72

Gelber, Jack, 106, 120

"The Genius" (Barthelme), 103–104, 105

Ghosts (Barthelme), 181

Gilpin, Helen. *See* Barthelme, Helen (née Moore)

Gilpin, Peter Randall, 3, 35, 37–38

Goeters, Georgia, 40, 50, 55, 180

Goeters, Herman F. "Pat": ad agency building, 125; anger at Don, 129; architectural firm, 102; Don and Don's father, 108; and Don's father as mentor, 17–18; *Forum* cover design, 78; and ideal relationship idea, 40; Mexican adventure, 12–14; separation of Pat and Georgia, 180; and television shows, 97; writing style, 27

Gollob, Barbara, 117

Gollob, Herman: career developments, 87; Don's campaign to get published, 147; Don's divorce from Helen, 157; and Don's third wedding, 159; early friendship, 15; new wife, 117–18; as publisher, 102; as roommate of Don's, 36; and W. Percy, 74; writer recommendations for *Forum,* 88

Grass Harp (Capote), 32

The Great Gatsby (Fitzgerald), 41, 94

Greenbloom, Saul (pseud. of Don), 78. *See also* Barthelme, Donald

Guggenheim Fellowship, 150–51, 153

Guilty Pleasures (Barthelme), 95

Guy's Newsstand, 50

Hang Down Your Head (McCormick), 111–12

Harper's Bazaar, 94, 98, 133, 146, 156

Harvest, 6

Hawkes, John, 106

Hayes, Mary Anne, 179–80

Heart's Needle (Snodgrass), 122–23

Helen's mother (Jewel Dawson Moore), 68–69, 186

Heller, Joseph, 106, 137

Hemingway, Ernest, 100–101

Henderson the Rain King (Bellow), 114, 115

Henry, O., 19

Hess, Thomas B., 128, 180

Hicks, Granville, 152

The Hidden Order of Art: A Study in the Psychology of Artistic Imagination (Ehrenzweig), 104–105

"The Hiding Man" (Barthelme), 20, 75, 88, 93

hippies, 167

Hirsch, Edward, 188

historical time, nontraditional use of, 96–97

Moore, Helen (Mrs. D. Barthelme) (second wife). *See* Barthelme, Helen (née Moore)

Moore, Odell Pauline (sister-in-law), 42, 125, 157

moral issues: and Catholicism, 10–12, 41, 59, 75; Don's handling of, 62; infidelity and military duty, 28; in *The King*, 191; lost children and medical research, 62

Morris, Gitta, 55, 118, 159, 180

Morris, Robert, 102, 110–11, 159, 180

motion pictures. *See* films

The Moviegoer (Percy), 73, 74–75

movies. *See* films

"Mr. Hunt's Woolly Utopia" (Barthelme), 98

music: Don as drummer, 10, 14; Don's love of, 24, 51; and Don's parents, 52; jazz, 10, 37, 43, 121, 133, 141

"The Mystery of Language" (Percy), 73

Natanson, Maurice, 45, 46, 47–48, 65, 71, 186

Nesbitt, Lynn, 151

networking, 86, 115

"New American Artifacts" (Barthelme), 111

New Criticism, dominance of, 99

New Orleans, 42–43

newspapers. *See Houston Post;* journalism careers

New World Writing, 113

New York: Don's teaching in, 174–75; Don's writing in, 146–49; fascination with, 143–44; first trip to, 113–18; moving to, 126–40

New Yorker: audience, 170; "Construction," 181; Don's stories in, 9; "Down the Line with the Annual," 95; First Reading contract, 148; "Florence Green Is 81," 94; "The Indian Uprising," 155; "Kierkegaard Unfair to Schlegel," 104; "L'Lapse," 133, 148; "Margins," 147; "Marie, Marie, Hold on Tight," 148; "On Angels," 82; "One Hundred Ten

West Sixty-First Street," 62; "Overnight to Many Distant Cities," 97; "The Piano Player," 148; "A Shower of Gold," 148, 149; *Snow White,* 164–65; "The Teachings of Don B: A Yankee Way of Knowledge," 181; "Visitors," 28

Nixon, Richard, 26

Notes from Underground (Dostoevsky), 101, 111

novels: *The Dead Father,* 175; development of, 153; first, 25–27; *Ghosts,* 181; *The King,* 188, 191; *Paradise,* 182; *Snow White,* 15, 140, 161, 164–65

"The Ohio Quadriology" (Barthelme), 147

Old Crow Ink, Inc., 125

"On Angels" (Barthelme), 82

"One Hundred Ten West Sixty-First Street" (Barthelme), 62

On Native Grounds (Kazin), 83

"The Ontological Basis of Two" (Barthelme), 150

Otis, Elizabeth, 72

"Overnight to Many Distant Cities" (Barthelme), 13, 97

"Pages from the Annual Report" (Barthelme), 97–98

Paley, Grace, 175

Paradise (Barthelme), 182

Parker, Dorothy, 5

Parker, Harley, 111

parochial schools, 10–12

Partch, Harry, 122

Pennybacker, Ruth, 6

Percy, Walker, 72–75, 76, 81, 107

Perelman, S. J., 5

perfectionism, Don's, 108. *See also* creativity

Phelan, Charlotte, 179, 182

phenomenology, 46, 71

philosophy, Don's interest in, 45, 46–47, 48, 71, 76, 149

Tokyo travels, 28, 31

"To London and Rome" (Barthelme), 147

Tolstoy, Leo, 46–47

Toner, Tom, 111

"Toward a Theory of Stalinism" (Bledsoe), 78

Tulane Drama Review, 106

Tyler, Parker, 82

unconscious as source of creativity, 106–107

undergraduate lifestyle, 20–21

undergraduate studies, scope of, 17

University of Houston: Don and Helen's first meeting, 2–4; Don and Helen's teaching careers, 172–73, 184; Don's father in faculty of architecture, 17; Don's resignation from, 88; Helen's departure from, 43; Helen's public relations job, 36; KUHT-TV, 44; Michener Fellowship in honor of Donald Barthelme, 191; origins of, 196n 1; overview of atmosphere, 4. *See also Forum*

University of Texas (1960s), 166–67

Unspeakable Parodies and Unnatural Acts (Barthelme), 170

"Up, Aloft in the Air" (Barthelme), 147

U.S. Army service, 22–34

V. (Pynchon), 106

Vandruff, Lee (nephew), 169, 185

Vandruff, Margo (sister-in-law), 39, 56, 131, 134, 145, 186

Vandruff, Roy, 39, 131

veterans of World War II, 4

"The Viennese Opera Ball" (Barthelme), 148

"Visitors" (Barthelme), 28, 31

Wagner College, 115

Waiting for Godot (Beckett), xiii, 46

Walker, Stanley, 85

wedding, Don and Helen's, 41–42

Weill, Kurt, 50

White Sulphur Springs, WV, 127

Williams, William Carlos, 81

wit, Don's, 15–16, 95

Wittgenstein, Ludwig, 47, 76

women: Don's character with, 16–17, 43, 45; executive glass ceiling, 164; Helen's desire for independence, 142; loan risk discrimination, 162; restrictions on careers for, 43–44

Woollcott, Alexander, 31

Wray, Dick, 168

Wright, Frank Lloyd, 7

writing: advertising copy, 98–99; daily process, 90–101, 103; Don's dissatisfaction with, 170; Don's early talent for, xiv; Don's search for perfection, 175; in Europe, 155; inspiration from mother, 8; journalistic, 18–20; New York production, 146–49; recognition of Don's, 173; 1980s developments, 181–82. *See also* novels; short stories

writing style: development of, 5–6, 95–97, 103, 106; ironic, 46, 95, 100, 104, 152, 165; journalistic, 19; lyrical, xv, 95, 97, 100; new creation of, xv; public vs. private elements, 17; revisions, 91–92, 103, 107, 108; satirical, 5, 147; as taken from life, 62. *See also* stylistic themes

Yates, Peter, 82, 122

Ye Olde College Inn, 124

The Zoo Story (Albee), 58, 111, 115

Zuruck an die Sache, 194n 4

HELEN MOORE BARTHELME is senior lecturer of English at Texas A&M University. Former professor at the University of Houston and Dominican College in Houston, she holds the Ph.D. from the University of Texas at Austin.

ISBN 1-58644-119-8

90000

9 781585 441198